12

DIVING
INTO
DARKNESS

DIVING INTO DARKNESS

A True Story of Death and Survival

Phillip Finch

St. Martin's Press ≋ New York

DIVING INTO DARKNESS. Copyright © 2008 by Phillip Finch. All rights reserved. Printed in the United States of America. For information, address St. Martin's Press, 175 Fifth Avenue, New York, N.Y. 10010.

www.stmartins.com

Picture credits: Dreyer family collection: p. 5 (middle); Phillip Finch: p. 1 (bottom left and right), p. 7 (bottom right), p. 8; Petrus Roux: p. 5 (top and bottom), p. 6 (top and bottom); Shaw family collection: p. 2; South African Police Service: p. 3, p. 4 (middle), p. 6 (middle), p. 7 (top).

Library of Congress Cataloging-in-Publication Data

Finch, Phillip.
    Diving into darkness : a true story of death and survival / Phillip Finch.—
1st. U.S. ed.
        p. cm.
    ISBN-13: 978-0-312-38394-7
    ISBN-10: 0-312-38394-0
    1. Deep diving—Case studies. 2. Extreme sports—Case studies. I. Title.

GV838.672.F56 2008
627.72—dc22

2008024271

First published in Great Britain as *Raising the Dead: A True Story of Death and Survival* by HarperSport, an imprint of HarperCollins

First St. Martin's Press Edition: October 2008

10   9   8   7   6   5   4   3   2   1

CHAPTER
1

On an afternoon in November 2004, David Shaw climbed a steep path up a mountainside that rose above Clearwater Bay in the New Territories of Hong Kong. His pace – hard, unflinching, non-stop – was typical of Shaw, a driven man who did everything with a purpose.

Shaw was fifty years old, a training captain with Cathay Pacific airline who helped to oversee the flight fitness of other Cathay pilots while flying the line's long-haul routes. He and his wife, Ann, both Australian, had recently celebrated their thirtieth wedding anniversary. With their two children at universities in Australia, the Shaws lived alone in the home that they owned, overlooking Clearwater Bay. They were prosperous, stable, settled: apparently typical of their circle of acquaintances in Hong Kong's English-speaking expatriate community.

Recently, however, those people had begun to understand that Dave Shaw was not like anyone they had ever known.

In October, he had gone on a diving trip to South Africa. In the past five years, after he learned to scuba dive during a family holiday in the Philippines, Shaw often flew around the world to dive, taking advantage of an airline pilot's flight benefits. Shaw's acquaintances imagined him at beach resorts, spending languid days on bright ocean reefs, swimming with tropical fish.

Harry (a pseudonym), one of Shaw's close friends in Hong Kong and director of a large Hong Kong business, had first met Shaw fifteen years earlier, when the Shaws had moved to Hong Kong and joined a small Christian congregation that included Harry and his family. He admired Shaw's intelligence and quiet confidence. Shaw spoke little, bragged not at all and accomplished much.

Shortly after Shaw returned from South Africa, Harry asked him whether he had enjoyed the trip. Shaw's answer was curious.

'I did,' he said. 'I went quite deep.'

Shaw referred Harry to a website address. As soon as Harry returned home, he opened the web page.

Welcome to deepcave.com, a website created by Dave Shaw, the opening page read. Written in the third person, the text described how Shaw had quickly moved from recreational scuba to more challenging, and more risky, pursuits:

Dave was introduced to diving by his son and immediately knew that technical diving was his area of interest. Following some penetration wreck dives in the Philippines, Dave decided

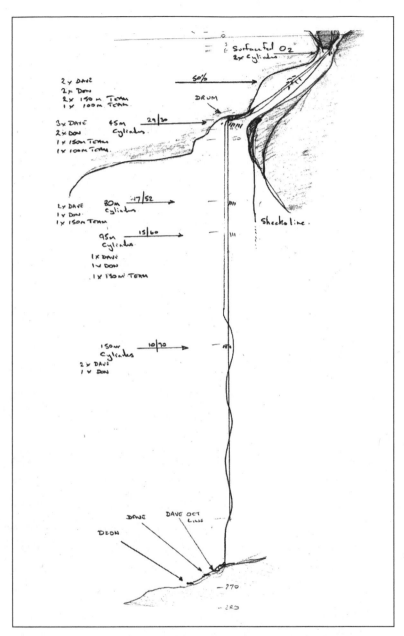

Diagram of Bushman's Hole by Don Shirley (May 2007) showing position of shot lines and placement of emergency cylinders and gas mixtures at each level. Drawn to scale.

All men dream, but not equally. Those who dream by night in the dusty recesses of their minds wake in the day to find that it was vanity: but the dreamers of the day are dangerous men, for they may act their dreams with open eyes, to make it possible.

T.E. Lawrence
Seven Pillars of Wisdom

and Megan Hughes, Andries van Zyl, Theo and Marie Dreyer, Dusan Stojakovic, Lo Vingerling and Gerhard du Preez.

Since I wasn't able to visit Cape Town and Iraq, Jack Meintjes and Stephen Sander cooperated with a series of emails that must have required much time and effort on their part; their passion was obvious.

Without Mary Martin's support, I never would have had a chance to do this book. Thanks, Mary. As he has been for the past 25 years, Mel Berger at the William Morris Agency was a source of unstinting faith and support. Cathryn Summerhayes in London placed the book when it seemed that this wonderful story might not find a home. My editor, Tom Whiting, showed unreasonable patience when dead-lines were stretched and broken.

I'm indebted to you all.

Phillip Finch
December 2007

Acknowledgements

I'm grateful to all those who made this book possible.

Ann Shaw, André and Don Shirley, and Gordon Hiles all opened their homes to me, received me with warmth and friendship, and answered every question unflinchingly – even when the topic was gut-wrenching. Don was endlessly patient in helping me to sort out technical details. André applied her formidable organizational skills to gathering documents and photos, and putting me in contact with members of the dive team and others. Gordon's video footage, generously shared, was invaluable.

Among those who sat for interviews and made themselves available for follow-ups later, in no particular order: Peter Herbst, Michael Vickers, Truwin Laas, Verna van Schaik, Nuno Gomes, Ernst Strydom, Petrus Roux, Lisa Shaw, Derek

To my mother,
Madeline Finch,
who has waited much too long for it

cave diving was worth exploring. Once completing the cave course in Florida, it has only really been cave diving that has been of interest since …

He is primarily interested in exploring. To be where no other man has explored before is the ultimate in his opinion. It seems that to achieve that goal, greater depths are becoming a must.

Another page on the site linked to reports of Shaw's notable dives. To anyone with any knowledge of diving, the dives were beyond extraordinary. They bordered on the unreal.

In October 2003 he accomplished two dives past 180 metres at Komati Springs, South Africa, including a critical equipment failure and what Shaw described as a 'near-death experience'.

In June 2004 he dived to 213 metres in one of the world's deepest underwater caves: Boesmansgat – Bushman's Hole – in South Africa.

During the trip just completed, Shaw had become the third diver in history to return from the bottom of Bushman's. His depth of 270 metres was a world record for the diving apparatus known as a rebreather.

During that dive, as he swam along the bottom, Shaw found the body of a young man who had disappeared ten years earlier while diving in the hole. Shaw had briefly tried to lift the body with the thought of bringing it to the surface, but he had become over-exerted. With his allotted time on the bottom running out, he was forced to leave the corpse behind.

His online dive report described the incident:

I was headed for what appeared to be a deeper section of the cave and was laying line as I swam. This was cave diving at its best. I scanned the floor as I went, taking in the scenery. It appeared the cave would not go much deeper. I sweeped right and left with my HID light as I moved forward ...

I was relaxed and could almost not believe where I was. I was slowly descending and reached a depth of 270m ... I swept left with my HID light, at an angle of about 30 degrees, and 15 m away I saw a body, as plain as day. This had to be the body of Deon Dreyer, who died on the 17th Dec 1994. Even following extensive searches his body had never been found.

He was lying on his back, arms in the air and legs outstretched. There was no shock on my part, but rather a decision-making process of what to do. Do I continue for depth or go to the body? The decision was easy really. I turned and was soon next to him. I needed to try and make a recovery of the body.

Time was critical. I was within seconds of my turn time and I needed to make a decision. I tried to lift him, but to no avail. I knelt next to him and tried harder. I was now puffing and panting with the exertion. This was not wise I told myself. I am at 270m and working too hard ... Time to go; I was one minute over my maximum bottom time already. I tied off my reel to him so that he could be found again, not even wasting time cutting the reel free. I followed my line back to the shot line and started my ascent.

Nearly all recreational diving takes places at depths above 40 metres. Many divers never exceed 30 metres. With his dive in October, Shaw had become the fifth sports diver in history to exceed 700 feet (213 metres) and survive; more men have walked on the moon. In five years of part-time diving, he had gone from rank beginner to one of the world's most accomplished and ambitious divers.

And he had done it without ever mentioning his feats to anyone in Hong Kong. Even Ann had had only a vague idea that he was going far beyond the norm.

Now, as Shaw crested the ridge at the end of his long climb, he encountered Harry, who had taken a more leisurely path to the top. The two men stood chatting for a few minutes, taking in the spectacular view of the bay.

Harry remarked on Shaw's strenuous push up the hill. Shaw explained that he was trying to stay fit for his next big dive. He said that he would be returning to South Africa soon, back to the bottom of Bushman's Hole.

Harry was surprised and dismayed. He was not a diver, but he knew that cave diving was among the world's most hazardous sports, and he guessed that Shaw's extreme cave diving must be unimaginably dangerous and challenging.

He knew, for sure, that Shaw had much to lose, a truly enviable life with a devoted wife, good health, all the money that he would need.

'What's the point?' Harry said. 'You've already done that.'

'Not like this,' Shaw said. 'Nobody has ever done anything like this. I'm going back to get the body.'

*   *   *

Bushman's Hole is about 500 kilometres southwest of Johannesburg, between the towns of Kuruman and Danielskuil, in the Northern Cape province of South Africa. It lies within the 34,000-acre Mount Carmel Game Farm, in the semi-arid 'green Kalahari', a region of scrub brush, sere grass and a rolling, rocky terrain.

From the lodge at the game farm, it is a drive of about fifteen minutes along a dirt track. The land rises and falls in gentle swells. You are upon the spot almost before you know you are there: it is, literally, a hole in the ground that seems to open up during the last few paces as you approach the rim.

Bushman's is a sinkhole. Like most sinkholes, Bushman's was created by the gradual dissolution of soluble dolomite in underground water. But Bushman's is a sinkhole in the way St Peter's Basilica is a church. It is huge and magnificent and almost without equal. The hole is roughly horseshoe-shaped, about 300 feet across at the top. Sheer walls of grey dolomite, topped with banded ironstone and streaked a rusty brown, fall nearly 75 metres straight down. The calls of birds waft up eerily from the chasm.

A steep rubble pile descends from the west end of the hole. The path down is rough, nearly hand-over-hand in places. The final step down is to the edge of a teardrop-shaped pool, about 10 by 15 metres. Most times, the surface of the water is covered by a green skim of duckweed, shockingly green. A slab-sided boulder, larger than an automobile, sits exposed in the middle of the pool. The spot is idyllic, cool, tranquil and hushed, and there is absolutely no hint of what lies below.

The large boulder sits atop an open seam in the floor of the pool. It partly obstructs the crevice – imagine a child's alphabet block sitting out of kilter in a bathtub drain – but below the surface of the water, at a depth of about three metres, are three openings. Two are large enough for a diver in full gear to enter without wriggling.

Immediately below the massive boulder is a rock-walled passage, tight at first but gradually opening up. Overhead, sunlight streams through the gaps. Below is utter darkness and nothingness. This is a twilight zone, and as you descend, the darkness closes in. The sense that you are leaving behind the world of light and life is reflexive and overwhelming. It requires no imagination.

This is the upper part of a bell-shaped chamber, one of the largest freshwater caverns on earth. From the surface of the pool to the deepest part of the sloping floor is about 280 metres. The circumference of the chamber has never been accurately measured, but a football field would fit at the bottom. In 2002 a team of divers tried to install a line around the wall at the 90 metre level. They brought 350 metres of line, and when they reached the end of their last spool, they still hadn't got back around to where they started, and they were forced to go back the way they came.

Any underwater cave is essentially a dead zone. The absence of light and air stifles most life (the exceptions are some micro-organisms and a few species of blind cave fish). For divers, the hazards increase with depth, so that the deeper reaches of Bushman's is one of the most perilous and inhospitable places on earth.

This would not have surprised the original inhabitants of the Kalahari, the !Kung-speaking Bushmen.

The sinkhole was one of the major features in this part of their range, a rare and inexhaustible source of water. The pool sustained them but it probably also terrified them. The Bushmen believed that waterholes were portals to an underworld of darkness and danger. In some Bushman rock art, death is represented by a human figure submerged in water. The Bushmen would have understood that to go beneath the surface of the pool was to enter another world: the realm of the dead.

*   *   *

On 8 January 2005, Dave Shaw returned to the bottom of Bushman's Hole and to the body of Deon Dreyer.

Shaw's day began with a 4 am wakeup in the room that he shared with his friend, Don Shirley, at the Mount Carmel lodge. After he had showered, Shaw called his wife, Ann, in Hong Kong. They spoke with their usual affection. Neither of them mentioned the dive that he was about to attempt. Ann didn't know – didn't want to know – the specific day he planned to dive.

'I'm going down to the dive site now,' he told her before they said goodbye.

Shaw joined Shirley for a light breakfast in the dining room of the lodge and then the two of them climbed into Shirley's pickup truck. Shirley pulled away from the lodge, heading east toward the hole. As he drove, Shirley punched up the volume on an iPod that was a gift from Shaw, who had loaded it with music including playlists that Shaw called DeepCave1 and DeepCave2. As Shirley drove through the desert, headlights piercing the darkness, the song that blasted through the truck's speakers was Led Zeppelin's 'Whole Lotta Love'.

The men had met about two years earlier, when Shaw first came to dive at Komati Springs, the flooded mine where Shirley taught courses in technical diving. Shirley was 47, a quiet and thoughtful Englishman who had moved to South

Africa in 1997 after a career in the British Army. He was married to a South African and was about to become a South African citizen. The country beguiled him. He found it beautiful and vivid, a land where life seemed to burn brighter than any place he had known.

Shirley was one of South Africa's finest divers and was the country's foremost instructor in tech diving. His log books showed thousands of serious dives. He had taught advanced techniques to hundreds of students, nearly all of whom revered him. In many ways he was a more accomplished diver than Shaw – certainly more experienced, though not as driven to push deeper and further. Shirley considered himself a facilitator, giving others the chance to accomplish what might otherwise have been beyond their grasp. That was how he approached his advanced teaching, and it was what he had done for Shaw. Shirley had organized all of Shaw's major dives in South Africa and had been his main support diver during Shaw's two previous visits to Bushman's. He was one of the few divers in the world qualified to follow Shaw to the depths that Shaw wanted to dive, and he would do it again today.

During the past two months Shirley had conceived an intricate plan for Shaw's dive to recover the body. The plan included eight support divers and a separate team of police divers, all entering the water at precise intervals after Shaw began his dive. Shirley and his wife, André, had organized all the details and logistics of the event, including a mobile recompression chamber, medics, and an on-site diving physician. All of this had come together while Shaw remained in Hong Kong.

Most dives – even the most thrilling and dangerous – are conducted in perfect obscurity. This one would be different.

Reporters from South African TV, radio and newspapers, stringers for international news organizations, and a documentary film crew were all on site. The discovery of the body had been national news, and the plan to recover it had become a major national story. Only the recent tsunami in Southeast Asia had received as much attention in the local press. The attempt seemed to affect people viscerally. The brave man who leaves his comfortable life to perform a hazardous task is a staple of myth in many cultures. And in bringing out a body that had lain so deep, for so long, Shaw would be retaking a prize that the cave had long since claimed as its own. In a real sense, he was trying to cheat death.

So perhaps the story tapped into the power of myth and imagination. Or perhaps the interest from the media was just by chance. For whatever reason, this would be, by far, the best-documented dive in history.

Bushman's is usually a place of silence and stillness. But today the place was alive as Shirley crested a low hill and dropped down toward the hole. Several large tents, and some smaller ones, were clumped between the dirt track and the edge of the hole. Dozens of people stood around the rim, many with electric torches. Others sat around campfires. A generator thrummed. Shirley parked near the rim. This was the limit of cellphone reception – no signal reached down into the hole – and when he left the truck, Shirley paused to call his own wife, André, who was at their home in the hills of Mpumalanga province, about 1100 kilometres east. Unlike Ann Shaw, André knew exactly what the two men planned to do today and exactly when they planned to do it.

Then the two men made their way down the steep jumble of boulders. Along the way, they passed a brass memorial plaque which the parents of Deon Dreyer had installed in the weeks after he disappeared.

Shaw's dive gear sat where he had left it the previous evening, on a flat shelf of rock against an overhanging wall. Shirley's gear was a few metres away, at the edge of the pool. While they dressed, others arrived at the bottom of the hole: support divers and their friends and family, the documentary producer, medics, a dive marshal, police divers and their retinue. The rubble pile became an amphitheatre, and boulders became perches.

In all its millions of days, Bushman's Hole had never known a morning quite like this one.

If the image of a diver that comes first to mind is of a lithe figure in a skintight wetsuit, a single scuba tank strapped to his back, banish the image. Shaw and Shirley were ponderous, vaguely menacing creatures as they stepped into the water. They wore bulky, inflatable, full-body drysuits to protect them during twelve hours or more in the water. They were festooned with gear: electronic handsets and dive computers on each arm, a black battery pack with a cord running to a lamp head that each man wore on his right hand, multiple aluminium cylinders slung at their sides.

The tanks were for emergency use, in case of the failure of the machines they wore at their backs: rebreathers, designed to capture their exhaled breaths and automatically replenish the oxygen. The rebreathers were shrouded in smooth black shells, carapace-like, with dark corrugated hoses dropping over the shoulders and connecting at opposite ends of a mouthpiece.

Shaw floated for several minutes in the shallows of the pool. One of the other divers handed him a rock-climbing helmet. Attached to the helmet were a torch and a blocky metal housing that held a video camera. Shaw had never before used such a thing, but he had agreed to wear it for this dive, with the footage to be used in the documentary film. Nobody had ever before performed such a task at such great depths, and Shaw wanted to show the world exactly what he had done and how he had done it.

He put on the helmet.

Shirley was in the water now, floating nearby. He had been the deep support diver during each of Shaw's monumental dives. Today he planned to follow Shaw down after 13 minutes, timed so that as Shirley descended, Shaw would be starting up with the body. The two would meet at about 220 metres. Shirley had never before gone to such a depth – fewer than a dozen sports divers ever had, intentionally – but he felt confident. Don Shirley had never started a dive that he wasn't sure he could finish.

At 6:13 am, with light now suffusing the walls of the pit, Shaw and Shirley exchanged a brief handshake.

'See you in a few minutes,' Shirley said. Shaw nodded and moved out into the middle of the pool. So quietly that he barely rippled the water, he dropped out of sight.

He followed a taut weighted rope, a 'shot line', letting it slide through the fingers of his right hand. At first the line angled downward at about 45°, following the roof of the cave. But at a depth of about 50 metres, the line dropped straight down, with the chamber opening up so dramatically that the walls seemed to fly out of sight. Shaw's high-intensity underwater light was blindingly bright and the water was absolutely clear, yet the walls of the chamber were now so distant that the light couldn't reach them. Shaw was truly in the void. The vertical shot line was his only reference.

Periodically he passed clusters of cylinders that had been clipped to the line, emergency breathing gas. One bunch at 80 metres. Another at 95. Occasionally he grasped the line and pulled himself down to hasten his descent.

He was calm. His movements were smooth as he angled his left forearm and turned his head slightly to check a digital display strapped to his left wrist. He looked at the depth and the running time. His rate of descent was increasing, ticking up towards nearly 30 metres per minute. At 150 metres, he passed the last set of three emergency cylinders, which he and Shirley had placed a few days earlier. Now, every second that he descended would carry him away from the security that they represented.

Seven minutes into the dive, he passed through 200 metres. He continued to drop.

Eleven and a quarter minutes into the dive, he reached the floor of the chamber. From the bottom of the shot line, a thinner strand of white nylon lay on the muddy floor. This was a guideline that he had placed during his record dive in October; the other end was tied off to Deon Dreyer's equipment. Shaw swam towards the body.

On the surface, Shirley floated above the entrance as he watched the sweeping second hand of a wall clock that sat in a cleft of rock above the pool. Twelve and a half minutes after Shaw's departure, Shirley's head disappeared beneath the water.

At almost that exact moment, 270 metres below, Dave Shaw reached the body of Deon Dreyer.

Shirley followed the shot line, descending at nearly the same rate that Shaw had. Shirley could see only blackness below him.

Shirley continued down. Somewhere past 150 metres, he saw a light below. This wasn't the intense glare of Shaw's hand-mounted light, but much dimmer, almost the glimmering of a star in the night sky. It was some distance off the shot line, about in the spot where Deon Dreyer's body should be.

The light wasn't moving. Shirley knew that Dave Shaw was in trouble.

Shirley reached 220 metres, his assigned depth. According to his plan, this was about where he expected to meet Shaw, coming up the shot line with the body. Shirley was already deeper than he had ever dived before. It wasn't that he avoided such crazy depths, not exactly: he had just never had a reason to seek them.

Now he had a reason.

He continued down, past 220. He was headed for the bottom.

Those above, at the surface and in the world beyond, had no way of knowing what drama was being acted out at the bottom of the hole. Their wives and families and friends, the other divers, the parents of Deon Dreyer – everyone who had a stake in the dive – all of them were completely unaware. The truth emerged only gradually, over hours and days, and when it became known, it stunned them all.

CHAPTER
2

Peter Herbst was one of the divers who followed Shaw and
Shirley down into the cave that morning at Bushman's Hole.
Herbst is a large man in many respects: burly, loud, profane,
vivid. He has a fervent appreciation of extreme diving, not
just the experience of it but what it represents and what it
brings out in those who do it. He relishes the spectacle of
remarkable people putting themselves into extraordinary
situations.

Herbst tells the story of the world's first 200-metre dive. It
was perpetrated by a German, Jochen Hasenmayer, in the
huge spring called Fontaine de Vaucluse, in the Provence
region of France. The dive took place on the night of 9 September 1982. Hasenmayer dove after dark because he had
been denied a permit to enter the spring, which is located in
a village of the same name.

Most big dives use auxiliary tanks that have been placed in advance, during shallower 'setup' dives. But since he was unable to do setup dives, Hasenmayer had to carry all his air and breathing gas. On his back Hasenmayer wore four large tanks on a rack which he had designed and built. He towed behind him a sled, also self-designed and self-built, with five more large tanks. The complete rig weighed nearly 450 kilograms. He had no support divers. Hasenmayer spent more than nine hours alone in 13°C water, with no light except those he carried. Because he was diving at night, he lacked even the overhead daylight glow that usually comforts and tantalizes cave divers during their long decompression stops. When Hasenmayer finally emerged, he was greeted by his 'crew': his wife, Barbara, who had waited for him all night in the darkness. They were the only two people on earth who knew what he had done.

Herbst loves that story. He savours the will and the steely passion that such an act must have involved.

'*That's diving,*' he cries, the way a wine lover might exclaim over an exquisite Cabernet. For Herbst such moments are the heady essence of a sport that, even at its safest and most benign, involves a conscious departure from the world of light and air.

Herbst is the owner of Reef Divers, a dive shop in the South African capital, Pretoria. Herbst trains dozens of new recreational divers every year. The act of submerging in water strikes many beginners as unnatural, and their first few shallow dives often require courage out of all proportion to the actual risk, which is minimal. Eventually, though, an ambitious diver may seek out truly precarious places and situations – usually great depth, caves, or both – where a mistake or simple misfortune can create drama of operatic dimensions.

There is the story of the Dead Man's handshake.

In the late 1970s, divers attempted to find an underwater connection between Kingsdale Master Cave and Keld Head, two cave systems in the Yorkshire Dales. Among them were a Yorkshire diver, Geoff Yeadon, and Jochen Hasenmayer (certain names and sites tend to recur among the legends of extreme diving). Hasenmayer set off solo one day into Keld Head. About an hour and a half later, when Hasenmayer failed to return on schedule, Yeadon went after him.

Nine hundred metres into the cave, Hasenmayer had lost his way in low visibility. He was running low on air when Yeadon spotted his light through a narrow gap near the roof of the cave. Yeadon attempted to squeeze through the gap but got stuck in the opening and was momentarily trapped before he managed to back out slightly. Hasenmayer swam towards Yeadon and floated at the other side of the gap. They were a metre and a half apart, but it might as well have been miles. Yeadon's own air pressure was dropping towards the halfway point and he knew that Hasenmayer's air must be critically low. Yeadon reached through the opening in a gesture of comfort. Hasenmayer took his hand and gripped it. Yeadon believed that he was shaking a dead man's hand.

Hasenmayer released Yeadon's hand and backed off. Though Yeadon had already reached the turnaround point on his air pressure, he remained at the gap and watched as Hasenmayer searched for another way around the restriction. Eventually Hasenmayer found a passage and the two men swam out together. Hours later, he and Yeadon were already plotting another penetration of Keld Head.

That's diving!

Extreme divers are almost always intelligent. They have to be: they survive by a cool accounting of risk, as measured against their own capabilities. It is a process that quickly weeds out the dullards. They crave control and try to leave nothing to chance. Luck, they believe, is malicious, and can be offset only by redundancy and fetishistic procedure. Though their surface lives may sometimes be chaotic, extreme divers are exacting and disciplined when they are in the water. They share the paranoiac's conviction that the worst will always try to happen, at the worst possible time.

This irrational attitude might not be so deeply held if it didn't prove so often true.

In 1983, Americans Sheck Exley and Ken Fulghum swam almost 1400 metres into an underwater lava tube in the Canary Islands. They had just turned around to head out when a malfunctioning regulator emptied the air from Fulghum's tanks. It was the most catastrophic of failures, at the most vulnerable point in any cave dive.* Fulghum now had no air. Exley had about two-thirds of his original pressure and a spare mouthpiece and regulator. In theory, Exley's remaining air was just enough to get both divers out alive; in reality, accelerated breathing in an emergency would probably exhaust the supply before they reached safety.

---

* Technical divers operate on the 'Rule of Thirds': one-third of air supply for descent, one-third for return, one-third for emergency use. This principle requires both members of a diving pair to turn around and head for the surface whenever either of them has used one-third of his supply of breathing gas. This allows both to reach safety from any point in the dive by sharing the remaining supply. But total loss of pressure is very rare, and nobody truly expects it to happen exactly at the turnaround point.

Exley understood that sharing air with Fulghum would probably result in the death of both of them. Yet he promptly handed Fulghum his own primary regulator and reached for the spare that he carried around his neck.

The two men began to swim out, connected by a seven-foot hose that ran from Exley's tanks to Fulghum's mouthpiece. Exley, who had helped to pioneer the technique, knew that the longest successful 'buddy breathing' rescue at that time was about 90 metres. Exley and Fulghum were 400 metres from a pile of white sand where they had cached two emergency tanks.

After 20 minutes, there was still no sign of the white mound in sight. My head throbbed with pain from the carbon dioxide buildup in my body caused by my efforts to conserve air. I checked my pressure gauge, trying my best to appear unconcerned to Ken. We had considerably less than 500 psig left, only a couple of minutes of air at that depth. We were going to die. I felt a profound sense of dismay and tried to resign myself to our fate. I wondered if anyone would guess what happened when they found our bodies.*

The air pressure continued to fall, until Exley and Fulghum were trying to suck air from empty tanks. Then the white sand mound came into view. Exley drew a last wracked breath and kicked toward the tanks with Fulghum beside him. Exley's chest pounded with spasms as he turned on the valve of the spare tank.

That's diving!

---

* Sheck Exley, *Caverns Measureless to Man* (St. Louis, MO USA: Cave Books, 1994).

Extreme divers are not thrill-seekers. This is a sport of controlled tension, not of cathartic release. A dive is an exercise in task management, patiently sorting through one after the other, and the payoff is not so much an adrenaline fix as the quiet sense of a job well done. The tasks are usually trivial: tying off a guide line, monitoring instruments, adjusting buoyancy. Many are mental. Nearly all of them appear to be simple, but even the simplest tasks are challenging in an underwater cave, or at great depth. And the consequences of failure – even something so simple as neglecting to check the reading of a pressure gauge – can have catastrophic consequences.

Summaries of some cave diving fatalities, all involving experienced cave divers:

During solo dive to test gear, died in mysterious circumstances just a short distance from the surface.

Equipment problem – a free-flowing valve led to a panic scenario and eventually blackout, possibly due to severe buildup of carbon dioxide due to fast swimming.

Lost line in poor visibility and ran out of air.

Drowned while making a rapid return from a bold exploratory push ... Became entangled in the line, possibly while changing to his reserve air supply.

Ran out of air after a sequence of stressful incidents.

Confused by the line arrangement, lost direction and ran out of air.

Found the line broken at a constriction, just over 244 metres from the surface. The out line was eventually located, but in the process a severe entanglement resulted. One of the divers ran out of air completely; the other still had a small amount remaining in his cylinders.

Ran out of air after severe line entanglement and (possibly) subsequent disorientation.*

In 1993 a team including Sheck Exley explored a spectacular cave system with five major sinkholes in the state of Tamaulipas, in northeast Mexico. The deepest of the five is Zacaton, 319 metres from the surface of the water to the floor of the chamber. Exley and another diver, Jim Bowden, decided that they would try to reach the bottom. They planned to dive simultaneously but separately, using individual 'shot lines' about 9 metres apart.

Exley's status in the sport is almost impossible to overstate. His first scuba dive was into a cave. He had more than 4000 cave dives, many of them explorations of amazing depth and length. He was admired both for his courage and for his judgment. He seemed to judge risk and anticipate danger unerringly. If Sheck Exley believed that a dual dive below 300 metres in a cave could be done, nobody questioned him.

---

* Martyn Farr, *The Darkness Beckons* (Diadem Books: London, 1994).

The attempt came on 6 April 1994. Exley began his descent several seconds after Bowden. Each carried several different tanks, containing air and various mixtures of specially blended breathing gas for use at different depths.

As depth increases, so does the volume of a diver's breath; at 250 metres, a dozen deep breaths can empty a large tank. Bowden and Exley had planned to conserve breathing gas by spacing out their breaths, inhaling in a measured pattern. But when Bowden reached 265 metres, he found that he was running dangerously low on gas, and he turned around.

At the surface, the support crews watched bubbles of exhaled gas billow up from the depths. Eighteen minutes into the dive, the bubbles stopped coming from around Exley's line.

Bowden spent almost ten hours in the water, slowly decompressing. Exley did not return alive, but two days later, his body surfaced while when the crew was pulling in his shot line. The rope was wrapped several times around his arms and the neck of one of his tanks. His wrist-mounted dive computer showed that he had reached 270 metres. Four experts, including Bowden, theorized that Exley had been overwhelmed by 'a probable cascade of problems' related to the fantastic depth, and that he had been unable to ascend.

They found that the entanglement in the shot line wasn't accidental; Exley had deliberately wrapped the rope around his arms, perhaps to stabilize himself while trying to work through his difficulties. Many cave divers have a different idea: they believe that Exley, aware that he was about to die, had the presence of mind to wrap himself in the shot line so that his body could be retrieved without risk.

And that is diving.

CHAPTER
3

There were times in their marriage when David and Ann Shaw could seem the unlikeliest of couples, almost a slapstick mismatch.

The day David took her sailing on St Vincent's Gulf, off the coast of Adelaide, was one of those times. They had been married about four years, living a near-itinerant life while he worked as an agricultural pilot in Western Australia and she finished the university degree she had put aside when she married at the age of 19. But recently life seemed to be more stable. They had a house of their own in Adelaide and David had recently bought a 40-foot ketch. He brought her out on the boat for a day; he hoped that she would learn to sail, so that they could spend many days and nights together on the water.

This was probably a long shot at best. Ann wasn't adventurous – at least, not in the usual sense. She also wasn't comfortable around water. She was a poor swimmer and even disliked having water stream heavily down her face when she took a shower. But she agreed to go with him.

Storms can come up hard and fast on St Vincent's Gulf. It happened that afternoon, and Ann and David got caught out in rough weather before they reached the harbour. He asked her to take the wheel while he lowered the sails.

'Steer it into the wind,' he told her. But the wind seemed to be coming from everywhere. While he struggled with the sails, the boat swung broadside to the waves. Water crashed in over the side. They lost steering and the boat drifted towards the rocks of a jetty. A small harbour rescue boat approached and threw them a line. David tied on the line – and it broke. The rescuers threw a second line. This one held, but the up-and-down bobbing of the ketch nearly swamped the small rescue craft. Eventually they were towed to safety. Ann was terrified. David was unflustered. The crooked grin that she loved was still, inexplicably, in place. He actually seemed to enjoy it!

Ann had many moments like that with David Shaw, as if she were going along for a wild ride while he galloped through life. David was a man of action, Ann was intellectual. He was bold; she was too often timid. David could be bluntly assertive, she was diffident. He was comfortable with the unexpected, gleefully meeting challenges head on; Ann sought quiet certainty.

Yet those who truly knew them realized that they were perfectly matched, an inevitable couple.

They understood and respected one another. Their mutual devotion was unquestioned. Ann was the daughter of a Baptist minister in Australia, David's paternal grandfather had been a pioneer Baptist minister, who died when David's father was only four. Ann and David shared a profound and highly personal kind of Christianity. Throughout their marriage, each would talk often of having received direction from the Creator; the phrase *I think God has told me that* ... was commonplace. It determined all the major decisions in their lives and many lesser ones. They were certain that their lives were divinely guided.

They had met at a Baptist youth camp in Australia. David – he was Dave to many others, but she would always use the more formal name – was 19 years old and an agricultural pilot. He had wanted to be a pilot for as long as he could remember. When he was a very young child, one of his playmates said that he wanted to have a farm. David announced that he wanted to *fly* on farms. And he did. Though money was tight, his parents scraped up the tuition for flight school. He received his commercial pilot's licence before his 18th birthday and began spraying crops. He had been an indifferent student, but in the cockpit he was a natural.

Ann was 17 when they met. She was shy and intensely bright, so accomplished academically that she had garnered some notices in the Western Australia press. She was especially adept at mathematics and economics, courses in which David had struggled, and she was already doing university-level work in both disciplines.

She was awestruck when she first saw him. He had a presence like nothing she had ever encountered. He seemed to notice her too: she was a pert and very pretty blonde. She saw him speaking to some of her friends and acquaintances,

people who might tell him of her academic accomplishments. This was a potential problem. Most boys were put off
by her intelligence and aptitude. It had already ended a couple of would-be relationships before they began.

She decided to confront the problem. Directness was out of
character for her, but this was a special case. She got him
alone, told him the truth and waited for his disappointment.

'I think that's wonderful,' he said. 'You should be proud.'

If she had had any doubt, it vanished at that moment. He
was, unquestionably, the one.

The next weekend, he asked her out on a first date. He
wanted to take her up in his plane. She didn't like flying and
she hated the idea of small planes even more, but she said
yes. She spent a petrified hour beside him trying not to show
her fright.

After that, he was with her as often as he could manage.
Every Friday afternoon, as soon as he finished work, he would
drive two hours to Perth, to spend the weekend with her.

They were married a year and a half after they first met.
David went through the formality of asking her father's permission to marry Ann, but the answer was foregone. Both of
her parents loved David and knew that he was right for her.
And their permission didn't matter anyway. Even at 20, David
was a man who would let nobody stand in the way of what he
wanted. And she would have followed him anywhere.

Her father performed the ceremony. There is a photo of
the newlyweds leaving for their honeymoon – in a small
plane. Ann smiles gamely as she poses outside the cabin
door. David is grinning like a pirate who has made off with a
king's ransom.

The first few years of their marriage, they lived throughout Western Australia and Victoria, mostly in rural areas, as David moved from one flying job to another, sometimes working as a charter pilot, sometimes spraying crops. Ann finished her university degree in patchwork fashion, picking up credits where she could. They lived mostly in small rental homes, but occasionally out of the back of a caravan. David sometimes worried that his parents were disappointed. With his religious background, he was a perfect candidate to fly for MAF – Missionary Aviation Fellowship – a Christian group that supports mission work in remote areas. But this was not for him, he said many times.

Though he disliked the uncertainty of the aerial spraying business, David loved the actual flying. Few forms of flying are so demanding, so constantly engaging: precision flying, low and fast, often passing beneath power lines and dodging low trees in order to spray to the edges of a field. Sometimes he would fly at night, so that the mist of the solution wouldn't dry up before it reached the leaves of the crops. Only once did she see him work. She was shaken by the sight of it and refused ever to watch him again. Sometimes he would be spraying so close to their house that she could hear the engine's drone, its rise and fall as he pulled up steeply at the end of each pass. Hearing it was all right. But she couldn't bring herself to watch.

There were incidents. Some she didn't hear about until later, like the night he cut a power line with the undercarriage of his aircraft. Others were too serious to withhold from her. One morning he brought his plane in safely after the loss of a rudder, an improbable feat of airmanship. Several years later, while flying into a morning sun, he lost sight of a steel stake sticking up above the vines where he was spraying. The stake clipped a wing, the plane crashed and burned. He walked away.

Yet she would be angry with those who called him a daredevil. She knew that it wasn't true: David was cool and calculating and was able to work through emergencies. He wasn't fearless. He just refused to let fear paralyse him. Still, she had to come to terms with reality: she understood that the day might come when he didn't return home. It was a fact, and it would be with her for as long as they were together.

After several years of a near-gypsy existence, David became the manager of an aerial spraying company outside Adelaide. The job promised stability. David was his own boss. They bought their first home and David bought the ketch.

Around this time, he began to talk about sailing around the world solo. David had long been captivated by stories of individual adventure. One of his favourite books was *Ice Bird*, a first-person account of a solo circumnavigation of Antarctica in a small sailboat by David Lewis, a 54-year-old physician from New Zealand. The voyage was a feat of will; Lewis was dogged and unreasonable, and refused to recognize the practical barriers to his quest. Some might call him a madman. *Ice Bird* is as much a story of commitment to a vision as of sailing. The first sentence of Chapter 1 reads: 'The personal dreaming of an Australian Aboriginal may be defined as doing that which is nearest to his heart – as fulfilling his own destiny.'

The book and the voyage both impressed Shaw. He wanted to do something similar, a solo transoceanic voyage, maybe even around the world. He devised a way to rig the ketch for single-handed sailing and he began seriously studying routes and currents. Ann was now pregnant with their first child, but took these plans almost as a matter of course. This was David: naturally he would decide to sail the world, single-handed. She didn't even find it especially remarkable. Except for her father, she had known few other men well, and she imagined that David was typical. Didn't all husbands, upon buying a sailboat, plan to do something like this?

His planning ended suddenly. One Sunday afternoon, David told Ann that God had spoken to him during the service earlier that day.

He told her, 'God wants me to fly for MAF.'

For both, this was an imperative not to be questioned. They rented out their house and sold the boat, and joined the missionary air operation in Papua New Guinea, where David was assigned to a remote mountain settlement. This was primitive bush flying, as hazardous as aerial spraying. He would fly into short strips tucked deep into valleys or cut into the side of a mountain, his final approach sometimes taking him over the scattered debris of wrecked aircraft.

Ann was seven months pregnant when they arrived. The town where the baby was born had only a basic hospital. The baby boy presented feet first, with arms wrapped around his head. The delivery was horrific: David held Ann around the arms, the doctor held the baby's legs, and for agonizing minutes, both pulled as hard as they could. 'Like watching your wife being tortured,' Shaw said of it later. They named the boy Steven. Though deprived of oxygen for forty minutes, he survived. All evidence of the brain damage disappeared after about two months. Both Ann and David considered this a bona fide miracle. Steven Shaw is now studying for a Doctor of Divinity in Australia.

A second child, their daughter Lisa, was born a year and a half later without complications.

The Shaws remained in New Guinea for more than three years. They briefly transferred to Tanzania, where David was to run a national programme for agricultural flying. But the few aircraft were a shambles and the pilots were unqualified. The Shaws found themselves in Nairobi. David had no job and the family had no place to live. They made their way to London, where they stayed for a time in a charity shelter before finally arriving in Australia, virtually penniless. Shaw immediately set about restoring his career. He worked for a time with an agricultural flying company in New South Wales, then as a charter pilot, picking up a series of certifications for increasingly complex aircraft.

He filed an application with Cathay Pacific. Cathay is one of the world's great airlines. Hundreds of hopeful young pilots compete to fill the occasional vacanies on its roster. But Cathay invited him and Ann to the company's headquarters in Hong Kong for an interview. David and Ann regarded it as an expenses-paid holiday. They came home without much expectation.

They had learned that when Cathay declines an application, the notice is by mail. When the company wishes to hire, it is by phone.

Several days after they returned home, the phone rang.

*   *   *

That was the end of their wandering and of their financial struggles. David's Cathay salary far exceeded anything he had ever earned. Ann became a maths teacher – later, an assistant principal – at Hong Kong's German-Swiss International School. David began to invest in real estate in Australia, the UK and the US. And he regularly moved up in grade within Cathay Pacific.

The Shaws joined a new Christian congregation. Here they met Harry and his wife, Pamela, whose two children were about the same age as Steven and Lisa. The Shaws' social life – what there was of it – involved mostly acquaintances from their church. But they were busy, and they were happy in each other's company.

Their first home in Hong Kong was a spectacular find, a waterfront property with views across the bay. For a time, David considered buying another sailboat. Through all his travels, he had kept his copy of Lewis's *Ice Bird*. He had brought it along to New Guinea and Tanzania and back to Australia; it sat now on a shelf in his home in Hong Kong. But the idea of a solo ocean voyage was far in the past. That was a dream for a younger man. If he thought about it, he kept it to himself. He decided that a sailboat was impractical: he wouldn't have the time to enjoy it. He settled for a kayak that he would sometimes paddle for hours around the islands that stud the waters off the New Territories.

The children grew, the family prospered. So that Ann would be closer to her job, they moved to Clearwater Bay and sold the waterfront place for a stunning profit. David became a senior check pilot, nearly as high as he could rise in the Cathay pilots' hierarchy. Their life was comfortable and assured. Their future – financial and otherwise – seemed to be as settled as futures ever can be.

*   *   *

The event that changed all their lives seemed insignificant at the time.

When Steven was about 16, he took a diving course through his school in Hong Kong. David saw a chance for a pastime that would allow him to spend more time with his son. In the summer of 1999, during a family holiday at a beach resort in the Philippines, he enrolled in a basic scuba course. After several days that included classroom instruction and training dives in a swimming pool and in the ocean, he was awarded an 'Open Water' certification, the sport's basic qualification.

David was captivated. Diving had many parallels with flying. It suited him in every way.

Like flying, it has clear requirements for training. Even at its simplest, it raises a bar that not everyone can surmount. That appealed to Shaw. He spurned the easy and the ordinary.

Divers are privileged to go places denied to others. It is a sport of arcane experiences, and even a trivial descent of 10 metres to an ocean reef puts the diver into an other-worldly environment. That was irresistible to the explorer in him.

Like flight, diving involves a practical grasp of science. Though never a scholar, Shaw was able to assimilate masses of technical data, a gift that had helped him to master the complex systems of modern airliners. Anyone who can digest the operating manual of an Airbus A340-600 will chew through decompression tables without a burp.

And diving, like flying, is a mind game that rewards cool self-possession and the ability to sort out difficulties calmly under pressure. It offers an infinite set of challenges to those who are willing to push their personal limits. Shaw began pushing almost immediately.

The hierarchy of sports diving is a pyramid, with ascending layers of complexity, difficulty and risk. The basic Open Water certification allows diving with a single tank of air, to depths that would allow a diver to return to the surface immediately at any time without decompression. In practice, this means about an hour at 20 metres, or about 20 minutes at 40 metres. Many divers are satisfied never to venture beyond 20 metres, the maximum depth of most ocean reefs. This is enjoyable recreation, uncomplicated and safe.

Various courses and certifications train the diver to dive deeper and longer, with more complex equipment. This is 'technical diving'. Most tech diving courses involve the use of specially blended breathing gases that allow divers to extend beyond depths that can be safely attempted on ordinary air. Nearly all tech diving involves decompression: stopping during ascent to allow excess gases to leave the body so as to avoid potentially crippling or even fatal decompression illness – the bends.

For most divers, the rewards of extended range don't justify the difficulties involved, and so the pyramid narrows with each layer of complexity. It narrows even further for 'penetration diving' into wrecked ships or caves, forbidden zones that demand knowledge, discipline, special equipment and exacting technique. At the apex of the pyramid are the few divers who go to the most difficult places and extreme depths, pushing to the limits of their equipment and of human physiology. They are beyond certification. They do not so much absorb knowledge as create it.

Almost immediately, Dave Shaw began reaching for the top of the pyramid, as quickly as anyone has ever climbed it.

His logbooks tell the story of a man in a hurry. He returned to the Philippines later in 1999 and enrolled simultaneously in two courses on the use of Nitrox, a system of adding oxygen to normal air. Nitrox allows divers to stay submerged longer without decompression, but it will also aid decompression. The courses introduced Shaw to fundamentals of circulatory physiology and principles of gas physics.

On the last day of the courses, Shaw did his first-ever decompression dive: down to 33 metres in the ocean, then slowly ascending to three decompression stops totalling ten minutes. He also exchanged the standard gear of the open water diver – a single tank strapped to the back of a buoyancy vest – for the tech diver's twin tanks with a backplate and webbing harness. He carried a third tank, clipped to his harness webbing, for use on his deco stops. He earned two new certifications. On the 23rd dive of his life, he left the bottom level of the pyramid.

Two months later he was back in the Philippines, returning to the resort area of Puerto Galera, which he reached by a ferry ride after a three-hour flight to Manila. He did eight dives in three days. Most were inconsequential. There was a faint tone of disdain for a dive in which he accompanied three recreational divers. *Dived with three others,* he wrote.

They stayed at 18M, I went to 28M, practiced shutdowns, etc. But near the end of the trip, he did his two deepest dives yet, one to 52 metres, the next to 54 metres.

Three weeks later, he was in the Philippines again, now visiting a group of wrecked Japanese ships, sunk in a raid in 1944. Several times, he followed his instructor as they entered the ships through hatches or bomb holes, to swim through the wreckage. *Significant penetration throughout the wreck,* he noted after one dive. *A number of tight passages and holes negotiated.* This was a training dive for a course in wreck diving, another new certification.

Three months passed before he was in the water again, back to the Philippines for yet another wreck course. It would have been sooner, if he could have managed it. Cathay granted him six weeks' leave a year, but he tried to spend at least half that with Ann and the children. He didn't care to dive in Hong Kong, so his only chances came when he used his remaining leave or when he was able to arrange a few free days in his schedule. His flight privileges with the airline allowed him to travel where he wished, and he had the financial means to dive as he wanted when he got there. Time was always the obstacle: for the next five years, he would scramble to find free days for diving.

With his opportunities limited, he tried to make every day and every dive count. In August 2000, about a year after his first Open Water training, he recorded six dives during a three-day visit to Puerto Galera, including three dives to 51 metres and a fourth to 61 metres, his deepest yet. The milestone required 38 minutes of decompression and was the 62nd dive of his career.

He then used two weeks of his annual leave for a remarkable visit to central Florida, an area that is a honeycomb of sinkholes and water-filled limestone caves. Shaw had arranged a series of consecutive courses, one-on-one instruction, with Bill Rennaker, an internationally known cave diving instructor.

The log book shows 21 dives in 10 consecutive days at several major sites: Ginnie Springs, Peacock Springs, Olsen Spring. Shaw completed the last of the courses within a week. He had three days remaining before his scheduled departure, and he filled the time by hiring guides for four more cave dives. The last dive in Florida – Number 85 in his log book – was a penetration of 900 metres into Peacock Springs. That was a substantial dive even for a veteran: a swim of more than half a mile each way, through flowing water, at depths up to 32 metres. For a newly minted novice, it was spectacular.

Shaw was enthralled. Cave diving was the underwater equivalent of the aerial spraying he had enjoyed as a young man, requiring crisp judgment and superb skills. At times Shaw would glide within inches of the muddy cave floor, using froglike twitches of his fins to propel himself without disturbing the silt. The tunnels and passages seemed impossibly remote from the rest of the world. He felt as if he were the first person on earth ever to see them. In fact, the caves were regularly visited, but only by cave divers. It was an experience denied to the less worthy. His ten days in Florida set Shaw apart, and he knew it. For the rest of his diving career, he would call himself a cave diver.

A misunderstanding with Ann took some of the shine off his elation.

He called her every evening (her morning) after the end of his day's diving. But on his last day, after the spectacular dive at Peacock Springs, a rush to catch his flight left him no time to phone home. Ann, in Hong Kong, grew distraught as the hours passed. She knew that his last dive must be finished, and she didn't understand why he hadn't called. She began to fear the worst. She was frantic until she finally called his hotel and learned that he had checked out.

She confessed her panic when he returned home. David was stricken; he didn't want to cause her anxiety. He promised her that he would never again miss a call. He also decided that he would no longer tell her the specifics of his trips, and for as long as he continued to dive, he was deliberately vague about what he was doing and when he was doing it, though he would speak of it later when returned.

The arrangement suited Ann. It was like the one time she had watched him spraying crops in Australia. There was no comfort in the details, and it was all really more than she wanted to know.

*　　*　　*

Over the next year and a half, Shaw returned twice more to central Florida, where he averaged more than two dives a day in the caves that spring near the Suwanee River, west of Gainesville. He arranged his flight schedule for several visits of three or four days to the Philippines. There Shaw picked up another important set of certifications, for the breathing gas known as 'trimix', which blends helium with oxygen and nitrogen so as to reduce the narcotic effects of air breathed at depth. Immediately after he completed that course, he recorded his first dive to 100 metres, a depth that many tech divers never attempt in a lifetime.

Shaw was now qualified in nearly every important aspect of sport diving. In three years, he had risen almost to the top of the pyramid.

Almost.

The man who had once dreamed of crossing oceans in a single-handed ketch still wanted to explore. Although he had racked up an impressive collection of dives in an impressively short time, Shaw hadn't yet truly breached the outer limits of the sport.

However, he had reached the limits of his equipment. From his first dive, Shaw had used the standard scuba breathing system, also known as 'open-circuit': breathing in air or other gas from a pressurized cylinder, then releasing the exhaled breath into the water as a cloud of bubbles. It's a simple method, using reliable equipment. It requires only that the diver monitor his tank pressure and return to the surface before exhausting his supply. The drawback is that increased depth means increased consumption. For his 100-metre dive, Shaw used four tanks: one for his descent and ascent, slung at his side; a back-mounted twin set of tanks for the ten minutes that he spent at maximum depth; and a cylinder with an oxygen-rich mixture that he used for shallow decompression stops. If he had gone deeper, or stayed longer, he would have needed more gas in additional tanks. The logistics of open-circuit are inexorable, and they would grind down Shaw's impulse to push into the unknown.

But there was an alternative. Within the past several years, a new 'closed-circuit' technology had become available to sports divers. The machine, called a rebreather, recycles gas rather than expelling it, so that total consumption is minimal. Two slim tanks, roughly the size of a man's forearm, replace a dozen large scuba cylinders. A rebreather will extend a diver's time and depth in the water, circumventing the logistical limitations of open-circuit scuba. The machine is about the size and weight of a tech diver's twin cylinders and it rides on his back as cylinders would. It is a marvel but it comes with three large caveats attached. It is relatively expensive, it is far more complex than standard scuba gear, and its safety is a matter of debate and controversy. It was even more controversial in 2002 when Shaw was considering it.

The expense was not a problem for Shaw and the complexity did not impress a man whose workplace was a jet-liner's control panel. As for the risk, Shaw believed that the dangers were overstated and in any case he had always been ready to accept some risk to get where he wanted to go.

In late August 2002, Shaw made two critical decisions. He took an introductory rebreather course in the Philippines. And he arranged an assignment to fly one of Cathay's longest routes, Flight 749 from Hong Kong to Johannesburg, juggling his schedule so that he would have three free days before he flew the return trip.

Shaw had learned of a technical instructor in South Africa who was using rebreathers to accomplish world-class dives, routinely reaching depths that were beyond the practical limits of open-circuit scuba. And that instructor was training others to do the same. Shaw wanted to meet the instructor and see for himself what was happening in South Africa.

The instructor was Don Shirley.

CHAPTER
4

He could remember the moment he first wanted to dive. He knew it exactly. It came on a visit with his parents to Wookey Hole, in an English village of the same name, in Somerset. The year was 1967, and Don Shirley was ten years old.

Wookey is a tourist attraction, a cave where visitors join guided tours to gawk at fantastic limestone formations. The cave consists of a series of chambers connected by sumps: water-filled tunnels that open as pools in the floor of the chambers. The first successful cave dive in England was through one of Wookey's sumps in 1935. On the day that Don Shirley and his parents took the tour, hidden underwater lights illuminated a large pool in one of the chambers. The water was absolutely clear and he could see the entrance hole at the floor of the pool, disappearing under a rock wall. To the boy the effect was magical. At that moment he wanted to be in the water, duck into that tunnel and follow it where it led. He wanted to be a diver.

It was an absurd impulse. In 1967, diving barely existed as a sport in England. Equipment was hard to find, and instruction was rarer still. Even if he had been able to find the training and the gear, it wouldn't have been in the family's budget. Shirley's father was a shop foreman; the family wasn't poor, but they lived frugally, in a working-class area of Egham, Surrey. The chances were remote that the boy would realize his juvenile impulse.

He grew into a tall and somewhat gawky teenager. He disliked team sports (a common trait among technical divers). He was a good student, with a technical bent. He also enjoyed drawing and architecture. When he was 16, he drew the building plans when his parents wanted to add a room to the family home, and he designed several similar extensions for neighbours.

He had no siblings, and when his mother took a job outside the home, he found himself spending hours alone in his room. He was sixteen years old when the British rock band, Pink Floyd, released its album *The Dark Side of the Moon*, in 1973. He had already decided that he wanted more from life than his parents' workaday existence, and the album's themes of alienation struck him. He bought the LP, the first stereo recording he ever owned, and he would often listen to it as he lay on the floor of his bedroom, headphones pressed against his ears.

One song in particular affected him. 'Time' is about the frittering-away of life:

You are young and life is long and there is time to kill today.
And then one day you find ten years have got behind you.

Ten years lost: he found it a frightening prospect. He promised himself that he would never let days, much less years, slip through his fingers.

A few months after his 17th birthday he faced a decision on his future. A university education was probably out of the question. He joined the British Army, both for career training and for the sports opportunities built into the British military system. He began training as an electronics technician. And though he had never learned to swim, he enrolled in a diving programme.

It was the start of a dual career. Over the next 22 years he rose to the rank of Artificer Sergeant Major in the Royal Electrical and Mechanical Engineers. He married at 23, raised two daughters, divorced in the aftermath of the first Gulf War. He also accumulated thousands of dives, taught hundreds of students, and led diving expeditions around the world. He was a member of the army team that discovered and first dived HMS *Pheasant*, a WWII destroyer that was mysteriously lost with all hands in the Orkney islands. Shirley was the first diver in the group to spot the wreck.

Shirley retired from the army in 1997, 40 years old. He had extensive experience in logistics and procurement, and many of his peers had gone on to lucrative jobs in private industry. But he imagined endless deskbound days of forms and spreadsheets.

And then one day you find ten years have got behind you.

He chose to dive. Originally he planned to lead diving excursions around the world with an Army friend and diving buddy, Mike Fowler, who retired a year earlier. But Shirley changed his mind during a visit to South Africa before his mustering-out. During that trip, he visited an inland dive site then known as Badgat, about 320 kilometres northeast of Johannesburg, in the province that had recently been renamed Mpumalanga, formerly the Eastern Transvaal.

From the day he saw it, Shirley knew that this was his future. It wasn't especially impressive from the surface: essentially a waterfilled pit about ten hectares in area. But it was set in classic African terrain, between a rugged range of hills known as the Barberton escarpment and the sprawling valley of the Komati River. And beneath the surface of the water was a diving dreamland: seven distinct levels of mine workings, a maze of flooded tunnels and passages, much of it unexplored since the day the mine's pumps were turned off and the water allowed to rise.

He knew that he could spend the rest of his life here; not just could, but would.

With Fowler as his partner, he secured a lease of the property. After his mustering-out in 1997, he came to Badgat to live and set up a centre for diving instruction. Shirley was qualified to teach nearly every course offered by IANTD – the International Association of Nitrox and Technical Divers, a worldwide certification agency based in Florida. Shirley secured the IANTD Southern Africa license which made it the IANTD headquarters for all of the southern part of the continent. With Fowler, he began to offer the first formal tech diving training in South Africa. They opened a small dive shop on site. Shirley thought that Badgat (literally, 'bath hole' in Afrikaans) sounded inelegant. He renamed the place Komati Springs.

It became a magnet for ambitious divers from around the world. The original shop and office, and Shirley's living quarters, were in a shabby building that had once been a farm bunkhouse and shed. On weekends, the place took on the appearance of a diving commune. Rooms in the building would fill up with divers. Other camped on the grass outside. They came for the training and diving, but Shirley himself was also an attraction. Soft-spoken, bright, forgiving, occasionally goofy: he inspired an almost cultish affection. *Everybody* liked Don Shirley. As a diver, he was superb: controlled, relaxed, economical in his movements. On training dives, he had a calming presence. He sometimes would quiet a jittery student with just a look, locking eyes with him, projecting confidence, then slowly raising an OK signal with a steady hand.

If Don Shirley said you could do it ... you could do it, no question.

During apartheid, South Africa had been isolated from the mainstream in technical diving, as in almost everything else. There was no standard of dive practices, and tech equipment was eccentric and often handmade. Shirley insisted that his students adopt a standard gear configuration and standard diving methods. He was also resolute in taking the macho out of diving. It was not a gladiator sport, he insisted, and he urged his students to cultivate sound judgment rather than bravado. He was qualified to train instructors as well as students, and the instructors that he certified, including Peter

Herbst in Pretoria, also adopted and taught the same practices.

Shirley's way was not only safer, but more effective. Soon many of his students were completing dives that previously would have been beyond their reach. After several years in South Africa, he had accumulated a core group of advanced divers who were loyal not only to his system but to Don Shirley himself.

*   *   *

Don Shirley knew that he had found his place in South Africa. He was living in one of the most beautiful places on earth, doing exactly what he wanted to do. He was thrilled by the sprawl of the Komati Valley and by the sublime African sunlight. No sunrise was ever quite the same as the one that preceded it. He would sometimes climb a ridge that overlooked Komati Springs and take in the endless golden hills, mottled with green. Africa seemed to throb with an intensity that he had never before known. When he returned for visits, England felt cramped and drab, in more ways than one.

At the end of nearly every day in South Africa, he knew that he had lived well and fully.

He had never enjoyed diving more. Komati Springs was a perfect playground, and it lay open to him any time. He liked the companionship of the South African divers; they were open and friendly, with a can-do attitude. He couldn't imagine being anywhere else. This was his life now and he loved it.

He lacked only someone to share it with. During his army days he had married young and helped to raise two daughters before his marriage ended in divorce. Since then he hadn't been seriously involved. As much as this existence suited him, he knew that most women wouldn't appreciate it: secluded and rural, revolving around diving and a flooded mine.

One night in 1999, Don took a glass of wine out to the veranda of the building where he lived and worked. A full moon lit the fields and trees and the distant hills. It was stunningly beautiful – and he was alone.

He reached for a phone and called André Truter.

André was in her early thirties, a striking beauty, independent and intelligent. She was a technical diver, cave-certified, and an open water instructor. They had first met in late 1996, at a divers' gathering in Mozambique, during Don's first visit before he moved to South Africa. André was then living in Pretoria with Peter Herbst and was co-owner of Reef Divers with him.

Don impressed her the way he impressed most people: friendly, a gentleman, a genuinely good guy.

A thoroughbred was how Don saw her.

Shirley became close to both André and Herbst. They often visited on weekends after Don moved into Komati Springs. Then Herbst and André broke up. Herbst's friendship with Shirley continued, but Shirley saw André less often.

He had her phone number, though, and he had recently heard that she was still unattached. With the glass of wine in hand and the moon large in the sky, he called her, and she answered. They spoke for a long time.

I want to see you, he said.

I would like that, she said.

They began to date, but the three-hour drive between Pretoria and Komati Springs quickly forced a reckoning: just how serious was this?

With his total lack of swagger, Shirley represented a departure for André. She was usually drawn to alpha male types with a touch of the rogue. Don was strong but in a quiet and unobtrusive way. She had to ask herself whether this was really what she wanted. She decided that she did. She moved to Komati Springs and they bought a thatched-roof farmhouse with an adjacent guest cottage, about five kilometres from the dive shop. The house overlooked the Komati Valley, and they often walked down to the river to picnic. They shared the house with his two dogs, and her three – André was an animal lover – and with two donkeys and four horses. André's mother, and later Don's father, both spent the last months of their lives in the little cottage, and when it was not otherwise occupied, Peter Herbst was a frequent guest there.

André changed his life and his business. She was energetic, computer-savvy, and organized. She took over the running of the dive shop and arranged all the logistics for the diving expeditions that he led several times a year. This allowed Don to focus on teaching and diving. He was acquiring a reputation for both. He had been an early convert to rebreathers and did most of his diving on the machines. He and several students and former students were routinely diving to 104 metres, the depth of the floor of the mine's seventh level, and several times Shirley had reached 120 metres while following an inclined shaft off that bottom level.

He made no effort to publicize these dives, but inevitably word got out. By 2003 Shirley was known throughout Africa and beyond, both as a diver and as one of IANTD's most respected instructors. He first heard of Dave Shaw in August 2002, through an email message in which Shaw described his diving background and his plans. This wasn't unusual. As his reputation grew, Shirley received email and phone calls from around the world, often from divers who exaggerated their accomplishments, and whose diving aspirations were far out of line from their true abilities.

Shirley had long learned that words didn't matter in diving. But no deception was possible under water. There, Shirley could spot a poseur almost at once.

Come to Komati Springs, he said.

*   *   *

Flight CX749 arrived on time in Johannesburg at 6.30 am on the morning of 7 September 2002. Shaw had arranged for a car and driver from the Cathay crew hotel, and he was on the road by 7.30 am. He slept part of the way but was awake to guide the driver the last few miles using directions André had sent.

The approach to Komati Springs is rough but beautiful: an unmarked turn off the blacktop onto a road of clay and gravel, then 9 kilometres through the rolling grasslands of the lowveldt. The dive centre sits in a hollow at the back side of a hill; the hole itself is on the other side of the hill.

Shaw arrived at 11 am. He had travelled with just his mask, fins and open-circuit regulators; he rented the rest, including a drysuit that was too large. He spoke for a while with Shirley, showed him his logbook. Shirley was teaching a student and he invited Shaw to come along on an afternoon training dive into the second level of the mine, about 27 metres deep.

Then Shaw dressed and prepared to dive. Shaw didn't know it, but he was already being evaluated. Shirley dived with dozens of strangers every year and he had to size them up quickly. It started before they ever entered the water. If a diver was slow or awkward in setting up his gear ... bad sign. A talkative person who grows silent as the dive approaches ... bad sign. Likewise a quiet guy who suddenly starts to chatter.

Shirley liked what he saw from Shaw. He geared up quickly. His demeanour never changed; he was relaxed, affable, easy-going. His logbook impressed Shirley, too. He had just 180 dives, barely out of novice territory, yet many of his dives were significant. He had done the right training with the right instructors. He had hit all the right notes.

The real test came when they climbed down the steel ladder from the edge of the hole, down into the water, and then descended to the entrance of the mine's first level. They did a 58 minute dive to 27 metres, the second level of the mine: nothing extreme by Shirley's standards, but demanding enough to expose any flaws in Shaw's technique. Shirley watched him closely. The water reveals all about a diver's abilities, if you know what to look for: the truth is there in nuances of movement, in the subtle timing of routine actions. It is in the pattern of breathing, it is in the eyes, on wide display behind the lenses of the dive mask.

Once more Shaw impressed him. He did everything right. The student struggled somewhat with his buoyancy control, sometimes kicking up silt when he sank too close to the cave floor. But Shaw had no problems. The rented drysuit was too large, potentially a problem in buoyancy, but he coped. His technique was flawless.

He did everything right, Don told André later.

That evening Shaw returned to Johannesburg. At the crew hotel he pasted Shirley's business card into a page of his diving logbook, noting:

A fun dive which would have been better with my suit. The mine has multi levels so plenty left to explore.

And he added:

Will be back.

CHAPTER
5

To find the real perils and drama in extreme diving, sometimes you have to look past the obvious.

In western Missouri, in the central US, a cave diver steps into a cool and clear spring pool, shaded by an overhang of limestone. He wears standard tech diving gear: a drysuit, a harness with a metal backplate; twin cylinders of compressed air, with redundant scuba regulators; buoyancy wings between his backplate and the cylinders; a primary light and two smaller backups. A smaller cylinder hangs at one hip, fitted with a regulator and mouthpiece. This tank is attached to his harness with spring-loaded clips and is filled with pure oxygen. He wades to the back of the pool, to a seam in the rock floor with a roughly circular opening approximately one metre in diameter, barely large enough to admit him and his equipment.

He dips his head and shoulders and enters the hole face first, using both hands to pull himself through. The beam from the primary light on his right hand shines down into a rough-walled shaft, shoulders-wide, running straight down as far as the light can reach. This would be a nightmare scenario for most humans: as soon as his hips clear the entrance, he is committed. There is no backing out, no room to turn around. He can only continue downward, enclosed by the dark-stained walls.

It's slow going. He's kicking against a strong outflow, and the walls are so tight that he bangs and scrapes against them as he descends. Fifteen metres. Eighteen. Twenty. The water is bone-chilling cold. Strapped to his left wrist is a dive computer, about the size of a tin of peppermints, with an LCD display. A counter on the display ticks off the depth, but he doesn't give it a glance. The number is immaterial. He is where he is and he has no option but to continue down.

The shaft begins to angle outward and it levels off horizontal. After a few more metres, the passenger opens up slightly. Here the passage is wide enough that, if he wished, the diver could turn around and return to the surface.

The depth here is 40 metres. He has spent the past seven minutes wriggling through a clenched fist of stone with nowhere to go except deeper. It's a nightmare scenario for most people, terrifying and surely fraught with danger.

Yet the hazards are mostly an illusion. The shaft is tight, but passable. The diver has ample air to breathe and his equipment is reliable. In the unlikely event that his regulator fails, a backup hangs at his neck. To an experienced diver, the trip down the narrow shaft is more tedious than perilous. Getting from top to bottom of that tight, dark passage is a mental trick, suppressing the terror that would seize most of us.

True danger does exist here, the kind that can snuff out a life like a burning match in a deluge. But it's not in the darkness, and it's not in the tight passage, and it's not in the mass of rock clamping down overhead. The peril is in the cylinder of oxygen hanging at his hip. If he breathes it at the surface, he'll feel clear-headed and suffused with energy; if he breathes it at six metres, it will help to flush the excess nitrogen dissolved in his tissues. But if he breathes it here at 40 metres, it will kill him as surely as a magnum bullet to the brain, and almost as quickly. He will convulse and drown before he breathes a second time.

It is impossible truly to appreciate the feats of extreme divers or to grasp the dangers they face without some understanding of gas physics and the physiological effects of gases when breathed in large doses. Tech divers deal with these realities constantly in planning and executing a dive: they understand the practical application of Dalton's Law of Partial Pressure better than most of us know the basic rules of the highway. This is a world of long and earnest discussions about Equivalent Nitrogen Depth and counter-diffusion; where the hours spent planning a dive, pondering Oxygen Tolerance Units and Maximum Operating Depth, will far exceed a diver's time on the bottom; where a difference in PPO_2 (partial pressure of oxygen) from 1.3 to 3.1 is a matter of heart-stopping drama and urgency.*

---

* The maximum safe partial pressure of oxygen is 1.6. A PPO_2 of 3.1 would put a diver at immediate risk of convulsion and drowning.

It's also a world where the word 'air' is seldom used. That's because advanced divers seldom breathe air at depth. Instead, they talk about 'gas', meaning an inert gas like nitrogen and helium, or a breathing mixture using those elemental gases in some combination with oxygen.

The following four paragraphs are the distilled essence of the science of diving, the absolute bare minimum required to understand what extreme divers do and how they do it:

1. All gases affect the body when breathed underwater, mostly in unfavourable ways; the greater the depth, the more profound the effect.

2. As depth changes, so does the required gas mixture, as divers try to balance the effects of each gas in the mix. Normal air is usually not ideal at any depth.

3. The greater the depth, the greater the pressure required to fill the lungs with each inhalation. On standard (open-circuit) scuba gear, this means increased consumption of gas. Greater depth means greater consumption.

4. Most dives require a plan for a slow ascent, stopping at precise intervals, in order to eliminate inert gases dissolved in the body's tissues. This is *decompression*. Longer and deeper dives require longer decompression. Failing to complete the decompression risks injury or death from decompression illness (DCI) – 'the bends'.

Deco and the virtual ceiling

On the surface, at sea level, our bodies and lungs are under constant pressure from the weight of the air that surrounds us: one atmosphere (ATM) or one bar; 1000 millibars or 1000 hectopascals; approximately 14.7 pounds per square inch. When a diver submerges, the weight of the water above him is added to the weight of the air. Every 10 metres adds one atmosphere of pressure, so that a diver at a depth of 10 metres is under two atmospheres (1 ATM water plus 1 ATM surface). At 30 metres the pressure is four atmospheres (3 ATM water plus 1 ATM surface).

The iconic example is an inflatable beach ball, blown up to full pressure at the surface – that is, 1 ATM of pressure – and pushed under water. Even at the bottom of a 3 metre swimming pool, the ball will begin to lose its shape. At 10 metres, the ball will appear flaccid and shrunken, as 2 ATM of outside pressure push against 1 ATM in the ball. But adding gas through a demand regulator – the way a diver breathes from a pressurized cylinder – will restore the ball's shape as the pressure inside the ball matches the pressure of its surroundings. The ball will retain its shape at any depth so long as it receives enough gas to equalize the outside pressure.

Breathing gas under pressure is how divers can descend to 200 metres or more without discomfort. Gas enters the lungs under pressure – the lungs essentially being the beach ball – and the body's tissues are equalized through the circulatory system.

But that comes with two penalties.

Increased depth means that a greater quantity of gas is needed to equalize the pressure. At 100 metres, the gas required to fill the lungs is 11 times greater than at the surface (10 ATM water pressure plus 1 ATM surface). If the exhaled gas is vented out into the water, as with conventional scuba gear, the rate of consumption is ferocious.

It also means that the surfaces of the lungs are exposed to a dosage of gases that is far greater than usual. From the lungs, inert gases – nitrogen, helium, or both – are dissolved into arterial blood. Because the pressure of the gases in the blood is greater than the pressure of the tissues, dissolved gases are forced into the tissues.

There they remain until the diver begins to ascend. Then the flow is reversed. When the surrounding pressure becomes lower, the pressure in the lungs and the arteries drops. Gases leave the tissues and return to the bloodstream and leave the body through the lungs. If the diver ascends slowly, this migration is a controlled seepage. If the pressure changes too quickly, the gases will surge out and form micro-bubbles in the tissues and in the bloodstream, not unlike the way bubbles of carbon dioxide are formed when the cap is removed from a bottle of carbonated drink.

The formation of bubbles creates decompression illness (DCI). In its milder forms DCI is painful but relatively benign: discomfort in the joints is one common symptom. Bubbles can also attack the spinal cord. Some early DCI sufferers were workers on the Brooklyn Bridge, who stayed all day in a pressurized compartment while digging footings for the bridge. When they returned to the surface, they often became hunched over with pain: hence the slang term for the disease: 'the bends'.

If the escaping bubbles become large enough – when, for example, a diver with highly saturated tissues ascends rapidly to the surface – the result may be an arterial gas embolism, mimicking the effects of a stroke or heart attack and causing paralysis or death. To prevent DCI, divers ascend according to a rigid schedule, stopping for different periods at various depths. Deep stops are shorter; shallow stops are always longest, often many times longer than the time spent at the bottom.

Deco is an obligation; it creates a 'virtual ceiling' that blocks a diver from reaching the surface until the debt has been paid off with time under water. Greater depth means greater decompression – often much greater. A 65 metre dive, with 15 minutes at maximum depth, might require more than an hour of decompression. A dive straight to 150 metres, with five minutes spent at that depth, would require more than four hours of deco, most of it between 10 metres and 3 metres.

A decompression schedule takes into account depth, time and the gases breathed during the dive. Every serious dive requires a unique decompression plan. Sophisticated dive computers, usually worn on the wrist, are able to calculate a deco schedule 'on the fly' by taking into account the actual conditions of the dive. But most divers also carry prepared tables as a backup; for their deepest dives, Shaw and Shirley used deco plans that they generated in advance, based on specialized software on PCs.

Toxic O₂, helium tremors, and the 'wah wah effect'

Oxygen is necessary for life. Oxygen kills at depth.

This is the great conundrum of gas planning for extreme diving. Pure oxygen can't be breathed safely below about eight metres. Beyond that, it must be diluted with some inert gas. Nitrogen and helium are the usual choices.

Air itself is a dilution: about 21 per cent oxygen, 79 per cent nitrogen, with some trace gases. It is also cheap and readily available, so for years it was the default breathing gas, even for advanced sports diving. But it is also a compromise, unsuited to really serious depths. A 21 per cent mixture of oxygen becomes potentially toxic at about 65 metres. At that depth, the ideal mixture is about 18 per cent oxygen. At 100 metres, the ideal mixture is about 12 per cent oxygen. At 150 metres, the ideal mixture contains only about 8 per cent oxygen. Normal air breathed at that depth would be lethal.

Air has another drawback as a breathing mixture: nitrogen breathed at depth is highly narcotic, and the greater the depth, the greater the effect. Symptoms vary with individuals, but usually include a narrowing of vision, disorientation, a slowing of thought processes. Many divers are unable to complete elementary arithmetic problems on a slate when breathing air at 45 metres. Often divers retain almost no memory of what they've done while deeply narcotized.

There are also psychological effects. How a person behaves while intoxicated on alcohol often predicts how he'll react to narcosis under water. Those who become morose and moody after a few drinks can experience anxiety and paranoia under nitrogen narcosis. Darkness and unfamiliar surroundings exacerbate the effect. For 'happy drunks', the experience of narcosis can include euphoria so profound that it saps the will to survive. Divers have been known to swim in languid circles, unconcerned, while the pressure in their tanks drops to zero.

Neither paranoia nor slack-jawed euphoria is desirable.

Some who dive truly deep on air report the perception of what seems to be a deafening howl. In an interview for aquaCORPS, a now-defunct tech diving magazine, veteran diver and instructor Bob Raimo described a dive to 110 metres on air:

> At one point I'm saying, this is about my tolerance. I was really getting narked, I'm at the limit ... I took one or two kicks and I went from being completely in control and just about capable of helping someone, into a complete head spin ...
>
> One thing that really scared me was this noise. When I couldn't read my gauges, I heard this noise *wah-wah-wah-wah* really loud. I didn't know what it was. When I heard the noise, I could not see my hand on the cable. All I could see was my gauge. I couldn't see anything else – everything surrounding the gauge was black ... I'm thinking: the next thing that's going to happen is that I'm gonna black out, and I said to myself, 'You're not gonna black out.'
>
> I haven't spoken to a lot of people about this, but at the worst point when I was really fucked up, I can understand how people give in to the euphoric feeling and die in deep water blackouts. Because as scared as I was, I felt fuckin' good. I don't know how you can say you feel good and think you're gonna die at the same time. But I can say this: I could have very easily said, 'Oh, fuck this.' And die.

To reduce narcosis, some helium is added to the mixture for dives below 40 or 50 metres, creating a blend known as 'trimix'. Helium isn't greatly narcotic; in fact, most divers associate it with enhanced clarity of mind. But it has drawbacks. It complicates decompression when mixed with nitrogen. It requires a strictly followed deco plan (nitrogen is more forgiving). It conducts heat extremely well and therefore tends to lower a diver's body temperature, a major problem during long decompressions when divers are often unable to maintain their core warmth.

And in high concentrations, during fast descents to great depth, helium can produce High Pressure Nervous Syndrome (HPNS), with narrowing of vision, dizziness and an involuntary twitching of the extremities. To avoid HPNS, divers are advised to limit their rate of descent. But that increases their time at depth, which increases their decompression obligation. Another way to offset HPNS is to add nitrogen to the breathing mix; yet the purpose of helium in the mix is to avoid exposure to nitrogen.

In short:

To buffer the effects of nitrogen, divers add helium to the mix.

To offset helium, they add nitrogen.

All this while maintaining a level of oxygen as high as it can be without risking convulsions and blackout.

It's a balancing act in search of the least dire effect. Those who feel that they tolerate narcosis well (and many do) will tend to reduce the helium content. Those willing to live with the consequences of helium will keep the nitrogen buffer as low as possible. But below 150 metres, with greater pressures driving the gases, the options become more limited, and some narcosis becomes unavoidable unless nitrogen is completely eliminated from the mix.

Extreme diving involves one more common gas that is potentially lethal at depth. Carbon dioxide, CO_2, is produced when the cells metabolize oxygen. We inhale O_2, we exhale CO_2. Dissolved carbon dioxide is always present in the blood, which carries it from the cells to the lungs, where it is released. When the levels of dissolved carbon dioxide rise to a certain level in arterial blood, the body automatically triggers the breathing cycle. In that sense, CO_2 is actually critical to life. But when arterial pressures of CO_2 are high enough – for example, when exertion at depth causes levels to spike – then CO_2 becomes a sedative and narcotic, powerful enough to cause a blackout.

Beyond 150 metres, beyond 200, humans enter a nether zone where the usual rules no longer apply: a place where compromises with physics and chemistry and human physiology are no longer possible, where even the act of drawing a breath helps to create the conditions for a tragedy.

CHAPTER
6

After his first quick visit to Komati Springs in September 2002, Shaw didn't dive anywhere for almost six weeks. Then in mid-October, he used ten days' leave for another extended trip to the karst caves of central Florida, his fourth visit there in the past two years. He dived with a local instructor, Fred Berg, who had guided him on most of his dives in Florida since Shaw finished his certification with Bill Rennaker.

As usual, Shaw made the most of his time. He logged 18 dives, twice a day on most days, a schedule that was possible because most of the dives were short enough and shallow enough that they required only a couple of hours' recovery on the surface. Typically the dives would last less than an hour and a half, including a few minutes' decompression. The divers might penetrate about 600 or 700 metres along the horizontal passages before one of them – often Shaw, but not always – reached the turnaround point on his gas supply. Such diving was remarkable for a 48-year-old man with less than three years' experience. Yet it was fairly routine by the standards of the locale and the sport. On most weekends, dozens of divers would enter the more popular holes and safely follow the same routes, reaching the same distances and beyond.

Shaw now had more than sixty dives in the local sinkholes and caves, and in some places he followed passages that he had seen four or five times already. As he gained more experience and learned to moderate his gas consumption, he might swim thirty or fifty metres farther before he hit the turnaround pressure on his tanks, but he was essentially diving the same caves over and over again. This was not so much exploration as tourism.

He did enter one cave that he had never before seen: Cathedral Canyon Spring, on property that Sheck Exley had owned outside the town of Live Oak, where he had taught mathematics in the local public school system. Exley had bought the property specifically to guarantee himself access to the cave, and in 1990 he managed a 3500 metre solo penetration of the system, a feat that immediately entered the sport's lore. Visibility at Cathedral is often too poor for diving, but on this trip Shaw caught near-perfect conditions and he was able to do three trips into the system with Fred Berg.

The cave was huge. In some spots, the permanent guideline stretched across chambers so large that the walls were beyond the reach of his cave light.

'A special dive', he noted in his logbook after his first visit. It was the 191st dive of his life.

*   *   *

Shaw's second visit to Komati Springs came on 7 November 2002, two months after the first. It was another 'drive and dive' trip, beginning with his 06.45 arrival in Johannesburg in the captain's seat of Cathay 749, meeting a driver with a car, where he slept much of the 320 km trip.

This time, he had brought his own drysuit and he rented a set of twin cylinders. Don Shirley was busy that day at the dive centre, but he gave Shaw directions to reach the fourth level of the mine, where the depth is about 51 metres, and loaned him a reel with line, for use if he wanted to swim off the fixed lines.

The dive was an embarrassment for Shaw. He wasn't able to find the vertical shaft that runs down from the first level, and while he was searching, he dropped Shirley's reel through a steel grate on the floor. He managed to retrieve it and finally surfaced after more than an hour at a maximum depth of 18 metres.

He had time for a second dive. Shirley sketched a quick map of the first level, showing the way to the shaft. This time Shaw found the way. Below the first level, visibility was as good as the clearest underwater cave, and Shaw spent an enjoyable 49 minutes working his way down to 51 metres, looking through the mazelike system of tunnels and rooms. His wrist seals leaked slightly, and he got cold during the ten minute decompression before he came to the surface.

That night, after the long drive back, he checked into the crew hotel in Johannesburg. He had one good dive to show for the effort and the expense. He liked Komati Springs, but nothing he had seen there so far would have led him to believe that his diving destiny lay in South Africa.

*   *   *

Shaw didn't return for five months.

He logged 43 dives during that time. The first 26 of those were rebreather-training dives at Puerto Galera in the Philippines, where he made several trips of two or three days in the free time between his flight duties during December 2002 and January 2003. Most of his dives were in the 40–50 metre range, practising drills at sites that he now knew well.

After his final day in Puerto Galera, nearly two months passed before he was back in the water. In March 2003, he flew to Mexico's Yucatan Peninsula, where he joined Fred Berg and his wife, Carol Berg, for a week of diving in the limestone sinkholes that honeycomb the area near the coast, around the town of Tulum.

These holes, known as cenotes, are some of the most inviting and least threatening underwater caves in the world. The water is warm and the depths are usually negligible: many caves are so shallow that tree roots grow through the ceiling. The passages tend to be roomy, current flow is light, and the walls and floors are often as white as confectioner's sugar, so that they seem to throw off a glow when they're swept by the beam of a cave light.

They're spectacularly beautiful. Most were originally air caves until they were flooded by changes in the water table and the level of the Gulf of Mexico, and they often contain amazing mineral displays that were formed by dissolved limestone dripping through the walls and ceilings.

The shallow depths allow virtually unlimited diving without decompression. Shaw and the Bergs racked up 17 dives in seven days, including some of the most popular systems in the area – Mayan Blue, Taj Mahal, Temple of Doom – places that thousands of divers have visited over the past two decades. His final dive of the trip was to the Cenote called Car Wash. It is perhaps the most heavily travelled of all the flooded caves in the Yucatan, a place where many hundreds of novice divers and cave diving students have left their ignominious marks, inadvertently breaking and scarring the delicate mineral formations as they struggle with their buoyancy.

It was an odd place to find Dave Shaw. For more than two years he had aggressively pushed his own limits, seeking out difficult training and dives that would stretch his limits. Ann was convinced that he enjoyed diving more for the challenge than for the intrinsic experience. But the Yucatan caves are all about the experience. They're interesting and engrossing – often amazing – but for a diver of Shaw's skills, they were elementary.

When Shaw began to dive, he'd had no trouble satisfying his taste for difficulty. Everything was difficult at first. Now true challenges were becoming harder to find. The well-worn caves of central Florida and the Yucatan could hardly placate the urge for exploration.

But exploration was an improbable goal in any case. He was 20 years too late for that.

In cave diving, exploration means 'pushing the line' – penetrating to the end of the furthest length of permanent guideline and then swimming beyond, into a place where nobody has ever swum, unspooling new line from a reel, creating a new guideline for others to follow. Or it may mean a traverse: finding a new connection between two different systems. But most of the realistic solo pushes and traverses had already been made, years before Shaw ever pulled on a dive mask; Sheck Exley's amazing penetration at Cathedral was the last of the great single-handed feats. Virgin cave still existed, but reaching it was a task for teams, with groups of divers caching stores of cylinders along the known route, sometimes weeks in advance, like Sherpas setting up base camps on the flanks of a Himalayan peak in preparation for a final push to the summit.

That approach meant spending weeks on site and endless hours devoted to organization and logistical detail. Shaw didn't have the time organize an expedition, nor probably the inclination. And he certainly didn't see himself as an interchangeable cog in someone else's organization.

One facet of sport diving was still open to him. Extreme deep diving has always attracted adventurous individuals who want to test the limits. It's relatively accessible in terms of expense and opportunity, and although a really deep dive usually requires some support in the water, the logistical demands aren't as great as for an ongoing expedition.

Most important to Dave Shaw, deep diving provided endless prospects for challenge. It would never become routine.

Shaw didn't explicitly set out to seek extreme depth. But he wasn't ready to become a cave tourist. He wanted to explore, if not virgin cave passage, then his own inner terrain. He didn't dive again for five weeks after he left the Yucatan. By the end of that time, his direction was clear – if there had ever been any real doubt.

He never again strapped on the twin scuba tanks that are the tools of the journeyman tech diver. Instead, he purchased a rebreather, the Inspiration, from the firm Ambient Pressure Diving, in Cornwall.

He never again hired a guide; thereafter, almost every important dive was a solo, and when he dived with someone else – usually with Don Shirley – it was as co-equal.

He never returned to Florida or to the Yucatan. If he wanted to take himself beyond the multitudes, the direction was straight down, and Komati Springs was the place to start.

* * *

The dive centre at Komati Springs is a low, whitewashed stucco building shaded by broad-leaf trees that give the place a somewhat tropical feel. Inside the building are a classroom, an equipment showroom, several dorm-style bedrooms, and a workshop. A tank filling station sits outside, on a roofed veranda, and on busy weekends the machine gun rapping of the compressor motor rattles off the walls almost non-stop.

Here the business of diving is conducted. Breathing gases are planned and pumped, dive plans calculated, equipment fussed over. Often one or more rebreathers sit on the sturdy bench outside the office, shrouds removed, innards exposed, as divers perform maintenance that is simultaneously routine and critical.

The actual dive site hole is about a kilometre away, hidden on the other side of a rocky knob. Divers load their gear into a vehicle and drive along a road of gravel and russet dirt that tracks along the base of the hill, past aloe plants that grow as tall as a man. Off to the right side, the road serves up a sublime view of the Komati valley, broad and serene. Then the road bends and dips, and it ends suddenly at a bare patch that overlooks the big water-filled crater that was the mine pit.

It is in fact a lovely spot. All traces of the mine's operation are long gone. The grounds around the edge of the hole have been groomed and replanted, and any signs of mining within the pit itself are covered by water, up to 50 metres deep in places. The water level is about 10 metres below the edge of the pit. A set of concrete stairs descends about halfway down to the water, and a steel ladder reaches the rest of the distance. A platform of steel mesh on pontoons floats beside the ladder, and after divers have entered the water they usually stop here to adjust their gear, pull on their fins, and make a last check of their equipment before starting down.

From the platform, students and novice divers head out into the open water of the hole. But cave divers descend about 12 metres and swim along the side of the pit. The water is clear, more like a spring than a pond, a year-round 16°C at the bottom, warming to about 25°C near the surface in the summer. A swim of a minute or two brings a diver to a grotto-like opening in the wall of the pit. At the back of the grotto is a rough-hewn tunnel, about two metres wide, descending at a gentle angle. This is the entrance to the multi-level maze of the flooded mine workings.

Dave Shaw came to know that tunnel nearly as well as he knew the ramp of his parking garage in Hong Kong. During a seven-month period beginning in April 2003, he returned to Komati Springs 11 times. Except for a few days of training at Puerto Galera, he dived nowhere else during that time. Every significant dive in his log began with his leaving the platform at the surface and swimming down into the tunnel. Before the year was over, he had become one of the world's most accomplished deep divers. And he had found a friend.

CHAPTER
7

Don Shirley was a rebreather evangelist. He believed wholly in the machines. He found unabashed joy in diving to remote places, and he saw rebreathers as a means for others to share the experience. Used with trimix gases, they were powerful tools to push back the practical limits of sports diving. He promoted rebreathers to his advanced students, and he took pleasure in watching veteran divers flourish on them after years of stagnating with open-circuit diving.

He saw it often at Komati Springs. The logistical difficulties of going long and deep on standard scuba are usually more than a weekend diver can manage, and a longtime open-circuit diver might repeat the same few dives several times a year, year after year, stymied by the practical drawbacks of the system. But that same diver would blossom on a rebreather, easily going places in the mine where he had never ventured before.

This was the future of diving, Shirley believed. And Dave Shaw represented the new generation of divers who were open to the technology. Under Shirley's influence, and with his help, Shaw saw the possibilities and began using rebreathers to open up depths that had previously been accessible only to a few elite explorers.

The question of whether deep diving *should* be more accessible was a subject for debate. Rebreathers themselves – and in particular, the Inspiration that Shirley favoured and that Shaw chose for his first machine – were also controversial.

To understand the debate, it's necessary to understand how rebreathers work and how they differ from open-circuit scuba.

Open-circuit is a one-way system. A first-stage regulator, attached to the valve of a pressurized tank, distributes high-pressure gas to a second-stage regulator with a mouthpiece. When the diver draws in a breath, the suction opens a demand valve, admitting gas at the same pressure as the surrounding water. When the diver exhales, the system expels the exhaled gas through the mouthpiece, out into the water, as a cloud of bubbles. It's gone and lost. Yet except for the addition of some carbon dioxide and the loss of some metabolized oxygen, the gas which goes out is identical to the gas that went in. If that gas could be recaptured, the CO_2 removed and some oxygen added, it could be used again, and again, and again.

That's what rebreathers do.

A closed-circuit rebreather is fundamentally a loop of flexible pipe, hanging around the diver's neck. Plumbed into the back of the loop is a canister filled with grainy chemical that absorbs carbon dioxide. A mouthpiece at the front means that this is a *breathing loop*, with the diver's lungs becoming part of the system. The lungs act as a pump, pushing gas around the loop and through the canister; an ingenious mechanical valve in the mouthpiece ensures that the flow circulates in one direction, with the exhaled breath – containing carbon dioxide – moving towards the scrubber canister, while the diver inhales only the purified gas from the canister.

The chemical filter is the heart of the system. The brain is an electronic module clamped to the top of the canister. Three sensors monitor the oxygen content of the gas in the loop. When the percentage falls below a level that the diver has specified, electrically operated solenoids inject small amounts of oxygen into the loop, replacing the oxygen that the diver has metabolized during the previous breath. A 'diluent' gas from another tank – air or a mixed gas – dilutes the oxygen and equalizes pressures within the loop to the pressure of the surrounding water. Electronic consoles allow the diver to monitor the system and set oxygen levels.

The advantages over open-circuit scuba are immense.

Because the loop is closed, the only gas consumed is the small amount of oxygen metabolized by the diver, an amount that stays constant regardless of depth. *In terms of consumption, there's no difference between breathing at the surface and breathing at 200 metres.* An open-circuit diver will consume 21 times more gas at that depth than at the surface. It is an axiom of diving that no emergency is hopeless so long as you have gas to breathe; with a rebreather, the gas is virtually limitless.

There are other advantages. By maintaining a maximum safe level of oxygen, the rebreather allows divers to reduce their decompression times.

And because it is constantly being moved through the lungs, the gas in the loop is nearly at body temperature, while gas breathed through a scuba regulator is usually much cooler. The warmth is significant on long immersions, where a drop in the body's core temperature can complicate decompression and can even become life-threatening.

There are drawbacks. Electronics can fail, and although divers can operate the machine manually, the procedure is tedious and demanding; in essence, a diver on a closed-circuit rebreather is staking his life on a system powered by batteries and immersed in deep water at high ambient pressure.

Also, the chemical scrubber can be used for only three to eight hours, depending on the size of the canister. When it begins to fail, CO_2 levels climb – insidiously so, since there is no mechanism for measuring the CO_2 in the loop. Rebreather divers are trained to monitor not just the electronic status of the machine but also their own sensations, watching for the onset of CO_2 buildup and for the symptoms of oxygen toxicity (if the machine adds too much oxygen) or hypoxia (if it adds too little).

In contrast, open-circuit equipment is reliable and undemanding. The equipment has been proved over millions of dives. Open-circuit divers need to watch only the tank pressure gauge, a depth gauge and a timer. But because standard scuba equipment becomes increasingly inefficient at depth, the usual system of two back-mounted tanks – the 'twinset' – imposes a practical limit. Diving below about 150 metres requires additional tanks, either mounted at the sides, at the back, or both.

For very deep dives, the configurations can be bizarre: racks of multiple cylinders, even dual racks, totalling five, six, seven cylinders, the setup so bulky that the diver couldn't do anything more than follow the shot line to the bottom and begin to ascend, and he would have to do that almost immediately.

Yet in 2003, the use of a rebreather for even standard tech diving – let alone extreme depth – was controversial. Critics claimed that rebreather divers were unpaid test pilots. Not all owners disagreed.

The rebreather that Shaw chose, and that Shirley used most often, was the subject of special scrutiny. In the two years after its introduction, at least eight divers perished while using Inspirations: a startling total, considering that fewer than 1000 units were in use around the world at that time. By 2003, the total was at least 15. Inspirations were easily identifiable by their blocky, neon yellow covers. Posters on Internet message boards, some of them Inspiration owners, began referring to the machine as YBOD – Yellow Box of Death.*

None of the fatalities could be directly related to the machine. Many were the result of diver error, though the relative complexity of the machines seemed to invite error.

The added demands were no problem for Shaw. Years of experience as an airline pilot had made him the perfect candidate for a rebreather. Scanning LED readouts, maintaining

---

* To some, more wryly, it was the Yellow Box of Debt, referring to the 2003 price of approximately £3000, and the ongoing expenses of maintenance.

mental checklists, staying alert for the electronic alarms that signalled a possible malfunction – he did this every working day from the captain's seat of an Airbus. Thousands of times, in simulators, he had calmly worked through task lists in emergency situations.

For Shirley, diving the Inspiration was a near-mystical act. He savoured the experience of unobtrusively slipping into dark, silent places, undisturbed by exhaled gas bursting through the exit valve; he described feeling at one with the machine, attuned to his own physiological sensations and to the rebreather's subtle workings, his body an organic component of the system. And while most rebreather divers were not quite so effusive, many did become reluctant to use open-circuit once they had come to appreciate the machines. In some cases they were slow even to go off the loop and use their open-circuit emergency tanks when the machine lost its electronics during a dive; they preferred to operate the rebreather manually, rather than to exhale gouts of bubbles half a dozen times a minute while the needle turned towards empty.

Some critics argued that closed-circuit rebreathers worked *too* well: not that they were excessively reliable but that they allowed divers to reach depths and run times that were beyond their ability and experience. And because the advantage of rebreathers increased with depth, the machines seemed at least subliminally to tempt the diver into greater depth, if only to fully enjoy the machine's capability.

It was almost a philosophical argument.

Open-circuit symbolized certainty and compromise; rebreathers, innovation and potential risk.

Open-circuit meant prudence; rebreathers denoted confidence.

Open-circuit represented the slow accretion of accomplishment, limits gradually pushed; rebreathers promised stunning advancement to those who would use the machines boldly.

A diver's choice of life support defined his approach to the sport. It could even be said to define his approach to life. Shirley and Shaw knew exactly where they stood on the scale.

*   *   *

The pages of Dave Shaw's diving log are studded with remarkable acts described in the laconic manner of a professional airman. He wasn't much impressed with his own feats and he was more likely to dwell on the minutiae of his gear configuration than on the events of the dive. But sometimes the circumstances are so gripping that even Shaw's casual phrases can't conceal the drama, nor his fortitude and commitment. His dive on 5 April 2003 was one of those times.

It was his first dive at Komati Springs in more than five months, and Shaw's equipment had changed since the last time Don Shirley saw him. Dave was geared up like a man ready to do some serious diving.

The most obvious difference was Shaw's new Inspiration rebreather, a powerful tool for deep, extended dives. Shaw's rig was also fitted with a small external cylinder: not for breathing, but filled with argon gas to inflate his drysuit. Because of its high density, argon is a more efficient insulator than air, and when pumped into a drysuit, it helps a diver to stay warm during long immersions. It was a sign that Shaw expected to be spending hours at a time in the water, doing the long decompressions that very deep dives require.

A third change was more subtle but just as telling: it was an outlet valve near the right knee of his drysuit, which had been added during the past several weeks. With a catheter condom attached inside, it allows a male diver to urinate into the water; it's an absolute essential during the extended deco stops that are mandatory for deep dives.

Shaw had all the new equipment when he arrived in Johannesburg from Hong Kong on the morning of the 5th. The Inspiration travelled as luggage in a plastic storage crate. Shaw had hoped to dive with Shirley to a level past 50 metres. But when Shaw arrived at Komati Springs around mid-morning he found Shirley occupied with a balky pump. Although Shaw did get his tanks filled after a delay of several hours, Shirley wasn't available to dive in the afternoon.

Although he barely knew the mine below the first level and hadn't seen it at all in almost half a year, Shaw decided to do the dive solo.

It would be his first cave dive with the Inspiration.

It would be his first time using the drysuit with the Inspiration (his training dives were all in the warm waters of the Philippines).

It was his first time diving solo with the Inspiration (all his previous dives on the rebreather had been with a very experienced instructor in Puerto Galera, Frank Doyle).

Shaw knew that piling firsts into a single major dive was an invitation to disaster. The cautious approach would be to ease into the new configuration. But Shaw would be leaving in less than 24 hours, and he didn't know when he would get his next chance to do the dive he really wanted to do. He didn't have time for prudence. He *never* had enough time. He decided to stick with his original plan to go deep: down into the 67 metre sixth level of the mine, if he could find it. He filled the rebreather's diluent tank and his bailout cylinder with a gas mixture suitable past 60 metres. A few minutes before 3 pm, he descended alone from the edge of the platform and made his way down to the entrance tunnel and into the mine.

He swam to the shaft that provides a direct descent into the lower levels of the mine. It was at the other side of a small square hatch, an opening with a steel frame. Months later, Shaw would come close to death in that hatch. But on this day, he squeezed through and dropped down the shaft. He was on his way down when an alarm from the Inspiration's controller caused him to slow his descent: oxygen levels climbed too high in his breathing loop, and he had to flush the gas from the loop to bring the level down. Finally he dropped until he reached the entrance to the sixth level, and he left the shaft and began to swim.

He stayed at that level for ten minutes, bottoming out at 69 metres. Finally the reality of the circumstances began to close in on him. He worried that his single bailout cylinder might not be enough to get him to the surface, and he felt a sense of isolation settle in his mind.

It was time to leave. He began to ascend. Two hours after he had started down, he pulled himself up onto the platform.

'It all went OK,' he wrote later in the log, 'but I was working a little hard due all the new stuff.'

It was Dive 249 in his logs.

For the first time, he had bid a flight schedule that let him stay overnight at Komati Springs, and he did a shorter dive the next morning before he returned to Johannesburg. But he wasn't able to dive again for another six weeks. At home, he used the Internet to research ways of improving the Inspiration. When he had three free days in mid-May, he flew to Puerto Galera for a series of short dives to test different configurations of the equipment. He tried fixing additional cylinders to the chassis, to extend its endurance. He meticulously recorded the effects of each new tweak, but after several different tries he still wasn't comfortable with the arrangement – speaking like a pilot, he said that it gave him an 'aft centre of gravity', pushing his legs down and raising his shoulders above the horizontal.

'Too unwieldy. Fighting to stay horizontal,' he wrote on his last day in Puerto Galera. 'This rig is a failure.'

Then he was back to Komati Springs, from a quick series of 'drive and dive' visits, one or two days, each time diving solo to the sixth level, 67 metres.

29 May – 66 metres, duration 1:29 solo

30 May – 67 metres, 1:24 solo

19 June – 67 metres, 2:32 solo

19 July – 67 metres, 1:22 solo

On the morning of 20 July – Shaw's 49th birthday – Shirley suited up and went along. It was their first time diving as a pair, and they both found it exhilarating. Shirley showed Shaw an alternate route down to the sixth level, and there they spent nearly half an hour exploring the tunnels and excavated rooms. Shaw found that with Shirley along, he saw more of the level than ever before. For Shirley, it was a rare chance to dive for the pleasure of it. Though he logged hundreds of hours a year, nearly all of his time in the water came as an instructor. Shirley loved teaching, but the responsibilities were grave. Even when he dived with friends, they were almost always former students, and he could never stop feeling watchful and responsible.

But Shaw had never been his student. They dived as equals, and Shirley could abandon himself to the sheer pleasure of what he called 'the dance': Shaw matching him move for move, effortlessly turning corners and slipping through passages, both transformed for a short time into creatures not quite of this earth, cruising through the maze with no point but the pleasure of it.

'Great dive!' Shaw wrote.

A standard part of all dive logs is a line for the signature of a trainer or a dive companion, to verify the details. In Shaw's book, the form read:

Instructor/Buddy Signature _____

When Shirley signed the page for that dive – it was Number 262 – he crossed out the first word of that line, and underlined the second in bold strokes.

*   *   *

After that dive, André Shirley always knew when Dave was going to visit. She could see it in her husband's face, his happy anticipation when the date grew close. Don and Dave were becoming friends.

It was a natural. The two men had much in common. Both were bright and inquisitive. Both were liked and respected. Shaw was more direct, more obviously driven, but both were genial and fundamentally decent men.

They grew closer when Shaw stayed for week-long visits in August and October, while continuing to schedule his drive-and-dive appearances. Usually when he stayed overnight – sometimes at the dive centre, sometimes at a resort in the nearby town of Badplaas, later in the Shirleys' guest cottage – Shaw would spend the evening with the Shirleys, and after dinner they would sit and chat.

Don and André welcomed the company. Though both loved their home and its spectacular setting, it was an isolated place. Friends passed through sometimes on weekends, up from Johannesburg or Pretoria for a weekend of diving, but when they stayed for dinner on Saturday night the conversation would usually turn into an ad hoc dive training seminar, with the visitors quizzing Shirley on some arcane aspect of technical diving.

Shaw wasn't like that. He preferred to talk about politics, pop culture, current events – almost anything but diving. He entertained with stories of flying, and Shirley told stories of the military. When they talked about diving at all, it was not so much technical details as their shared passion for the sport. Don had long felt isolated: not just geographically but by what he could do and where he could go, and what he had

experienced, all of which were beyond most people's reckoning. The cave is where I live wasn't some fatuous overstatement. For Shirley, it was literally the truth: his visits to the depths were some of the most profound experiences of his existence, and he could share it with almost no one, because unless you could go there as well, you had no chance of empathy. And almost nobody could go where Shirley went.

But now he had Shaw. Dave understood. Dave knew. Because where Don went, Dave could go.

And he was about to go beyond even that.

CHAPTER
8

Though he had dived there constantly for more than seven years, some parts of the flooded mine were still a mystery to Don Shirley. He knew the upper levels very well, but the deeper sections defied easy exploration.

Shirley still didn't know how deep the mine was at its deepest part. He knew where that deepest part was: it was an inclined shaft that descended from the bottom of the seventh level. But he didn't know how far down it ran. A guideline ran part of the way down that incline, to a depth of 152 metres. From that point, the passage continued angling down. Nobody had been deeper.

In August 2003, Shirley organized a week-long gathering of six advanced divers, including Shaw, at Komati Springs. In some ways the project was a prototype for the team that he would assemble at Bushman's Hole a year and a half later, with divers from five different nations, all on Inspirations. The objective was to push the end of the line as far it could go: to 'hole out' the deep incline. Shaw, Shirley and a Canadian diver, Glenn Campbell, were to do the big push together.

Shaw had never before been part of such an ambitious and complex dive. On the final setup dive, Shirley, Shaw and Campbell planned to swim to the end of the line in the incline, at 120 metres, and drop three tanks of emergency gas – 'bailout cylinders' – that they would use for the final dive, two days later. Other divers had already placed different mixtures higher up on the route. This was classic expedition-style diving, simplified by the fact that the dive centre was just a short drive away, with all the divers using rebreathers. Though Shirley didn't know how deep the incline would run, he had mixed the deepest bailout gas as a '6/70,' just 6 per cent oxygen, 70 per cent helium, safe for use as deep as 200 metres. The mixture was labelled on each bottle, black marking pen on duct tape. A second label showed the depth at which each tank was supposed to be placed during the setup dives.

Shaw had never before been below 100 metres, so the setup alone was heady stuff. The three divers dropped straight down the main shaft, the same route Shaw usually used for his regular trips to the 67 metre sixth level. But this time they continued down to the bottom of the shaft, 107 metres, and then swam for four minutes down a horizontal passage in the bottom level. The inclined shaft was offset from the tunnel, and easy to miss, but Shirley knew the way. He led them down. The shaft sloped at a continuous 35°, falling two feet for every body length that they swam. This demanded some exquisite diving skills. Touching bottom is anathema for cave divers: it inevitably means raising a cloud of silt that cuts visibility to near-zero. Scraping the ceiling with tanks or a rebreather is also bad form, a shabby way to treat life-support equipment. The three divers had to adjust their buoyancy with every breath to stay within the narrow zone between the ceiling and the floor.

They reached the end of the line, remained for about a minute, then dropped the extra cylinders and started back the way they had come. The greater depth meant greater decompression: nearly three hours, after a 20 minute trip to the end of the line. At 3.18, it was an hour longer than any dive Shaw had ever done.

Shirley scheduled a full day's rest, giving them nearly 48 hours to recover before the big push. On the morning of the dive, as he checked out the rebreather before going down to the water, Shaw found two problems with the Inspiration. First he repaired a leaking hose. Then one of the three oxygen cells failed as he was doing his final checkout of the electronics. These critical pieces measure the O_2 level in the breathing loop. Shaw replaced the cell, checked the machine one more time, and climbed down the ladder to the water.

Shirley, Shaw and Campbell gathered in the water, floating at the side of the platform. They fitted their masks, checked the readings one last time on the rebreathers' electronic handsets and switched on the lamps of their cave lights.

Shaw's torch wouldn't come on. He waggled the switch of the battery pack at his right hip. But the lamp stayed dark.

Shirley immediately called off the dive.

Like many serious divers, Shirley (and Shaw) followed a 'three-strike' rule: any three unforeseen problems will force a dive to be postponed for at least 24 hours. It's partly superstition – 'Fate is sending a message, and we'd better pay attention' – but there's a sound practical basis. Diving requires mental focus and a period of mental preparation. Shaw could have replaced the light in a few minutes, but the third mishap put him past the arbitrary threshold.*

The three divers climbed out of the water and went to rest and wait.

But the delay didn't end the problems. And the next day, the mishaps took place underwater. As Shaw and Shirley and Campbell approached the entrance tunnel, gas bubbles began to appear from one of the fittings of Shirley's rebreather. Don swam on a short distance, then aborted his dive. They had all agreed beforehand that if anyone had a problem before they reached the bottom level, the other two would continue on.

They stopped briefly; Shirley gave a goodbye wave and Shaw and Campbell swam into the tunnel. Once again they entered the long vertical shaft and dropped toward the bottom. But they were slower than they should have been, and when they reached the new end of the line at 148 metres, they had no time left to push on. Instead, they turned to begin their ascent and decompression.

---

* Peter Herbst, the Pretoria instructor, calls it the 'three-on-a-match' rule: at night, in WWI, soldiers in the trenches were said to be wary of lighting three cigarettes from a single match, because keeping the fire burning long enough for the third cigarette might give a sniper time to take aim on the flame.

Still it was a notable day for Shaw: 148 metres (another computer showed 152), 3 hours and 59 minutes. For Campbell, it was memorable in another way; soon after he surfaced he complained of pain in his shoulder and elbow, so Shirley drove him to Pretoria for treatment of what was diagnosed as a Type One decompression injury. Though Campbell and Shaw had followed the same profile, staying together the entire time, only Campbell was affected, and after a day of rest, Shaw and Shirley finished off the week with a 108 metre dive, laying line down another shaft that had never been explored: another shaft with no end in sight.

Shaw returned six weeks later to finish them both.

* * *

In planning to take the Inspirations beyond the 150 metre depth, Shaw and Shirley were entering unknown territory in more than one way. Nobody knew how the rebreathers would hold up under the pressures of such depths.

The machine's operating manual contained this:

40 m – max. Depth with air diluent.

100 m – max. Depth at which all rebreather parameters are proven: CO_2 endurance, O_2 control and work of breathing.

110 m – max. Depth at which the work of breathing has been tested using trimix diluent.

150 m – max. Depth at which the work of breathing has been tested with a heliox diluent.

160 m – Depth at which all components are pressure tested during type approval (not during production).

WARNING! Diving deeper than 100 m carries the following additional risks.

Deeper than 100 m: CO_2 endurance unknown.

Deeper than 100 m: Onboard decompression invalid.

Deeper than 130 m: Depth gauge inaccurate.

Deeper than 160 m: Structural integrity of components unknown – the air cavity within the buzzer will implode eventually, and other components may fail.

Shaw and Shirley and others routinely flouted the 100 metre recommendation every time they reached the bottom of the main shaft at Komati Springs. Nobody was known to have used the machine as deep as 150 metres on an actual dive. The manufacturer had pressure-tested a prototype to 160 metres, but individual machines weren't tested before sale.

At 150 metres, the surrounding pressure is 16 times greater than normal air pressure at the surface, and the effects of such constant pressure can be unpredictable. Depth or pressure gauges can seize up, the needles sticking in place. Any part with an air cavity is especially susceptible. The glass face of gauges can crack and flood; if the glass is even slightly scratched, that scratch will become a failure point, with the glass cracking inward along the exact line of the defect. On the Inspiration, one of the most vulnerable areas was the alarm buzzer, located near the top of the unit, at the diver's left shoulder. It contained a small sounding chamber where the pressure wasn't equalized, so that at 150 metres, 16 atmospheres of pressure were pushing against one atmosphere inside. The chamber would give way at some depth, but nobody could say when.

Shaw arrived for a week of diving on 18 October, which was a Saturday morning. Don Shirley was busy with a trimix class, but he had already blended several cylinders of gas according to a plan that he and Shaw had worked out by email. While he was preparing to dive, Shaw met Lo Vingerling, a Dutch-born 57-year-old developer and businessman who was up from Johannesburg for a weekend of diving. Vingerling was a good friend of Don and André, one of Don's early students, and an Inspiration owner. He was a well-liked man with a vivid history; his friends tell a story of Vingerling escaping from Mozambique during that country's civil war, driving a Jaguar across the border at high speed with one of the armed factions in hot pursuit.

Shaw met him when they ran pre-dive checks of their rebreathers side by side on a bench at the dive centre. Shaw invited Vingerling along on the setup dive, and Vingerling carried in a couple of tanks. Fourteen months later, Vingerling would be one of the support divers during the attempted body recovery at Bushman's Hole.

Shaw did a second, deeper setup dive on Sunday morning, dropping three more tanks, the deepest at 122 metres, part way down the incline.

On Monday he made a short trip to 68 metres to reposition tanks. It was his third consecutive day of diving: he was essentially acting as his own support crew.

90

At 9.18 on Tuesday morning, he set off on the big push. Don Shirley was nearby, floating beside the platform, and would follow him in by 15 minutes so as to meet him near the bottom of the main shaft as Shaw was returning.

Shaw carried two bailout tanks with deep mixtures. And he had a reel, wound with 150 metres of cave line, clipped to his harness. He swam directly to the entrance tunnel, through the first level, to the steel-framed hatch that was the entry to the main shaft. The hatch was too tight for him to enter with both tanks; he removed one, pushed it in ahead of him, and then squeezed past the restriction.

He started down the shaft. On his 148 metre dive with Glenn Campbell in August, he had descended at about 16 metres per minute, a rate that left him no chance to add new line. Now, diving alone, he reached the bottom in nearly half the time. He turned down the horizontal corridor at 107 metres, keeping his torch beam on the taut white string that ran a few centimetres above the floor. He was moving quickly, more than ten minutes ahead of schedule. He turned left at a 'T' in the line and started down the inclined shaft. He had decided earlier that he would turn the dive at a maximum depth of 182 metres, or when his running time hit 30 minutes – whichever occurred first. Less than 20 minutes after he left the platform at the surface, he reached the end of the line at the 148 metre depth. He had at least 10 minutes to continue.

He quickly unclipped the reel, tied off to the end of the line, and headed down the slope. He dropped toward the 160 metre depth ...

... and continued past. The Inspiration was now deeper than anyone had ever taken it. He was focused and intent, checking the depth and oxygen levels on the handset displays, occasionally adding gas to his drysuit to counter the increasing pressures at depth: now 17 times greater than surface pressure and increasing. He listened. The sounds of the rebreather's operation are hushed in a normal environment, almost imperceptible against normal background noise at the surface, but Shaw had no trouble picking them up in the silence of the cave: the tapping of the oxygen solenoid, the gentle gush of diluent gas entering the loop. It all sounded good.

He passed through 170 metres.

Now 180.

Up ahead, he could see the end of the shaft. He was still just at 21 minutes of running time. But 182 was his turn-around depth. He slowed his descent, stopped, tied off the line on a protruding knob of rock and cut the reel free. He had laid 85 metres of new line. He began to ascend.

Shirley met him at the bottom of the shaft, checked that he was OK, and returned to the surface. Five and a half hours later, Shaw climbed out of the water. Nobody had ever taken a closed-circuit rebreather deeper in a cave. And he had done it solo.

In his log book, it was dive number 283.

*   *   *

Finally, the next day, he rested. And he and Don Shirley talked about repeating the dive, this time together. The emergency cylinders were all still in place, down to 122 metres, and would have to be removed anyway. Shirley would carry in one more tank, his emergency gas between 122 and 182 metres.

When they ascended, they could both remove cylinders and bring them out.

Cave divers almost never swim side by side. Even in areas where the passage is wide enough to permit it, they prefer to keep the guideline directly beneath them, where they can reach down and hold the line between their fingertips in case of a silt-out or a light failure. This means that in any but a solo cave dive, there's a leader and a follower. First diver into the cave becomes the leader.

Shaw and Shirley would alternate leading from dive to dive. Batman and Robin, they called it: 'You be Batman today,' one or the other would say as they floated at the surface beside the platform. Then they would usually switch roles the next time. It was a way of acknowledging an equal status. Equal, but different: Shirley was by far the more experienced diver, but Shaw was proving more aggressive and driven.

On this day – it was 23 October 2003 – Shirley led as they retraced Shaw's route from two days earlier. Again down the main shaft, along the corridor, down the incline. Past 160 metres, following the line Shaw had put in two days earlier.

Shirley described it later:

The descent was going well. Dave and I dropped into the tunnel; all was quiet, no noise from bubbles. Bright lights, crystal clarity in the water, and crystal clarity in my mind. We were 'flying'!

At 180, Shirley saw the end of the line. He floated down, covering the last few metres to the wall at the end of the shaft.

With his depth readout showing 186 metres, he waited for Shaw to join him.

But Shaw had stopped his descent, and was headed up.

His Inspiration was crippled. It happened just as Shirley approached the end of the line. Shaw – following a few feet behind Shirley – heard a thump. The Inspiration's master control handset, strapped to his left wrist, went blank. The secondary console, on his right wrist, began flashing.

Shaw waggled his light back and forth, a distress signal, trying to catch Shirley's attention. But Shirley was looking the other way, still headed down to the bottom.

Shaw turned and started back up the passage. As he swam up, he was able to restart the master console by repeatedly turning it off and on, but he knew that something was wrong. From behind his head he heard an unsettling sound, a pinging that he later compared to distant sonar. The buzzer chamber on the rebreather had imploded under a pressure of 19 atmospheres. It disabled the alarm that would warn him if oxygen didn't stay within the safe range.

That alone didn't greatly concern Shaw. He could always monitor the oxygen levels himself, so long as the rebreather's electronics were still functional. But he worried that the pressure would force water through the crack and into the electronics.

Below him, Shirley had turned his dive and was now following him back up the incline. He caught Shaw during their first decompression stop, at 126 metres, still in the incline. They continued together, along the corridor at the seventh level, but as they reached the bottom of the main shaft, both of the handsets on Shaw's machine blinked and went dark.

Shaw turned the blank faces of the headsets to Shirley. The damage didn't surprise Shirley; his backup torch had imploded at almost the same time.

Shaw faced a decision. He could go off the Inspiration and begin breathing from an open-circuit scuba regulator; he was carrying two bailout tanks, each with a regulator filled with gas suitable to at least 30 metres, and more tanks were waiting along his ascent route. The tanks and the regulators were there for a moment exactly like this.

But he could also continue to use the rebreather in 'semi-closed' operation. Although the electronics were disabled, the chemical scrubber wasn't affected and would continue to absorb carbon dioxide. Shaw could breathe from the loop until the oxygen was depleted, about three or four breaths. Then he would have to empty the loop, venting the depleted gas into the water by exhaling forcefully through his nose, where it would discharge around the edges of his mask. Then, with the loop exhausted, he would recharge by pressing a valve button on his right side, just above his waist, injecting gas from an offboard tank.

The drill went like this:

Breathe ... breathe ... breathe ... breathe deep ... VENT ... button ...

Depending on his breathing rate, he would have to repeat cycle every 30 or 40 seconds for at least the next three hours.

The decision was immediate. He would stay on the rebreather. Part of the choice was comfort; he preferred the warmer gas from the rebreather. Gas consumption also figured in his choice. Even though it was disabled, the rebreather would use only about a quarter of the gas of the open-circuit scuba (although there should have been enough gas for both he and Shirley to ascend on open-circuit if necessary).

There is another explanation: once divers become accustomed to rebreathers, they are often reluctant to revert to open-circuit scuba in all but the most extreme emergency. The complexity of manual operation didn't intimidate Shaw. He was sure that he could ride the crippled machine all the way to the surface; he was so confident that he never really considered the alternative.

From the bottom of the main shaft, he ascended to his next deco stop. Shirley had gone slightly deeper than Shaw, so his ascent was slower. Soon a gap of more than 10 metres separated them, and as they climbed, the distance between them increased. They were, essentially, beyond one another's aid.

Shaw continued his ascent, following the rebreather drill.

Breathe ... breathe ... breathe ... breathe deep ... VENT ... button ...

At 68 metres, he plugged one of the cached emergency tanks into the plumbing of the Inspiration.

A slow climb up the shaft, with deco stops every three metres, required about two hours. Finally he found himself at the entrance of the first level. This was the other side of the narrow steel-framed hatch. He was still travelling with two bailout tanks, slung at his left side.

For two hours he had been following the rebreather drill:

Breathe ... breathe ... breathe ... breathe deep ... VENT ... button ...

Now the narrow hatch required him to remove one of his bailout tanks. He unclipped a tank with a mixture of 35 per cent oxygen that he had picked up earlier. He swung it upward, pointing the bottom of the cylinder toward the hatch.

Breathe ... breathe ... breathe ... breathe deep ...

He pushed the cylinder ahead of him, through the hatch, to the other side. Then he began wriggle through ...

... VENT ...

With head and shoulders poking through the hatch, he reached for the button to inject gas into the loop.

He couldn't find the button. It was out of reach, somewhere behind him as he squeezed through the restriction.

His lungs were empty, the loop was empty. He was desperate for a breath. He groped for the open-circuit regulator on the tank that he had just pushed through.

Later, in an email message, he described the moment:

Things were getting desperate. I took an involuntary part 'breath' and swallowed some water. I quite calmly then decided I was about to drown and seemed to cope with that thought without panic. That water ingestion I think did give me incentive for another minute of no-air time though! Anyway ... I eventually found the regulator, took some calming breaths of glorious 35% gas, sorted out the tangle and went back on the loop in semi-closed mode again. Talk about a near-death experience!

He finished the ascent without incident, after operating the machine manually for three and a half hours. Total time of the dive was seven hours.

It was number 284 in his log.

'Quite an exciting dive!' he noted in the book.

*   *   *

He had two more days remaining in his week of diving, and he wasn't done yet. He borrowed a replacement head for the Inspiration, and after resting on Friday, he set off early Saturday morning to explore a shaft off the sixth level. He added new line as he followed it to 139 metres, where it ended at a wall.

He emerged from the six-hour dive with pain in one shoulder. Sudden pain in the joints or muscles at the end of a dive is a strong indication of a decompression injury. Don Shirley was waiting at the platform when Shaw surfaced, and they discussed what Shaw ought to do. The nearest chamber was in Pretoria, three hours away. Shirley recommended in-water recompression, a technique called the 'Australian Method' in which the injured diver resubmerges, breathing 100 per cent oxygen, then very gradually rises to the surface again.

Shaw reluctantly fitted his mask and descended to six metres. The pain quickly disappeared – another classic sign of a decompression injury. The Australian Method usually calls for treatment to start at nine metres, but Shirley shortened it because Shaw's oxygen exposure was already high after the long decompression he had just finished. Shaw rested on a shelf that was part of a fixed scaffold beside the platform.

Shirley stayed with Shaw at the scaffold. André filled several squeeze bottles with water and hot broth that she dropped down on a line, and Don prodded Shaw to drink from the bottles. André contacted the South African office of Divers Alert Network. DAN is a global medical group that insures divers against DCI and coordinates their treatment. A DAN physician now told André that Shaw should be treated at a chamber if the pain continued after the in-water recompression.

Shaw surfaced after two and a half hours in the water; the time was now 2 pm, and he had been under water almost continuously since 6 am.

The pain didn't return at first. Shaw removed all of his gear at the floating platform and climbed slowly out of the water, up the ladder. Shirley drove him to the dive centre and put him to bed, breathing oxygen. But over the next hour, the pain crept back, and in the late afternoon Don drove him to Pretoria.

Shaw took a series of three recompression treatments over the next three days. The first, on Saturday night, was six and a half hours, ending at 3.30 Sunday morning. Between treatments, Shaw stayed with Peter Herbst at his house above the Reef Divers shop in Pretoria. It was the first time they had met, and almost at once Herbst began to joke with him – about the injury, about his beachbum attire, about his Aussie accent – a rough-edged teasing that Herbst calls 'chirping'. Herbst chirped hardest at those whom he liked and respected. He liked Shaw right away and he was greatly impressed by the diving.

On Saturday night, Herbst went along to the hospital with Shaw and Shirley, and was witness to an incident that he still remembered and laughed about years later, a classic *That's diving!* moment. Before Shaw climbed into the chamber, a technician asked him how deep he had been gone during the previous week.

Shaw rattled off the series of depths: '67, 122, 182, 181, 140.'

'Feet?' the technician asked.

'Metres,' Shaw said.

It was one of the most spectacular weeks of deep cave diving ever recorded. And Shaw had done most of it solo, with only incidental support.

The accomplishment went almost unnoticed, even within the insular world of tech diving. Shaw wrote a report for his web pages, but the site got little traffic. Don Shirley wrote an article about his dive to 186 with Shaw, published in a South African diving journal about a year later, but by then it didn't matter. In the months to come, Shaw would far surpass even his own feats, and this time people would notice.

CHAPTER
9

The first scuba divers ever to enter the water at Bushman's Hole arrived at the Mount Carmel farm some time in the late 1970s. Who they were, and exactly when it happened, has never been recorded. They almost certainly drove several hours to get there, and probably used basic scuba equipment, intending to do nothing more than swim and dive in the surface pool. Only a geologist who knew the classic hourglass shape of sinkholes would have guessed that a huge cavity lay below.

The water level in those years was at least 10 metres higher than it was at the time Dave Shaw and Don Shirley dived there; the huge exposed boulder that would be so prominent in later photos of the pool was completely under water, and the edge of the pool extended into the rocks at the base of the rubble pile. It would have been just wide and deep enough to provide a fun, easy dive, splashing around for a day in cold and clear water.

Small groups of divers arrived sporadically over the next few years. Early on, someone must have dived to the bottom and investigated the openings into the cavern below. Soon the word was out. Charles Maxwell, who explored many caves in southern Africa during the 1970s and early 1980s, published a dive report on Bushman's, noting that he had been to 60 metres in the cavern and that there was no bottom in sight.

Nuno Gomes read that report. Gomes was an engineering student at the University of Witswaterrand in Johannesburg, and chairman of the Wits Underwater Club. With a friend, Peter Verhulsel,* he travelled to the coast for a dive on a shipwreck, but they found that the weather was too rough for ocean diving. Gomes remembered Maxwell's dive report. The two students decided that they would try to find the place. After a drive of several hours, they arrived at the town of Kuruman, 60 kilometres east of the hole, and began asking directions. Finally, in a bar, they found someone who told them the way.

The farm was then a cattle ranch, owned since 1954 by a family of famers and ranchers who lived about 300 kilometres away. Gomes and Verhulsel found the resident manager,

---

* In 1984, Verhulsel died in an especially grim cave-diving accident. He wandered off the line while following Gomes and a third diver, Malcolm Keeping, at Sterkfontein, an extensive but shallow cave system near Johannesburg. Gomes and Keeping searched the cave for three hours, but found nothing. Six weeks later, searchers discovered Verhulsel's body in a dry section of the cave. He had climbed out of the water and survived for three weeks before he perished alone in the darkness.

who gave them permission to dive. Their gear was more appropriate for ocean diving than for caves – they had a single torch between them – but they entered the cave and went to 70 metres on air, beyond the throat of the cave and deep enough to sense the vastness of the place.

Gomes was fascinated. Over the next several years he often returned, doing 90 metre 'bounce' dives – descending and then quickly returning to the surface with little or no time at maximum depth. All these dives were on compressed air. Like many deep-diving specialists, Gomes seemed to have a preternatural tolerance for both narcosis and high pressures of oxygen; the sport eliminates anyone who lacks these qualities. Gomes was able to do 90 metres on air while feeling that he was still in control, but most of his diving companions were badly narcosed as they approached those depths, and they could sense the onset of blackout. Then one of his friends lost consciousness at 90 metres, and Gomes had to rescue him, staying with him on ascent to make sure that his mouthpiece stayed in place.

At 90 metres, they were beyond the limits of air.

Gomes began experimenting with trimix, adding helium to air in order to offset narcosis and reduce the proportion of oxygen. He wasn't able to find decompression tables for trimix, but he obtained US Navy tables for compressed air and heliox – oxygen diluted with helium – and he drew from both to create his own trimix schedules, taking into account the 1500 metre elevation at the site.

Gomes successfully tested the new tables during 60 metre dives at Wondergat, an underwater cave northwest of Johannesburg. In early 1988, the day after he received his graduate degree, he dived to 100 metres. Twenty-four hours later he staked his life on his self-designed schedules. Without the customary day of rest after a major dive, he went to 123 metres with Dian Hanekom. They measured the depth from markings on the shot line; they had no gauge that would operate at that depth.

Nuno Gomes continued to experiment with gas mixes, and gradually the world became aware of Bushman's. Sheck Exley arrived in August 1993 for an expedition. Four years earlier, Exley had set the world depth record with a trip to 264 metres at a Mexican spring cave, Nacimiento del Rio Mante. Now Exley intended to try for the bottom of Bushman's, and possibly beat his own record. He enlisted Gomes as one of his support divers.

Exley and Gomes became friendly during the days leading up to Exley's climactic dive. Like everyone else who knew him, Gomes found Exley to be modest, easy-going and friendly. South Africa at the time was a backwater of diving knowledge, and Gomes saw an opportunity to learn from the very best. Gomes hung around Exley as much as possible, making mental notes of how he approached the dive, absorbing all that he could. Exley designed a decompression schedule using a laptop computer with software that incorporated the latest decompression research within its algorithms. Gomes was fascinated, and Exley traded him a copy of the software on a diskette in exchange for Gomes's Casio dive watch.

For the big dive, Exley ran a shot line beside the one Gomes had used in 1988, straight down to the bottom. He descended without knowing how deep the bottom was. Exley was famously resistant to the narcotic effects of nitrogen, but he was less tolerant of the helium in trimix. At about 210 metres, with only blackness beneath him, his vision began to blur, and he experienced some involuntary muscular twitching, the first symptoms of helium-induced High Pressure Nervous Syndrome. He continued down. His vision deteriorated further and the trembling became so violent that he had trouble operating the inflation valve for his buoyancy wings, but he continued down. By the time he reached the bottom, his entire body was shaking. After a struggle, he managed to inject air into his wings, and he rose towards his first decompression stop. The HPNS symptoms slowly abated but didn't disappear until he passed 120 metres. When Gomes saw him leave the water, about eight hours after he had gone in, Exley looked grey-faced and drained. His depth gauges averaged at 263 metres, one metre short of his own world record,

Afterwards, Exley offered Gomes his gear to repeat the dive. Gomes wasn't ready to try the bottom yet, but he did do a 177 metre dive, down the line and back up, wearing only a wetsuit. It was his longest dive yet, four-plus hours in the 19-degree water, breathing 19-degree gas. Though it was far from freezing, it was cold enough to rob him of body heat, and he felt that only adrenaline had got him through his decompression. When he was done, Gomes understood why Exley had seemed so ashen at the end of his dive. Years later, in an interview, he described it this way: *With every breath, you give up a little bit of the life inside you. You're dying by degrees. Even if nothing goes wrong, you'll die if you stay down long enough.*

He had been down only half as long as Exley, and 80 metres shallower. Still, Gomes felt that he now knew what a trip to the bottom would require – the logistics, the equipment and decompression, the mental approach – and he decided that he would prepare to do it himself. But in April 1994, he learned of Exley's death at Zacaton.

For Gomes and for almost every other serious diver in the world, this news was sobering and incomprehensible, a genuine God-is-dead moment. If the best could die doing this, the very best who ever did it, what did that mean for everyone else? For a time, Gomes considered abandoning deep dives. But he relented, and returned to Bushman's for a 231 metre dive that left him with mild symptoms of decompression illness, not severe enough to require a visit to a chamber.

He continued with plans to reach the bottom of Bushman's, not only to match Sheck Exley's feat, but to exceed it if he could.

The topography of the bottom was still mostly unknown. Exley's dive established the depth at the point where he landed but he saw only the small area where his light penetrated, and then only for a few seconds while he was wracked by spasms. Gomes wanted to know whether the floor was level and, if not, whether he could beat Exley's mark by hitting the bottom at a lower spot. He arranged for a sonar depth-measuring device, small enough that a single diver could operate it while swimming.

Gomes and five support divers spent ten days at the hole in late September 1994. Gomes learned that the floor of the cave remained relatively level for some distance across the bottom, at a depth of about 250 metres, then began to slope away to a depth of 285 metres or more. By following a line straight down from the surface, Exley had dropped in near the head of the slope.

After a week of preparation, and with five support divers scheduled to go in behind him, Gomes set off on a deep solo dive, using Exley's shot line. His main gas supply was a pair of large cylinders that he mounted at his back. His plan was to descend until he reached the bottom or the pressure in the main tanks reached 120 bar (1700 PSI). Twelve minutes into the dive, and with the bottom still not in sight, he checked the pressure gauge and saw that just 110 bar remained. Yet he decided to continue down. Two minutes later, just 10 metres short of the bottom, he added gas to his wings, slowing his descent and stopping. He felt some tremors of HPNS, but nothing he couldn't manage. He glanced down and got a quick look at the bottom – he wore four torches mounted to a helmet – and then he began to ascend. The first cylinder of decompression gas was at 130 metres. When he reached it, his main gas supply showed just 40 bar of pressure, enough for perhaps a dozen breaths at that depth.

He emerged from the water feeling well, but his hearing was badly impaired: it was as if he had tin cans over his ears. He knew that this was probably a sign of a decompression injury. He lay down and breathed oxygen for three hours, and in the morning he was driven to Pretoria, for a week of sessions in a recompression chamber.

Frans Cronje, the DAN physician, suspected that Gomes had been affected by a specific decompression injury, an inner ear counter-diffusion, caused when helium, leaving the tissues, is blocked by heavier nitrogen. It is thought to be common among divers decompressing from very deep trips on trimix. If so, Gomes had been very lucky: an inner ear DCI usually disrupts the balance mechanisms of the ear, inducing immediate vertigo while the diver is still under water. Cronje believed that any diver breathing trimix below about 200 metres was at great risk for the injury, but nobody knew for sure, in part because so few divers had returned from such great depth. A diver struck by vertigo while decompressing would almost certainly die; alone, unable to maintain balance while floating, he would roll and gyrate, tumbling away from the shot line, disappearing into the void. Even if his body were recovered, the injury wouldn't be apparent. It would be just another unexplained fatality, and the history of deep diving was full of those.

In time, Gomes recovered 95 per cent of his hearing. He was certain that the problem was an inner-ear DCI, and he knew that he had escaped with his life.

Yet he made plans to return to Bushman's for another attempt at the bottom.

* * *

Nuno Gomes was now the best-known diver in South Africa. With his prominence in the sport and his effervescent personality, he had collected a coterie of admiring divers whom he counted on for assistance. Among them were three cave divers, John-Wesley Franklin and brothers Bergerd and Dietloff Giliomee, members of a diving club. All three were trained for trimix, and Dietloff Giliomee was the club instructor. In late 1994, Franklin and the two Giliomee brothers planned a week-long expedition to Bushman's in order to position a new shot line and to continue the sonar sounding of the bottom. They would do three major dives, including one to 150 metres. They decided that they would need some shallow support and they asked two young divers from their club to join them. Though they weren't trained either for cave diving or for deep diving, both had impressed Dietloff Giliomee with their diving ability.

The young men's names were Robbie MacPherson and Deon Dreyer.

Deon was 22 years old, the first-born of a prosperous family living outside the town of Vereeniging, about an hour west of Johannesburg. He was adventurous and he loved sports. He had been a shooting champion in school – once missing a national rifle team by a single point. He drove open-wheeled race cars and he had been an enthusiastic diver since he was 18. Theo and Marie Dreyer doted on their son. Though he was planning to be engaged to his long-time girlfriend, he still lived at home with his parents, and with his younger brother, Werner.

Before the trip to Bushman's, he joined the others for a weekend of diving at Wondergat, the popular cave northwest of Johannesburg. He did two 60 metre dives to the end of the passage, and he impressed Dietloff with his skills. At Bushman's, Dietloff planned to have him to place some shallow decompression tanks, no deeper than 33 metres. It was well within his abilities, based on what he showed at Wondergat.

Deon was busy the next week, working hard at the family business, selling and installing two-way radio systems. He had several long days that week. Marie fretted that he would be too tired to dive on the weekend, and the night before he was supposed to leave for the hole, she asked him again whether he was sure he wanted to make the trip.

'Ma, stop nagging,' he told her. 'This is a great honour, and I want to do it.'

The team gathered and set up at Bushman's on Saturday morning, 17 December, and when they were done they dressed for a preliminary 'build-up' dive, to acclimatize themselves to the depth and the conditions. The plan was to drop down the shot line as a group to 70 metres; then the three most experienced divers would descend an additional 10 metres, while Deon and Robbie MacPherson waited at 70. Although Franklin and the Giliomees planned to use trimix for the deep dives, they would all be on air this time. But Dietloff didn't consider the dive especially challenging. They would all stay on the line, and the cave entrance was directly overhead.

Dreyer and MacPherson didn't need to come along on this dive. Their support dives to 33 metres later in the week wouldn't require any build-up. But it was their first time at Bushman's, and they had come to dive. So they dived. Deon paused at the edge of the water, as usual, for a quick prayer. Then he joined the others in the pool.

Dietloff led them down the line, keeping the descent slow. He stopped at 70 metres, they all gathered around the line, and Franklin gave Deon and MacPherson a stay-here sign. The three cave divers descended another 10 metres, long enough to inspect briefly a crack in the nearby wall that might serve as an anchor point for a new shot line. Then they returned to MacPherson and Dreyer at 70 metres. Both of the new divers seemed OK, and the five of them began to rise up the line.

Their slow reaction to what happened next, and their confused memories of it, are typical of the thickheadedness induced by nitrogen narcosis. At 70 metres all seemed normal. At 60 metres, Deon and Robbie MacPherson exchanged hand signals. At 50 metres Dietloff Giliomee noticed a light below. He thought that someone had tied a torch to the line. For a while, everyone in the group seemed uncertain about what was happening. 'An eternity of confusion followed, which could have lasted tens of seconds,' was how Dietloff phrased it later in his statement to police.

Dietloff did a head count and realized that someone was missing. He asked Robbie MacPherson where Deon was; MacPherson answered with a puzzled shrug. Dietloff looked to Franklin, who showed him a cut-throat gesture.

Dietloff started down towards the light, with his brother behind him. But as he hit 60 metres again, Dietloff realized that the light was at least 40 metres below them and was disappearing fast. He halted, and stopped his brother from going farther.

Afterwards, Dietloff Giliomee remembered that he hadn't seen any bubbles from below during the entire episode. It meant that Deon must already have been dead when he sank, having drowned after losing consciousness between 50 and 60 metres. Dietloff Giliomee thought that a CO_2 blackout was the most logical explanation, but that's doubtful, since he didn't exert himself during the dive. More likely, he was sensitive to the high partial pressures of oxygen that are incurred from breathing air deep.

The question could never be answered and in any case it was moot to those who loved him. For Marie and Theo Dreyer, all that mattered was that Deon was gone.

✳   ✳   ✳

For a parent, the death of a beloved child is a nightmare made tangible. Marie Dreyer was living the nightmare, but it didn't seem quite real. Not without a body. She had the vivid memory of her son saying goodbye, leaving the house and going to dive. And then ... nothing. People told her that Deon was dead: she heard the accounts, and at a certain logical level she accepted that it was true and she acted as if it were true. But a part of her resisted it. She didn't feel that he was dead; she kept expecting him to drive up and walk through the front door.

Several days after the accident, they were contacted by the owner of an ocean-going Remotely Operated Vehicle, who offered to bring the rig to Bushman's, in order to locate the body and possibly retrieve it. They accepted eagerly, and after Christmas they drove to the Mount Carmel farm to watch the operation. Divers lowered the machine down through the opening and helped to feed the umbilical as an operator guided it down to the bottom. Marie and Theo Dreyer watched a video monitor at the surface, showing the feed from the onboard camera, the view lit by powerful flood-lights. Theo was certain that they would soon be seeing Deon's body.

A day went by and they saw nothing except the desolate floor, with rocks occasionally breaking through the otherwise featureless expanse of mud. It looked like a lunar landscape. Another day of searching turned up nothing. The ROV operator tried to run the machine in a grid pattern, in order to cover every square metre of the floor systematically. Divers checked the roof of the cave to be sure that the body hadn't floated to the surface; they found nothing. A third day of searching: nothing.

To Theo, it was a spirit-breaking exercise. Marie was crushed; he was crushed. He didn't think they could take much more of this. At the end of a fourth fruitless day, Theo called off the search.

In January 1995, about a month after the accident, Theo and Marie planned a service at the site. They booked a hotel in Kuruman for their family and friends, and arranged for a bus to bring them all to Bushman's. The farm's owner, Andries van Zyl, allowed them to install a brass memorial plaque on the wall, just off the path into the hole, in a spot where any visitor could see it. The inscription, in Afrikaans, read:

DEON DREYER
7.8.1974 – 17.12.1994
Met liefdevolle herhinnering aan
ons seun wat net sonskyn en
lag in ons lewe gebring het.
Jy is net 'n kort tyd aan ons geleen
en dié tyd vir ons vreugde
Theo Marie + Werner

(With loving memory to our son who only brought sunshine and laughter into our lives. You were loaned to us for a short period, this time of our joy).

Deon Dreyer and the story of his death became part of the country's diving lore. The plaque was partly responsible. A dive at Bushman's requires multiple trips to haul gear between the rim and the pool, with divers passing the plaque every time.

Deon Dreyer wasn't the first fatality at Bushmans. In 1993, Eben Leyden, an experienced South African diver, ascended too quickly from 60 metres, suffered an arterial embolism, and died at the surface. His accident was barely remembered among divers. Other underwater caves in South Africa have taken more lives than Bushman's; at Wondergat, so many more have died that there is no accurate count. But Deon Dreyer was different from Eben Leyden and all the dozens of others. All those bodies were brought out of the caves. Only Deon's was never recovered. Swallowed up by Bushman's, so far out of reach that even an ROV couldn't find him – that was the stuff of legend.

Marie Dreyer never completely reconciled herself to the fact of his death. She became frustrated after joining a grief therapy group, when others in the group told her that she had to let go. She didn't want to let go – she couldn't. She gave some of Deon's favourite shirts and sweaters to a young man who worked in their shop; seeing him in the clothes made her feel good because it reminded her of her son. Deon's girlfriend remained close to the family. She didn't date for several years. Then she told Marie one day that she had met someone special. She introduced him to the Dreyers, and after her marriage she brought her first child to Marie.

For others, these events and the inexorable passage of time might have provided some closure, or at least some distance. But Marie and Theo found that the pain never want away, and Marie never truly accepted that Deon was gone forever. Without the body, she probably never would. As improbable as it might be, she couldn't shake the notion that he had made his way up out of the cave and wandered off, and that one day he would return.

He was out there somewhere. Deon wasn't dead: he was just overdue.

*   *   *

Nuno Gomes continued planning for a dive to the bottom of Bushman's – not only to match Exley's dive in 1993 but also to surpass Exley's still-standing world record of 264 metres from Nacimiento del Rio Mante. In August 1996 Gomes assembled a team of eight divers with a chamber and a physician. In logistical scope, it was nearly a match for the project that Shaw and Shirley would mount eight and a half years later, though it didn't receive nearly as much attention.

After the four days' exploration with the ROV, the floor of the cave was now better known than ever before. It confirmed Gomes's sonar readings. He now knew for sure that one end of the sloping floor was at least 25 metres deeper than the plateau at the other end. But a line dropped straight down from the cave opening – the approach that Exley had taken, and that Gomes himself had followed so far – brought a diver to one of the higher areas.

Gomes didn't want to swim down to reach the greater depth; in fact, the idea of lingering at 260 metres, much less performing any exertion, was anathema to him and to any-one else who understood the harsh realities. Even momen-tary existence at that depth was a threat to life; to swim along a 260 metre floor the way he might travel in a 40 metre cave was unthinkable.

No – his maximum depth would be whatever he found at the bottom of the line. The trick to greater depth would be finding a way to drop the line into the deeper area of the cave.

He conceived a plan to position a plastic barrel over the deep end. When filled with air, the barrel was so buoyant that it clung to the roof of the cave. Gomes and his support divers then threaded the weighted end of a guide line through a ring attached to the barrel. The weighted rope dropped straight down into the darkness and came to rest at a depth of about 280 metres.

With the end of the line in place, the divers removed the rope from the barrel and brought the other end up to the cave entrance. Now, rather than dropping straight down, the rope ran off at a 7° angle, starting at the cave entrance and ending at one of the deepest parts of the cavern. It was a guideline direct to a world record, if Gomes could reach the end and return.

In 1994, on the dive where he nearly reached the bottom, Gomes had come close to exhausting the deep gas in his two tanks. For this dive, he carried a total of seven tanks, including a huge rig of four tanks that he mounted at his back, filled with trimix.

Gomes didn't use the powerful handheld lights that were popular among tech divers. He had doubts about their reliability at great depth, and he didn't want his right hand tethered to the large battery pack. Instead, he wore a helmet where he had mounted four inexpensive plastic-body torches, available at any dive shop. The arrangement had always worked well for him. But on his final dive of the expedition, two of the torches went dark as he approached the bottom, swimming beside the angled line. He was dropping fast, with nitrogen narcosis increasing and helium tremors beginning to appear. The bottom loomed up suddenly in front of him, and he saw that the rope was laying slack in the silt, inviting entanglement. With no chance to inflate his wings, he glided over a short ledge and crashed onto the floor on all fours, burying himself in deep mud as clouds of silt suddenly reduced visibility to zero.

He tried to stand, staggering under the bulk of the seven cylinders. He feared becoming caught in the slack rope, but he didn't want to lose it either; it was his route to the surface. He kicked and tried to rise out of the mud, but he couldn't get free, and the effort made him dizzy. He was stuck at the bottom.

He forced himself to stop, relax, control his breathing. He wore two identical buoyancy wings at his back, between his body and the rack of cylinders. Each of the devices had a lifting capacity of 45 kilos when fully inflated – Bushman's was no place to run short of buoyancy. He injected air into one of the two wings, until it could hold no more. But he remained stuck at the bottom. He inflated the second of the wings, and he kicked, popping free of the mud.

He rose up above the cloud of silt, caught the guideline and began his ascent. His two computers showed an averaged maximum depth of 283.5 metres.* He had beaten Exley's depth record by nearly 20 metres.

Gomes's record stood for five years until British diver John Bennett returned from a 308 metre dive along a deep ocean

---

* When two devices show slightly different readings, the depths are customarily averaged.

wall near Puerto Galera, the same resort area in the Philippines where Dave Shaw did much of his training. Bennett lost the record two years later when another Briton, Mark Ellyat, went to 313 metres off Phuket, Thailand.

In 2005, at the age of 52, Gomes attempted to take the record back in the Red Sea. He dived open-circuit as always, using the same massive four-tank setup that he had used for the record dive at Bushman's, and the same helmet with the four inexpensive torches. Though he was forced to turn the dive sooner than he wished, he still reached 318 metres.

He never tried another deep dive at Bushman's Hole.

*   *   *

For eight years after Gomes's record dive, nobody else tested the depths beyond 200 metres at Bushman's Hole.

Small groups of divers would sometimes trek there, usually on weekends, and Don Shirley brought groups of advanced students and experienced cave divers for visits of several days or more. The most ambitious diving during that time was an attempt by six divers, including Don Shirley, to explore the walls of the cavern above 100 metres, using rebreathers and battery-powered 'scooters' – torpedo-like craft that an individual diver can use for propulsion, controlling it from behind. On one dive, a team of two tried to circumnavigate the cavern at the 86 metre level while stopping to attach a guideline. They used an entire 350 metre spool of line and were forced to turn back and retrace their route along the line. They believed that they were still about 100 metres short of completing the circuit when they ran out of line.

None of this would have happened without the consent of Andries van Zyl. He was the owner of the property where Bushman's is located, and he controlled access to the hole. Andries had taken over the farm from his father and had converted it from a cattle ranch to a 5000 hectare game farm that he called Mount Carmel Safaris. Andries and his wife Debbie, a schoolteacher in Kuruman, lived on the property with their children. They had converted an old farmhouse into a comfortable lodge. Ranch hands' living quarters became tasteful guest rooms.

Like many others, Andries felt an affinity for the hole. He sensed that it was a special place. Sometimes, when he drove past, he would park his truck and get out and stand at the edge, taking it in. He made little income from divers, nearly all of whom camped out along the rim during their visits.

During Exley's expedition, and Nuno Gomes's visits, Andries would sometimes join the divers in the evening as they stood around a fire pit, talking about what they had done and what they planned to do. Andries wasn't a diver, but he became knowledgeable of the sport. And the more he knew, the more he liked the divers and appreciated their feats and their courage. Especially the really deep stuff, where survival seemed to be almost a matter of chance, a coin flip to live or die. He would watch them working out the decompression tables, calculations on which they would stake their lives. He would see them the night before a big dive, smiling and laughing, and then next morning going off into the unknown.

Somebody like that could dive on his farm any time.

CHAPTER
10

Don Shirley's most vivid memory of his first trip to Bushman's Hole was not of depth or gas mixes or equipment. It was of a certain exquisite moment, a sight that brought emotion to his voice whenever he talked about it, even ten years after it happened.

It came near the end of a weekend of diving with members of a diving club called Boing-Boing-Boing. At the time, in 1997, it was the country's largest group of technical divers; its members were enthusiastic, brave, but unconventional by the emerging global standards of technical diving. The name of the group was an acronym – *Breathers of Oxygen and INert Gases* – but it also referred to their penchant for 'bounce' dives, quickly down to considerable depth and then straight back up. That style of diving didn't appeal to Shirley, but he went for the chance to meet some of the divers and spread the word of safe practices. And he wanted to see Bushman's.

Full membership in the club required a 100 metre dive. During that weekend Shirley escorted a prospective member on an initiation dive to that depth, and he accompanied others on shallower dives. At the end of the weekend, he wanted to look around in the cavern, so he slipped down through the opening for a solo trip. He descended to 50 metres, far enough that he had only the dark emptiness of the cavern beneath him, with the cave entry above.

He turned and looked back towards the entrance. Two divers floated above him, hanging motionless in the water. One was at 30 metres, the other about 10 metres higher. Both wore helmet-mounted torches, creating a brilliant halo of white light around the head of each man as he floated in the blackness. Above them were the three openings near the surface, bright shards set against the blackness, with shafts of sunlight lancing through.

Shirley was stunned by the beauty of it. He dived for many reasons, but this was the most fundamental – the chance to visit remote and stunning places from which almost everyone else on earth was barred, to collect these rare experiences that elevated life above the trivial and mundane. He found emotional resonance in diving.

To some who didn't know him well, Shirley's approach could seem whimsical. He occasionally mused about placing a team of divers around the wall of the cavern at a certain depth, each diver with a high-intensity lamp, so that for the first time the immensity of the space would be apparent. And to be a diver in the middle of the void, surrounded by the distant lights – wouldn't *that* be a sight to remember!

He was truly passionate about the sport, and it was the truest passion – the kind that comes from the heart. His technique was impeccable, he was comfortable at depth, he could calculate deco schedules and gas mixes as well as anyone, and he had the touch for equipment that you would expect of an electronics technician. But for Shirley, diving was not about deco schedules or gas mixes or about gear. It was not about depth, it was not about technique, it was not about numbers. Diving for Shirley was about the rare richness of feeling that the sport provided him, a quality that was so hard to find in workaday life. And if you didn't get that, you didn't really grasp diving. At least not diving as he understood it.

His trip to Bushman's with Dave Shaw in June 2004 was that way. Most people would look at it and see only a spectacular new entry on the world's list of notable dives. But to Shirley, it represented much more – and in a sense, much less. When he looked back on it later, he saw three carefree pals on a lark. He saw frost on tent fabric and ashes puffing as he blew on embers to revive a dying fire, and the wind firing sand that stung exposed skin. He saw goofy laughter as they toted crates of equipment down to the bottom of the hole and then trudged back up for more. It was the kind of rough-edged diving holiday that dive buddies have been taking together for decades, except that this time in the normal course of things, one of them became the first diver ever to take a closed-circuit rebreather beyond 200 metres.

Just a group of friends diving for the sheer pleasure of it, Shirley remembered later, *and doing things others only dream about.*

Shaw arrived for the trip at the end of May. He had been sending gear ahead for two weeks. Other Cathay pilots would bring it in a piece at a time, and put it into storage at the crew hotel in Johannesburg. It was packed and loaded and waiting for him in a car when he arrived.

The trip began with a couple of shakeout dives for Shaw at Komati Springs. Then Shaw and Shirley loaded gear into the back of Shirley's small pickup truck – known throughout South Africa as a 'bakkie' – and into a trailer. There was plenty: three rebreathers (Shirley brought one as a spare), 15 diving cylinders, five larger storage cylinders of helium and oxygen, a Haskel booster pump, drysuits and regulators, a generator. They also brought camping equipment; June was high season for visiting hunters at the lodge. Shirley liked it that way.

> I prefer camping, as you experience the outdoors and all the vibrations that go with it ... If you don't experience the hole that way, you have missed a lot. Even when some of my divers stay at the farm house I still prefer to camp. When you use the accommodation, it is just not the same.

The load formed a heap that rose above the level of the truck's cab. Shirley wedged it together and strapped it down, and with the truck riding low under the load, they trundled out and down the highway to Pretoria. They brought with them Sipho Nkozi, one of Shirley's employees, trained in gas mixing and one of the first black Africans with a meaningful job in the country's dive industry. They stayed overnight with Peter Herbst, and early the next morning Herbst – his bakkie likewise heaped with gear, including a compressor and scooters and a black cast-iron cook pot – joined them for the eight-hour trek to the hole.

They arrived in mid-afternoon and spent the rest of daylight setting up camp along the east rim of the hole. It was a cold night, near freezing, and they started a bonfire that they would keep burning day and night throughout the trip. They spent most of the next morning hauling gear down to the bottom of the hole – only the compressor and the five large storage tanks stayed at the top – and then finally they were ready to dive.

After the failure of his Inspiration rebreather at 180 metres the previous October, Shaw knew that he needed another machine if he hoped to go deeper. But no other closed-circuit rebreather in production was capable of even the same depths as the Inspiration. So Shaw found one that was not in production. The Biomarine Mark 15.5 had been designed and built under contract to the US Navy (most likely for use by Navy Seals; the stealth of rebreathers, emitting no bubbles, has military implications). There were few in civilian hands. The Mark 15.5 was regarded as the finest rebreather in existence, capable of extended depths and running times. It was no longer being manufactured, and even when it was made, it was never made in great numbers. The size of the market for such a specialized item was exceedingly small, because few divers ever felt the need to use the machine anywhere near its limits. But the few who did own and use one were reluctant to let go of it. So a Mark 15.5 was hard to find, and when you found one, it was expensive.

Shaw tracked down one, owned by a collector. The man was actually selling another exotic rebreather, a CisLunar, but Shaw worked out a deal for both machines, buying two so that he could get the one he really wanted.

In fact what he really wanted was not the whole Mark 15.5 but its internal plumbing and the large radial scrubber which was more efficient than the Inspiration's canister, with a greater capacity that allowed longer duration. He upgraded nearly all the rest. He replaced the hoses and mouthpiece with parts from an Inspiration. He replaced the Mark 15.5's electronics with an aftermarket unit, known as a Hammerhead, which used two wrist-mounted controllers milled from a thick block of acrylic; Shaw filled the cavities with oil to resist compression at great depths.

Besides the chassis and cover, all that was left now of the original machine was the scrubber canister and the internal plumbing. But that's all he had really wanted. One of the problems of rebreathers at serious depth is an increased work of breathing. Gases thicken under pressure, increasing the effort required for the lungs to push gas around the loop and through the scrubber. Shaw hoped that the Mark 15.5's large radial scrubber and generously proportioned hoses would allow him to breathe more easily in the places he wanted to go.

A diver's gear is a manifesto, if you know what to look for. Shaw's purchase of the Mark 15.5, and his modifications, were a statement of purpose. He intended to go to depths that few sports divers had ever attempted, and none ever with a rebreather.

They had arrived on a Friday afternoon. His first dive at Bushman's came Saturday, after they had carried down the gear. They began to do the usual preparations that precede a major dive. Shaw and Shirley went to 60 metres on that first dive. They found lines left by Exley and Gomes, but dropped a new one and placed the first five of what would be 11 bailout cylinders. Herbst placed some oxygen cylinders in the shallows, just beneath the cave opening.

The following day, Shaw placed two more bailout tanks, one at 80 metres and another at 120. On Monday, Shirley and Herbst took scooters down to about 50 metres.

The diving was by far the most orderly part of the week.

Bits and parts had been left behind. Some were trivial, some crucial. Shaw lacked an adapter to fill his rebreather's onboard tanks. A fourth diver, Ben McGarry, was due to arrive on Sunday. Shirley and Herbst peppered him with text messages, a growing list of items he should bring. A compressor motor quit on Sunday evening, and one of Herbst's employees was dispatched to buy a replacement and bring it to the hole. The motor, when it arrived, didn't fit the mounting holes, but Shirley and Herbst fixed it with wire and plastic tie wraps.

The weather was brutal. Cool days gave way to frigid nights, clear skies sucking all the warmth from the earth. The wind blew. Herbst did most of the cooking, using propane burners on a folding table, and he had to rig a shelter around the stove to keep wind from blowing out the flames. Sand migrated under clothes and into sleeping bags. Shaw one day did his deco calculations in his tent, using a hard shell valise for a desk. He was bundled in a down jacket, numb fingers tapping the keyboard of a notebook computer.

To Herbst, this was the kind of shared experience that creates a bond. He and Shirley were already close, and in the few days they camped at the rim above Bushman's, Herbst felt Shaw, too, becoming a friend. In the evenings they would sit around the campfire – hefty logs served as wind-breaks and back rests – and they would look up at a sky so clear that it seemed smeared with stars, and they would talk and chirp and laugh. Nearby down in the pit was the water and the cleft entrance to the cave, never far from the mind. They were brought together by the water and what they did there and hoped to do there. It excluded most of the world. Almost nobody else could know firsthand the sensation of slipping through the opening and descending into the cave and then finding yourself suspended over that black void. Somehow this arcane knowledge brought you closer to those few others who shared it. Nobody could do it and not be touched in some way, and once it had touched you, you were never the same.

*   *   *

On Monday evening, Shaw sat with the others around the fire and went over the plans for his big dive in the morning. He told them that he planned to reach 200 metres. Shirley would meet him on his ascent at 120 metres, 29 minutes into the dive; Herbst at 60 metres about fifteen minutes later; and McGarry at 21 metres, half an hour after that.

Even with advances in equipment and gas mixing and deco planning, 200 metres was still a formidable depth, rarely achieved. Beginning with Jochen Hasenmayer's fabled 'sneak dive' at Fontaine de Vaucluse in 1982, there had been fewer than 30 successful dives to that distance; in 2004 there would be four – two by Shaw. Some people talked about 150 metres as the threshold of what was really known and tested. At around 200 metres a diver exceeded the limits of the easily predictable. Anything could happen.

Shaw actually planned to go even deeper. His deco calculations were based on a maximum depth of 220 metres. He didn't know how he would feel about going the full distance, and he wanted the freedom to come up short without seeming to have failed. Only Shirley knew the truth.

Don approved of the plan, and he approved of the dive. In general he was wary of those who sought depth for depth's sake. He sometimes called it 'soap on a rope' diving: for some record attempts, divers would descend a shot line hung with tags denoting certain depths, and when a diver had reached his limit he would pull off the nearest tag and bring it to the surface as proof of his feat. Shirley considered it more stunt than true diving. Shirley himself didn't dwell on depth as such. Depth was something that happened when you were going where you want to go.

Dave was like that, he thought. Although he was obviously pushing for depth, he wasn't fixated on it. This dive wasn't about 200 metres or 220. It was preparation. Dave had an explorer's spirit, Shirley thought. He intended to accomplish something unique, and this was just something that he needed to do along the way.

Shaw calculated a total dive time at seven hours, most of it in decompression, and he was in the water early. Shirley went down ahead of him, to shoot video of him entering the cave and swimming past at 15 metres; then Shirley went back to the surface to wait for his scheduled descent, and Shaw continued down.

Shaw didn't inflate his buoyancy wings, and only added argon gas to his drysuit in order to relieve the squeeze from the pressures of the depth. Without any added buoyancy, he dropped quickly past 50 metres – more quickly than he had planned. He had not been below 121 metres with the new rebreather: that was on his last training dive in Puerto Galera. Now he silently swept past 121, past 150. He continued to plummet.

At 185 metres – past his own personal depth mark, from the previous October at Komati Springs – he pressed and held the button that opened the wings' inflator valve. The rush of air was loud, and the wing gave out muted popping noises as onrushing air opened up parts of the bladder that the pressure had squeeze shut.

Shaw continued to drop. He clamped down on the inflator button; air continued to gush into the wing – 15 seconds, 20 seconds – but it didn't seem to have any effect. He was still dropping fast. He passed through 200 metres and he noticed that his vision was narrowing. When he looked at the displays of the computers and the Hammerhead controllers on his forearms, it was as if he were peering down a tunnel.

After half a minute of inflating the wings, his descent began to slow. When he stopped falling, now floating and neutrally buoyant, his depth read 213 metres.

He turned slowly, looking around, pointing his light outward to where the walls should be. He saw nothing but water. *This place is huge.* He realized that he was breathing easily, with no more effort than if he were at six metres. This was exactly what he had hoped to get from the new rebreather. He considered dropping down to 220 metres, just to know that he had done it. But that would require him to dump air from the wings, and fill them again, and he decided that he didn't want to do that: 220 was just a number, and he would be back.

He arrived safely at the surface about an hour later than he had planned. A slow descent added to his decompression debt, and as the afternoon dragged on, with Shaw floating for two and a half hours at three metres, Herbst dropped down a slate that brought a grin to Shaw. It read:

> Going to town for burgers. Pls bring up batteries and charge them when you are done.

'There were no drum rolls,' Don Shirley said later, remembering the late afternoon when Shaw eased up to the surface at the end of his deco. He stretched the last three metres over several minutes in an almost superstitious gesture of appeasement to the gases that might still remain in his tissues. Shirley and Herbst were waiting for him. They took his bailout cylinders, and helped him out of his rebreather. Shaw walked a few steps to a tarpaulin shelter that they had rigged for shade. There he sat and sipped warm drinks for the next two hours. He remained in his drysuit, in case he needed to go back into the water for recompression. But he felt no pains or twinges, and with the sun low in the sky and the hole completely in dark shadow, he changed into his clothes, including the pair of jeans that he seemed to wear all the time – Peter Herbst sometimes kidded him about being so destitute that he could afford only a single pair of pants – and he slowly made his way up to the top, where Herbst was cooking a meal in the cast-iron pot, and he sat with the others around the campfire.

Two days later they hauled the gear back up to the rim. They broke camp, loaded it all again and slowly drove out to the highway with the two bakkies riding low under the weight.

Dave Shaw would be back, but it would never again be so simple.

CHAPTER
11

When he boarded a flight home later that week in Johannesburg, Dave Shaw left behind the few people in the world who knew him as an extraordinary diver, and understood how much he had accomplished in such a relatively brief time.

Nobody in Hong Kong had even a glimmering of it. Ann was aware of his website. The pages got so little traffic that she would sometimes access the site eight or ten times during a day just to give him a thrill when he checked the traffic statistics. But if she read the dive reports which he posted there, they made no impression. 182 metres, 213 metres ... they were just numbers to her, and she didn't imagine that her husband, nearing his 50th birthday, actually did anything noteworthy when he disappeared on his trips. She knew that his diving was dangerous, but she didn't realize that it was extraordinary. Their daughter, Lisa, had the same reaction when she heard about his records: *If Dad is doing it, how hard can it be?*

But his diving companions in South Africa knew as little about his personal life. He would occasionally tell flying stories, and they knew that he was looking forward to his retirement from Cathay Pacific in 2009, so that he wouldn't have to scrape together days for diving. They knew that he had a wife named Ann and two grown children. They had absolutely no inkling of his religious commitment, his sense that in both great and trivial matters he was guided by divine will, clearly expressed, and by his conviction that putting one's destiny in the hand of God was the only way to ensure a proper outcome in life. They would have been astonished to hear him say with total conviction: 'I believe God told me ...' or 'I think God wants me to ...' Yet these phrases were frequently spoken in the Shaw household.

The Shaws' lives were busy, and when they were together they were satisfied with their own company. But when they did socialize, they drew most of their friends and acquaintances from their church. It was a congregation of about 200, associated with an established Episcopal church for legal purposes, but doctrinally separate. Services varied from week to week – traditional, modern, sometimes charismatic. The pastor was Michael Vickers, a former businessman from England who had experienced a radical and sudden conversion in his late twenties. Now about forty, he was square-jawed, dynamic and fit. He played amateur rugby and was informal and affable, but completely committed to his religion and to the congregation.

It was a church without a church building. The congregation rented space on Sunday mornings where it could be found, usually in the area of Clearwater Bay and the nearby town of Sai Kung, in Hong Kong's New Territories; in 2004, Sunday services were often held in the gymnasium of a Chinese middle school. Vickers did much of his office work from a favourite table at Jaspas, a popular café in Sai Kung.

Vickers had come to Hong Kong in 1998, hired from England to replace the long-time pastor who had been with the church since its founding. Vickers and David Shaw didn't really connect right away. But over time, Vickers was impressed by Shaw's sincerity and faith and his quiet charity among the congregation. More than one member had survived a rough patch through the Shaws' largesse. Shaw was steady, capable and completely reliable. Dave had a way of making things happen, and when he made a commitment, you could consider it bankable.

Vickers wanted to build a proper church. It was a topic of much debate among the congregation; real estate in Hong Kong is scarily expensive. But Shaw weighed in on Vickers's side, and with his friend Harry, David took on the job of finding and buying a suitable property. Shaw felt called to do it, divinely directed. The money didn't actually exist – the congregation barely managed to pay Vickers's modest salary – but Shaw was confident.

If God wants us a build a church, the money will take care of itself.

To those who knew them, Ann and David were as devoted as any couple in the congregation. If they weren't gregarious, it was because they were happy in one another's quiet company. Their children's departure from home left no emptiness in their lives: it meant more time for each other. David's duties as a training pilot meant that he flew shorter routes than many of Cathay's senior pilots. He might get one extended international trip a month, with several legs, but most of his destinations were within a few hours of Hong Kong, day trips or at most overnight. Ann could count on spending at least half her evenings with him. For the wife of an international flight captain, it was a rare luxury.

Every year, they would take a two-week holiday together during Ann's summer break. David liked unconventional travel and was fascinated by the extreme points in countries: the lowest, the highest, the most distant. In 2003, they visited Norway for two and a half weeks, including a week north of the Arctic Circle, travelling without an itinerary, just driving and stopping where they pleased. One evening they took an 18-kilometre hike to the northernmost point in Europe. They didn't leave until after lunch, and they returned to their hotel late night, yet still in daylight.

About a month after he returned from his first trip to Bushman's, the Shaws took their 2004 summer holiday together, this one to Finland and Russia. They travelled by train to St Petersburg. Ann became ill on the train, and while she rested at their hotel, David went out exploring and met a local guide who did walking tours of the city. Shaw hired him for the rest of the visit, and he took them around the city, using buses and streetcars – not the normal tour, but it suited the Shaws.

On this holiday their baggage was misdirected, and wasn't waiting for them at Heathrow. The Shaws decided to go on without it and spent the rest of the trip living out of a single valise with clothes they picked up along the way. The luggage was waiting for them when they returned to Finland on their way home and they took it back to Hong Kong without ever having opened it. So this would always be remembered as the 'no-baggage' holiday: the trip when Ann learned to appreciate Russian ice cream and Russian public toilets, the trip when David stepped in to protect Ann from an obnoxious drunk at an underground station, when they learned St Petersburg from the ground up.

Memories like these made a marriage. Ann had nearly 30 years of such memories with David, and she hoped – she expected – to have many more.

When the holiday was over, David still had several more days of his annual leave for the year. He used it for the last week in October, for his return to Bushman's Hole.

* * *

It was an opportunity seized.

For months Verna van Schaik, a 35-year-old business analyst from Johannesburg, had been preparing for an attempt at the women's world depth record during the last week in October at Bushman's. van Schaik planned a two-week visit to Bushman's, with half a dozen or more support divers performing the usual setup before her record attempt. Don Shirley had agreed to be the team's principal gas-mixer – a substantial job, since van Schaik and her team were all using open-circuit scuba equipment.

Shirley knew that Shaw was ready to extend his depth in the hole. The problem was logistics: a trip to Bushman's always required serious planning and organization. Shirley realized that everything Shaw needed for a major dive would already be in place when van Schaik completed her dive. Shirley suggested that he and Shaw could serve as van Schaik's deep support divers; in return, van Schaik would keep the setup in place for a few extra days so that Shaw could attempt his own deep dive.

Van Schaik liked to have support divers with her as much as possible, as deep as possible. She agreed, and Shaw made plans to travel to Bushman's.

This time, he was going to the bottom. Shirley never had much doubt of that, but Shaw confirmed it on 11 October, in an email message with detailed instructions for the gas mixtures he would need. The list included three tanks filled with a mixture of just 4 per cent oxygen and 80 per cent helium: a mix for extreme depth. He wrote:

> How deep? We will see but I will be looking for the bottom so I have planned everything for 300m, but expect the dive to be 280m or so. I would appreciate it if you kept the aim to yourself as much as is possible, or to those who need to know, to keep my superstitions happy.

Van Schaik planned to dive on 25 October. Shaw arrived at the hole two days before and did an 80 metre dive to place some cylinders and test his gear. It was his first time in the water since the 213 metre dive in June. Van Schaik successfully completed a dive to 221 metres, a world record depth for a woman and the deepest cave dive ever by a woman. Shirley and Shaw met her at 150 metres, after placing bailout cylinders for their own dive, which they planned for the 28th.

One night around that time, Shaw dreamed that he was diving to the bottom of Bushman's Hole. In his dream, as he was swimming just above the sloping floor, he found the body of Deon Dreyer. The body lay on its back, arms outstretched, as if reaching up towards the roof of the cave.

Shaw didn't tell anyone about the dream until later. But among those who knew him, nobody doubted the story. Apart from being honest, Shaw was simply too straightforward to make up such a tale.

And he had more practical concerns. He was going to a place where just two others had been before him. Both had barely survived. His worry wasn't just the depth of the floor; Shaw didn't know what he would find when he got there.

At Bushman's a shot line to the bottom must start through the entry cave that leads from the surface, angling down to the top of the huge bell-shaped cavern. Shaw's line would run along the roof of that initial passage, down to the end at about 45 metres. At that point was an air-filled drum, with a metal ring. The shot line ran through that ring and dropped straight to the floor of the cavern, hitting the bottom somewhere between Sheck Exley's line and the angled shot line of Nuno Gomes.

If it hit the bottom. Shaw and Shirley weren't certain. The line had been installed by one of van Schaik's crew, using weights at the end of a rope about a centimetre in diameter. But nobody was sure that the weighted end of the rope actually reached the floor. If it didn't, and if Shaw came down too quickly, he might plummet past the end of the rope where it hung above the floor. If he wasn't cautious, Shaw might also find himself floundering in mud and silt, as Gomes did.

Silted out at 260 metres, out of contact with the guideline – it was a nightmarish possibility.

But Shaw didn't just intend to reach the bottom and start back up. He would carry a hand reel loaded with white nylon cave line: a primary piece of equipment for all cave divers, but something that nobody – not even Exley and Gomes – had used at the bottom of Bushman's. When he reached the bottom, he intended to tie the end of the string to the shot line and swim away, seeking the deepest part of the cavern. He was going to *explore.*

Nobody, not even the fabled Sheck, had ever done such a thing. Not at 260-plus metres.

That explained the uncertainty about depth in Shaw's message to Shirley. He didn't know how deep he would end up, or how long he would be down there. He calculated a variety of deco plans, based on depths between 260 and 300 metres, with bottom times from three to five minutes. Every second he spent at the bottom would add about 75 seconds to his deco debt. An extra minute would tack on an hour and a quarter.

He began his dive almost exactly on schedule at 6 am; he expected to be submerged for about twelve hours, and wanted to finish the dive while some daylight still remained in the sky.

He dropped quickly, but as he approached 250 metres he added gas to his buoyancy wings to slow down. His cave light found the floor, and he saw the last few metres of the shot line in a tidy coil, on a floor that seemed more rock than silt.

He settled and stopped. The bottom of Bushman's Hole was less than a metre away, close enough to reach out and touch. Shaw's breathing seemed effortless. He felt only slight nitrogen narcosis. The helium tremors that wracked Sheck Exley so badly at this depth were totally absent. Perfect.

He floated just above the bottom, tied off his reel to the shot line, and swept the light around to check the slope of the floor. The light cast a tight, bright patch in the blackness.

He headed off towards the deep end, reeling out the cave line while he scanned the barren surface. He was doing something truly difficult and improbable, something previously undone. It was the reason he had started that long climb up the pyramid, the culmination of five years' devotion to his sport, and although others had striven longer, perhaps nobody had ever wanted it more.

*   *   *

Up at the surface, there was trouble. Don Shirley's rebreather was malfunctioning.

Shirley was supposed to follow Shaw down the line at an interval that would allow him to meet Shaw when Dave was on his ascent – the usual deep support scheme that they had followed during all of Shaw's major solo dives. This morning, Shirley was to meet Shaw at 150 metres. By their calculations of Shaw's ascent rate and dive plan, that required Don to start his dive 38 minutes after Dave left the surface.

But when Shirley stood in the pool, waiting to start his descent, one of the rebreather's wrist-mounted consoles suddenly lost power. The console controlled the basic operation of the machine, analysing the gas in the loop and maintaining the oxygen level. Shirley quickly diagnosed a faulty battery, and changed it where he stood. But, improbably, almost at the same time, two more problems occurred: one of the rebreather's three oxygen sensors suddenly failed, and a rubber O-ring began to leak.

Derek Hughes was Verna van Schaik's team manager, an entrepreneur and an accomplished underwater photographer. He was videotaping the dive today. After shooting Shaw coming through the cave at about 15 metres, Hughes had returned to the surface and was standing in the pool waiting to tape Shirley's departure. Shirley was able to change the battery in the water, but the new problems required him to drop his bailout cylinders, pull off the Inspiration, and open it up on the ground at the edge of the water.

Someone ran to get Shirley's tool kit and quickly Don was hunched over the machine, the cover removed and the innards exposed.

Hughes came over to see if he could help. The scheduled time for Shirley's departure was coming up in a hurry.

Hughes was in a drysuit, and although the tanks on his back were filled with a mixture too rich for deep diving, he did have a twinset up at the top, pumped with a trimix blend suitable for 100 metres. One of the Mount Carmel employees was nearby, helping with equipment, and could have the tanks down at the bottom in a few minutes.

Hughes spoke up and offered to do the support dive. He told Shirley that he would meet Shaw at 100 metres instead of 150.

Sitting nearby was Hughes's fiancée, Megan Jarvis, an attorney in Johannesburg. She was dismayed to hear

Hughes make the offer. His deep diving made her nervous, and she wasn't mentally prepared to have him do a big dive today.

But Shirley declined the offer.

Hughes persisted.

'Leave the Inspiration, do the dive with my twinset,' Hughes said.

Shirley shook his head, and continued to work on the rebreather.

Megan Jarvis was struck by the sight of Don hunched over his rebreather, tools arrayed around him. The machine was in pieces, and the pieces weren't so impressive. Batteries, O-rings, spanners ... *these guys stake their lives on such ordinary things*, she thought.

Shirley worked calmly, but with purpose, and within a few minutes the pieces were back together and he was lifting the Inspiration onto his back.

He descended on schedule.

*　*　*

Down at the bottom, Dave Shaw was exploring.

He was moving just above the sloping floor, using slow and measured strokes of his fins. He didn't want to stir up silt, and he wanted to avoid exertion that would generate CO_2; at this depth, under this pressure, that could quickly cause a blackout. He had swum about a minute, down to about 270 metres, when the beam from his cave light caught an object to his left. It was a wetsuit, filled out in human form. Shaw realized at once that it was a body – *the* body. This had to be the mortal remains of Deon Dreyer.

142

Shaw had a quick decision to make: continue deeper, or go to the body.

He changed direction and headed for the body. It wasn't a matter of mere curiosity; he had something else in mind. This was how he put it in his dive report: 'The decision was easy really. I turned and was soon next to him. I needed to try and make a recovery of the body.'

The body lay exactly as he had seen in his dream, supine, arms outstretched. The twin tanks at the back seemed to be buried in the mud, along with the cave light's big battery canister.

Later Shaw wasn't able to recall all the details of what he had seen. He remembered the position of the body, and he remembered the skull, still attached, fleshless but with the dive mask in place. He had never before encountered a body under water, and Don Shirley thought that he might have been somewhat shocked at the sight, though Shaw disagreed. Some narcosis might have been in play; his mixture was the equivalent of breathing air at 45 metres.

Shaw believed that he might be able to bring the body out on the spot, hauling it up with him as he ascended, handing it off to Shirley when they met at 150 metres. He grabbed the body and pulled. The body didn't budge. Shaw reduced his buoyancy and sunk down on his knees to the floor, and he pulled some more, putting effort into it.

The body didn't budge.

Though he didn't say so later, he may have persisted in this attempt for a minute or more, because when he checked the elapsed time on his dive computers, he saw that he was a minute behind schedule; he had allowed himself five

143

minutes on the bottom. Shaw also realized that he was panting from the exertion – something he had specifically promised to avoid.

Shaw tied his cave line to the body. He attached it to the manifold, the steel tube that connected the two tanks at the back (though he didn't remember this detail later). To save a few seconds, he left the reel on the body, rather than cutting it free with the knife that he always carried. Then he followed the string back to the shot line, and he began his slow return to the surface. His first decompression stop was at 221 metres, exactly the depth Verna van Schaik had reached two days earlier.

He met Shirley at 140 metres and wrote on a slate:

270 M

FOUND BODY

Shirley raised his eyebrows behind the lenses of his mask, and he shook Shaw's hand.

What occurred next – or, more exactly, what didn't occur – offers insight into their relationship and their shared mindset. The two deepest emergency cylinders on the line were at 150 metres. Nobody else was scheduled to dive that deep, so the tanks were no longer needed after Shaw had passed them. According to the dive plan, Shirley should have picked up those tanks and brought them out, beginning a process known as 'cleaning the line.' Shaw would have brought out the next deepest set of tanks.

But none of that actually happened. Instead of descending the last 10 metres to get the tanks, Shirley headed back to the surface, leaving the 150 metre tanks on the line. Shaw, likewise, left in place the next set of tanks. They removed no cylinders that day. Though no other messages were passed on the slate, two words 'FOUND BODY' told Shirley everything. Dave would be going back for the body.

Of course. *They left the tanks because they both knew that they might repeat the dive two days later, to bring the body back.*

As Shirley put it later: 'I knew Dave, and I knew me.'

Hours later, after Shaw surfaced, he sat quietly with Shirley at the bottom of the hole, drinking water and occasionally taking oxygen as a precaution. He had lost 2°C from his body core and was wrapped in a sleeping bag.

When they spoke, they decided reluctantly that a quick return to fetch the body probably wasn't feasible. Not because they couldn't do it; they were both certain that Shaw could safely repeat the dive and find a way to bring out the body. But the discovery of any corpse is potentially a police matter. They would have to perform the ultimate 'sneak dive' and then plead ignorance after delivering the body to the surface.

Probably not very smart, they concluded. But they had no doubt that they could pull it off, just the two of them.

During that conversation, Shaw told Shirley about his dream. Although Shirley had understood at 140 metres that Shaw would want to bring back the body, Don realized as they spoke that Dave seemed to have a connection to the body, as if he had been given the job of bringing it back, and had embraced the task; this was *his* job, *his* body.

Neither of them mentioned the possibility of simply leaving the corpse where it lay. The only questions were *when* and *how*, not *whether*. Yet bodies have been allowed to remain underwater in places that are far more accessible than the bottom of Bushman's Hole. Most serious wreck divers are aware of other sunken ships where bones and skulls can be found among the silt-covered detritus. Probably the best-known is the liner *Empress of Ireland*, which sank quickly to a depth of 45 metres in the St Lawrence River, following a collision. More than 1000 passengers died, and nearly all went down with the ship. A salvage operation was mounted to recover mail and valuables, but there has never been a serious effort to retrieve the bodies. The wreck was considered their final resting place.

In comparison, Bushman's is as remote as the far side of the moon. It could well have been regarded as a gravesite; in fact, when they considered the possibility of dying during the recovery dive, both Shaw and Shirley would discourage any attempt to recover their remains. Each man believed that the bottom of Bushman's was a proper tomb for a diver.

That evening, Shaw made three phone calls from Andries van Zyl's office at the Mount Carmel lodge.

One was to Ann. Another was to Theo van Eeden, a police inspector and diver who was a long-time member of the diving scene in South Africa and at Bushman's; in 2005, he would be a member of Nuno Gomes's team for the world record dive in the Red Sea. Van Eeden had taken Dietloff Giliomee's sworn statement after Deon Dreyer's disappearance, and had a long-standing interest in the case. Shaw told van Eeden where he had found the body, and how he had tried to free it from the mud.

Shaw's third call was to Marie and Theo Dreyer.

'I want to bring back your son,' he said.

Marie Dreyer, recounting the conversation later, recalled feeling joy at Shaw's request, as well as a sense of dread when she thought about the risks involved. But she could not refuse an answered prayer: she agreed to the attempt, and so did her husband.

Good thing, Don Shirley thought. He would not want to be the person who tried to stop Dave from bringing back the body of Deon Dreyer.

It was dive 330 in Shaw's diving log. The entry for that page read, in entirety: *World Record 270M. Ran Reel.*

* * *

The two-man dive to recover the body wasn't just idle musing. Shirley was certain that they could have done it. Dave would descend to the bottom and start back with the body. Don would meet him as usual at 150, where he would take the body away, relieving him of that burden. An unspoken 'well-done', a quick grin that you really couldn't see behind the mouthpiece, then Don would be off with the body and Dave would resume his slow, solitary trip up the line. Up at the top, Don would phone the police. Hello, we have something here for you. Dave would have been alone nearly the entire time, twelve hours, but he could handle that.

Dave didn't require anyone else's presence. He didn't need company to pluck up his spirits in the lonely depths; good thing, because on most dives he was alone nearly all the time until he reached 20 or 30 metres. He didn't need help switching gases in his rebreather or handling the tanks that he carried with him. Dave had his gas, he had the rebreathers, he had his own inner resources. He looked after his own survival. He would have finished his deco, and by evening they would have been sitting together among the boulders, joking and quietly satisfied.

Two friends diving for the sheer pleasure of it, doing things others only dream about.

They could have done it, no question. Quick, direct, simple.

But the chance to do it quietly vanished quickly. News of the discovery spread quickly, bringing attention to Shaw and Shirley to a degree that they couldn't have imagined. On his last day at the hole, Shirley did a quick dive to hide the upper end of the shot line, so that it wouldn't be disturbed, and he left it there for the next time they would need it.

CHAPTER
12

The attempt to recover the body began as a dive, but it soon became a project. It involved elements which Shirley and Shaw knew only in passing, if at all: public relations, bureaucratic manoeuvring, documentary film production. The actual dive became as complex as any single sports dive in history.

Superficially the recovery dive resembled Shaw's two previous major dives at Bushman's, with Shaw first into the cave. After some interval, Shirley would follow Shaw down and meet him during his first deep decompression stops. Other divers would follow Shirley and meet Shaw further up the line.

But if the operation went well, Shaw would be bringing back the body as he ascended. That was a potential distraction as Shaw switched tanks and tracked his deco times. Shaw handled his equipment as adroitly as anyone Shirley had ever seen, but Don didn't want him to carry the body any longer than necessary. Shirley imagined a separate support team for the body, bringing it up in a relay.

So there would be a 'technical team' and a 'body recovery team', several divers each with different maximum depths. Each diver would enter the water at a precisely planned time keyed off Shaw's descent, with the job of meeting either Dave or the body at a given depth. Descent rates and deco plans had to be managed to the minute, especially for the deeper rendezvous. Regardless of his own assignment, every diver would be ready to assist everyone else. Shirley thought of this as 'rolling support', with divers passing one another on the line: some going down, others on their way up, an intricate overlay. In theory, the overlapping dive profiles would ensure a safer dive; but there was also the danger that a single problem could cascade into a series of difficulties. Several of the divers would be engaged in major dives simultaneously. Shirley settled on four divers going to 150 metres or beyond (including Shaw and himself) and two more as deep as 100 metres. This was serious diving, and any mishap would be potentially life-threatening.

Shirley decided that every diver on the team must use a rebreather. Rebreathers cut down deco requirements and allowed support divers to stay down longer; on open-circuit, the 150 metre divers would have barely enough time to hit their depth and start their return, and they would need to carry so much gas for their own use that they really wouldn't be able to support anyone else. And rebreather divers and scuba traditionalists don't mix well. Procedures are different, and if a diver on a rebreather needed help with his rig, an open-circuit diver probably wouldn't know how to help.

There was also an element of techie pride. Shirley believed that the dive wasn't feasible on open-circuit: only on a rebreather. This would be a display of the power of the machines.

Shirley's Inspiration became even more powerful about a month before the dive when Shaw sent him a Hammerhead controller, like the one Shaw used on his machine. The Hammerhead was a replacement for the original electronic hardware, including the audio alarm chamber that was believed to be the point most likely to fail under pressure. Without this limitation, Shirley could now meet Shaw even deeper. He decided that he would make his support dive to 220 metres, nearly 40 metres farther than he had ever gone before. And he would be ready to go even deeper.

Now he needed divers – and Inspiration owners – to fill the support roles.

He knew that he could count on Lo Vingerling and Peter Herbst. Both were his personal friends. When Herbst heard that Shaw had found the body, Herbst immediately sent Shirley a text message: *When do we fetch him?* Vingerling was capable of a 100 metre dive. Herbst had never been deeper than 80 metres.

Stephen Sander was another friend. Sander was a veteran of the wild and unconventional South African tech diving scene of the early '90s, and Shirley had met him on Don's first visit to Bushman's. On that trip Sander had saved another diver's life. When the man's regulator failed at 150 metres,

Sander brought him to the surface, sharing gas with him the whole time. That impressed Shirley. Sander had become his student and adopted all the standard techniques that Shirley taught. Sander dived more safely now, but he was as brave as ever. A good man to have around. He was qualified to go anywhere Shirley needed him to go.

Mark Andrews and Dusan Stojakovic came as a pair. Most tech divers like to dive solo. Andrews and Stojakovic were in the minority: they preferred to do the more difficult dives as a pair. Stojakovic was 50, an executive at a pharmaceuticals firm. Andrews was eight years younger, a businessman. Together they could handle a support dive to 150 metres.

Gerhard du Preez, 30, was a former student of Shirley, now working as a paramedic in Saudi Arabia. Du Preez hadn't done much deep diving since he left South Africa, but Shirley knew that he was a skilled diver, and Don liked having a medical technician in the water.

Truwin Laas, 30, was an explosives expert who worked in the South African mining industry. Laas had taken several advanced courses with Shirley and was also a trained paramedic.

Before Shaw left South Africa, he and Shirley discussed scheduling the dive for 17 December, the tenth anniversary of Deon Dreyer's death. But Shaw had no more annual leave for the year and he had to petition Cathay Pacific for the time off. While he was still in South Africa, he asked Ann to contact one of Hong Kong's English-language newspapers with the story of his record and the discovery of the body. He hoped that the publicity would help persuade Cathay to sponsor the operation.

None of Shaw's friends and family, including Ann, had ever really grasped the reality of his diving ambitions. Now the truth was out. Shaw also arranged for a letter from Theo Dreyer, asking for the airline's cooperation. But Cathay officials weren't moved. They dismissed the idea of sponsorship and refused to extend Shaw's leave for the December dates. The airline did agree to carry Shaw's excess baggage without charge, and allowed him to take two weeks advance leave in the first part of January.

Shaw would leave Hong Kong late evening 1 January, arriving in Johannesburg on the morning of the 3rd – a Monday. Shirley calculated a schedule for the setup dives, and he settled on the date of the big dive.

It would be Saturday, 8 January.

*　　*　　*

Before the dive could take place, Shaw and Shirley needed the permission of the South African Police Service. Though there was no suspicion that the disappearance of Deon Dreyer was anything but an accident, police still controlled how (or whether) the body would be removed, and by whom.

Ordinarily the recovery of a body would be the job of police divers. The SAPS trained and maintained teams in each South African province. They usually dived in shallow water – rivers, ponds, even ditches – under conditions of zero visibility: 'black water' diving. It was grim work, and it kept them busy; Theo van Eeden, the police inspector who stayed interested in the Dreyer case, had recovered more than 500 bodies during his career.

The police divers operated under basic commercial diving standards, with a level of training that limited them to a depth of 20 metres.

Most of the time, work performed under water is the task of a commercial diver, an occupation that compares to sports diving approximately as piloting an Airbus across an ocean compares to flying an aerobatic display in a biplane. Sports diving and commercial diving operate in the same environment, under the same physical laws, but the approaches are radically different. Commercial diving is conducted under strict occupational safety rules. The availability of breathing gas is never an issue; divers are usually supplied with gas from the surface, and are almost always in voice contact with a topside operator. Decompression takes place in a submerged chamber or bell. On a major job, divers may stay for days in a pressurized chamber resembling a small submarine, venturing out to work and then returning to the chamber to rest and eat; when the job is finished, the chamber will be hauled to the surface, still under pressure, and the divers locked inside will slowly decompress over several days, supervised by a diving physician. The ready availability of breathing gas, and the opportunity to decompress in a chamber, allow commercial divers to work at depths of 350 metres and more.

Essentially, commercial diving involves the brute application of resources to mitigate danger as much as possible. Sports divers – especially extreme divers – accept far more risk in order to dive unencumbered.

The recovery of a body from 270 metres below the surface would usually be a job for commercial divers. In order to be allowed to attempt the dive, Shaw and Shirley had to

154

convince the police that they were a better choice. When Shaw returned to Hong Kong, that job fell to Shirley. He made his case at a meeting in Pretoria with police officials and national health and safety officials.

With help from André, Don prepared a brief in which he argued that the narrow opening prevented a bell or chamber from being lowered into the cavern. Without a controlled environment for decompression, the dive couldn't be conducted according to commercial standards, and if the safety standards couldn't be followed, the law forbade commercial divers from taking part.

Shirley argued that he and Shaw were uniquely qualified to organize the operation and perform the dive; they had demonstrated their capabilities in October. He submitted a preliminary version of his dive plan.

Superintendent Ernst Strydom was in charge of the SAPS diving teams,* and he favoured allowing Shaw and Shirley's group of divers to do the recovery. But he wanted a team of police divers involved as well, to ensure the proper chain of custody for the body and the equipment.

The panel agreed to the plan, on condition that police divers would be included in the operation, operating at their maximum depth of 20 metres in order to receive the body after Shirley's body team brought it up from the depths. The police would bring a mobile decompression chamber to the site.

Shirley was delighted. He had been trying to locate a mobile chamber. Even with planning and careful execution, every serious dive involves a risk of decompression injury,

---

* Strydom was also in command of the SAPS hostage negotiation unit.

and with several major dives taking place simultaneously, the odds were increased that somebody would need treatment at the site.

But the panel also demanded that Shirley have a diving physician on hand to supervise any treatment. Shirley spoke to Grant Jameson, a leading commercial diver who knew Don and André. Jameson recommended W.M.A. 'Jack' Meintjes, a Cape Town physician and an authority on decompression, who was also a commercial diver.

Meintjes agreed to take part.

*   *   *

Until the discovery of the body, Shaw and Shirley had pursued their sport in near-total obscurity. Shirley had written articles for diving publications in South Africa, and Shaw was known on Internet forums devoted to tech diving and rebreathers. But neither had ever been recognized by name in any mainstream newspaper or magazine.

That changed instantly. The discovery of the body was literally front-page news in the *Star*, a large and influential English-language newspaper with a national circulation. Other outlets picked up the story, and interest grew as plans for the body recovery became known. Eventually André Shirley collected a stack of press clippings several centimetres thick. The broadcast media, especially radio, covered the story just as closely.

Nobody involved in the dive – nobody involved in any sports dive, anywhere – had ever seen anything like it. Nuno Gomes received occasional coverage of his major dives, but nothing comparable to this.

In late November, Marie and Theo Dreyer became uncomfortable with the publicity, fearing that the dive would become a spectacle. Shaw called them from Hong Kong and promised them that the recovery would be discreet. He had already decided to restrict press access at the site, partly out of sensitivity to the Dreyers, but also from sheer practicality. Reporters couldn't be allowed into the hole; amazingly, the place was just too small to accommodate them all.

*   *   *

Gordon Hiles sensed right away that this dive was going to be different.

Hiles was an independent documentary filmmaker in Johannesburg with long experience in South African media. In the mid-1970s, he was a member of the first documentary production unit in the country's national broadcast system. He was a diver and underwater photographer, and had been at Bushman's with Derek Hughes during the last week in October to shoot what he hoped would become a documentary video on Verna van Schaik's record. He met Shaw there for the first time, and they briefly discussed the idea of collaborating on a documentary about Shaw's own diving. But it went no farther than that, and Hiles returned to Johannesburg the day after van Schaik's dive.

Afterwards, when he saw the press coverage of Shaw and his finding the body, Hiles realized that this story would far eclipse the interest in van Schaik's dive. He had never seen anything like it.

Before Shaw returned to Hong Kong, he met Hiles in Johannesburg. Hiles taped an interview and they discussed a film to document the recovery dive. More than once, Dave and Don had sat together in the evening after a day of diving, and talked about the fact that nobody outside their very close circle knew what they were doing. They could not have been more obscure if they had tried to keep it secret.

But that changed with the discovery of the body. Now people knew who they were. Shaw told Hiles that he was interested in a documentary that was about more just than the upcoming dive. He wanted to convey the true sense of what he and Shirley did, and how they did it. Hiles liked the concept. He told Shaw that he would need full access and total cooperation from everyone involved in the operation. Shaw agreed, and Hiles mentioned the possibility of Shaw taking a camera with him and recording his work at the bottom of the cavern. This would be a real coup, he told Shaw: not only to recover a body from 270 metres, but to bring back video. Hiles had hoped to do the same with Verna van Schaik, but it never happened.

Obviously, Shaw wouldn't be able to film his work actively – he would literally have his hands full. Hiles suggested a camera mounted to a helmet. Shaw agreed to consider it. They left open the financial arrangements, but Shaw told Hiles that he would purchase a camera in Hong Kong and have it sent ahead to Johannesburg.

At first Hiles considered using a miniature camera feeding video via cable to a recorder that Shaw would carry somewhere on him. But he thought that was impractical. He decided to use a compact video camera in a housing. Hiles was aware of no commercial housing that would withstand the pressure at 270 metres, and if one did exist it would be far too expensive for his limited budget. But Hiles knew a machinist in Johannesburg, Greg Raymond, with a computer-operated milling machine. Raymond was Hiles's friend, and he agreed to produce a housing.

Shaw purchased a camera in Hong Kong, and sent it to Hiles: it was a Sony HC20, a popular consumer model that recorded on mini-DV tape. It was slightly larger than palm-sized. After taking measurements from the camera, Hiles and Raymond used a computer-aided drawing program to design a housing to fit. Raymond machined the body from a solid block of aluminium that Hiles had kept for years in his garage. The housing used a Plexiglas lens port and viewing port, it had an external control to operate the recording switch, and it sealed with two hex-head screws.

Hiles was confident that the housing would withstand the pressure at the bottom of Bushman's. If anything, he thought, he had made the walls slightly too thick. The housing looked slightly bigger than he had imagined.

He decided that he would let Shaw make the call.

In December, Hiles and Shaw worked out the details of their contract. Hiles wanted to be reimbursed for the production costs before the profits were distributed. Shaw wanted any income to be split from the first money earned. He wrote in an email:

> Without either party, nothing would be happening, so we depend on each other in this enterprise. So it all comes down to risk, and the benefit of that risk. The principal divers take a risk doing the dives. The production company takes a risk that the resultant project will not sell. So we are all investors. What is

worse, investing your life, or investing some money? Personal question that I do not expect an answer to!

The diver's risk is short term but significant. The production team invests time and money. As far as I am concerned, that makes the risk or investment good enough to be equal. Well, in all honesty, I think the divers' risk is higher ... The divers invest in full their capital when they do the dive.

Shaw won the argument.

*   *   *

David had always withheld the details of his diving from Ann, in part because Ann had always resisted knowing. But there was no avoiding it now. For the first time, Ann was going to hear it all.

He brought her to Sai Kung, a waterfront town in the New Territories that they both enjoyed. Their first home in Hong Kong had been nearby, and even after they moved to Clearwater Bay they frequently came here for the shopping and restaurants. It's a lovely place, clean and tranquil, situated beside a sheltered harbour. They ate lunch at their favourite restaurant – Jaspa's, the same place where Michael Vickers was a fixture – and then they walked along the wide esplanade which follows the shoreline for more than a mile.

He told her about Bushman's and about finding the body, about cave diving and rebreathers. What he did had some dangers, he told her. But it wasn't as dangerous as it seemed.

She asked him questions.

What if your mask implodes? *I carry a spare.*

What if your rebreather quits? *I bail out straightaway to the gas I'm carrying.*

What if you get a hole in your drysuit? *I'd probably get cold, but it's not a big problem.*

He could deal with every foreseeable problem, he told her. The real risk was the one you did not expect, and the unexpected was always a possibility.

But he believed that he could do this, and that he would be coming back from it. God had a job for him, and the job wasn't yet finished – the congregation still didn't have a church building of its own.

She knew that she could force the issue: ask him not to do the dive, ask him to quit diving altogether. And he would do it for her. He loved her and respected her that much. But that would be a betrayal. Since the first time they met, they had always accepted each other exactly as they were. For her, he would walk away from the dive; if she insisted, he would walk away from diving altogether, but he would never be the same. He needed this. Deprived of his challenges, David would no longer be David, but instead a diminished version of the man she had always loved.

Their stroll along the waterfront lasted more than an hour. Before it was over, she did not just give her consent; in a small but important way, she had become an active participant in the project.

*   *   *

Her contribution involved the body.

Even before he returned to Hong Kong, Shaw began to consider how the body might be brought to the surface. If he had been able to pull it loose during his dive, he would have had to carry it by hand or tie it to the shot line, to be pulled up later. Now his options were wider, but when he discussed it with Shirley, they quickly realized that the answer depended in part on the condition of the body.

What would happen to a body over 10 years in 19°C water, in an environment of complete darkness? The exposed tissues of the head had apparently long decomposed, but what about the limbs and trunk, covered by the wetsuit? Was there any chance that some solid flesh remained?

Shirley consulted several physicians and pathologists. None could give him a definitive answer. Each said that the best possibility was that the flesh was completely gone, and a skeleton was all that remained.

This created a difficulty. Some way had to be found to contain the bones, which would likely spill out from the open wrists and cuffs of the wetsuit when the body was lifted.

Shaw thought that a body bag was the answer. But a standard body bag would be difficult to handle under water, and Shaw wanted to keep his effort to a minimum. Further, he had to deal with the tanks, apparently stuck in the mud. Soon he conceived of a bag and a plan to use it.

He imagined a tube-shaped sack, open at one end. A mesh bottom would allow water to flow through, minimizing drag. He would slide the bag over the legs of the body, up to about mid-thigh, then cut the body loose, using a knife or shears to remove the material of the buoyancy vest that bound it to the tanks.

Once the body was free, he could lift it enough to finish sliding it into the bag, then close the top with a drawstring.

162

Drawstrings around the area of the knees and the chest would help to hold the body in place. The top would close with another drawstring. Once secured, the bag and the body could be carried or even clipped off to a diver's hip.

All this was predicated on the body remaining in place after Shaw cut it loose. But Shaw couldn't imagine otherwise. The wetsuit would have long lost its buoyancy, the Neoprene material having been crushed for a decade by the relentless pressure. And a skeleton will not float. When he mentally rehearsed the procedure – and he surely did dozens of times, if not hundreds – Shaw always saw himself working with a stable body. He had no reason to visualize it otherwise.

The bag which Shaw imagined did not exist. Ann volunteered to make it.

Like all new Cathay pilots, when Shaw was first hired, he was issued a dark silk sleeping sack for use when he went off duty during long haul flights. Shaw had never used his, and the shape and light weight seemed ideal for his body bag. It wasn't quite long enough, and he coaxed another from a pilot friend who also never used his sack.

From the two bags, Ann created a single elongated tube that she cut to length. She enclosed one end of the tube with net from a fishing supply shop in Sai Kung. She sewed in the drawstrings, and attached Velcro tabs so that the bag would hold a compact shape but would deploy easily under water when Shaw was ready to use it. She was squeamish about allowing him to test the bag by drawing it up over her head. But she tested it on David, on the floor of their dining room and in a swimming pool.

She liked being a part of what he was doing, and knowing the details didn't bother her as much as she had thought. His accomplishments and his ambition made her proud. She compared him to the brave pilots in aviation's early days, flying aircraft that weren't well-proved, pushing forward on guts and skill and sheer will. She resented Cathay's reluctance to support him, and she complained to a company official whom the Shaws knew personally.

It's a dangerous sport, the man told her. *The wrong image for an airline.*

'If it wasn't for people like my husband, you wouldn't have an airline to run, because there wouldn't be any aeroplanes,' she told the man. 'We would still be getting around in a horse and cart.'

*　*　*

For a couple of years, Ann and David had discussed updating their wills, which were created when the children were much younger. Now Lisa and Steven were grown, responsible enough to handle money without a guardian or a trust, but Ann and David had put it off; there was always something else more pressing or at least more interesting. In December, however, Ann insisted on following through. She didn't want David to think that she was concerned about the upcoming dive – and, in fact, she did expect him to return – but the updating was overdue and she wanted it taken care of.

On 7 December, they visited a solicitor to have it done. It was their thirtieth wedding anniversary. A few days later, the papers were ready to be signed.

Ann was unaware that David had made some arrangements of his own. In late December he met Michael Vickers at the pastor's usual table at Jaspa's, and after they had discussed some church business Shaw talked about how Ann should be notified in case of an accident. He said that he would give Vickers's phone numbers to a trusted person in South Africa. If you get a call, he told Vickers, you will know that I'm not coming back. And he asked that Vickers take Harry and Pamela when he delivered the news. Shaw didn't seem especially concerned, not morbidly preoccupied. Vickers just got the impression of a loving husband looking after his wife. It was completely in character.

'The documentation you sent was very good,' Shaw wrote in an email to Don, referring to the materials the Shirleys had prepared for their meeting with police.

> I gave it to my wife to read. She was impressed. I have cheated on the dive date with her. She is a bit worried as normally she only learns about my dives after the event. She thinks the main dive will be on the 10th. With a bit of luck I can ring her and tell her it is over before it has happened if you know what I mean!!

At Komati Springs, Don and André were now working full time on organizing the dive; Don quit giving classes around the second week in December.

The mobile chamber was welcome, but it created a couple more tasks. It required large quantities of helium and oxygen, far more than Shirley had on hand for diving purposes. Because helium was not produced locally, and must be imported in very heavy tanks, the gas is expensive in South

Africa.* Shirley hoped to find a sponsor for the gases. Theo Dreyer volunteered to help, and persuaded Afrox, the country's largest supplier of commercial and medical gases, to donate the gas on condition that it would be used for medical purposes and not for diving.

Shirley was also concerned with the mechanics of getting an injured diver from the surface of the water to the chamber, which would have to be parked up on the rim. In severe cases, decompression injury must be treated as quickly as possible. Minutes can be critical. Manhandling a diver on a litter basket up the steep path to the top would be slow and torturous, and might make the difference between a full recovery and a crippling injury, or even death.

A possible solution came from Truwin Laas, the explosives engineer whom Shirley had approached to join the dive team. Laas knew that every big mine employed a rescue team trained to extract injured miners from shafts. One of Laas's friends, and his diving buddy, was Reán Louw, captain of the Proto rescue team at the Modikwa platinum mine, in northern Mpumalanga. The mine owners agreed to release the Proto team for the dive. The publicity was paying off; everyone seemed to know about the operation and wanted to be a part of it.

One after another, the divers for his proposed support team all agreed to make time for the dive. Around New Year's weekend, most came to Komati Springs for practice dives at the depths where Shirley intended to use them.

---

* Helium is produced by distillation of natural gas. The United States is the world's largest source of the gas, accounting for about 80 per cent of global production.

Shirley gathered equipment. The dive would require about 25 emergency cylinders on the shot line, each with a scuba regulator. It was more than Shirley had in his shop inventory. He ordered tanks and a batch of his favourite regulators, Scubapro Mk25/XS650, and he asked the other divers to bring as much personal equipment as possible.

In an email to the support divers, he wrote:

> This will be an amazing dive in terms of logistics and team work alone, not to mention the 'epic' nature of the dive. The backup and support we are receiving will probably never be repeated.

*   *   *

It was a good Christmas season at the Shaw home. David and Ann had several days together. Lisa was at home for a long break between semesters at school.

Lisa was 21, in her fourth year at university, finishing a course in applied science. She was intrigued by her father's diving and asked him to tell her more.

At first he was reticent. Lisa thought that he wasn't deliberately opaque; he was simply a private person by long habit. But she persisted in getting him to open up. 'It was like prodding him with an electric prod' – and eventually he opened up. He described his dives and his plans for the recovery at Bushman's.

Lisa devoured it all. She told him that she wanted to go along the next time he went for a big dive. There wasn't time to make plans for the recovery dive, but the next one after that.

'It's not much,' he told her. 'I just go down deep and then sit around for twelve hours until it's time to come up again.'

'I don't care,' she said. 'I want to be there.'

She wasn't sure, but she thought that this pleased him, that one of his offspring showed some interest in his passion.

'Maybe next time,' he said.

*   *   *

Dave planned to leave on the evening of 1 January, flying out on Cathay Flight 749 after a day at the Cathay offices. His last free day was 31 December, and he spent it packing equipment and loading it into Ann's car, which had fold-down rear seats and more room for cargo. It made a hectic day, and they were asleep in bed before the arrival of the New Year.

The next morning David drove off to work and Ann drove her gear-laden car to school. One of the teachers had been killed in the southeast Asian tsunami after Christmas, and the principal, a German, wanted a native English speaker to help compose a letter to parents and statements to the press. She finished in time to pick up David at the Cathay offices and drive him to the airport. They parked, unloaded and checked 120 kilos of luggage, and then went in to a coffee shop together.

She thought that she was holding up all right. Then he took her hand and said, 'Don't fret.'

'Of course not,' she said. But inside she collapsed. It was something about what he said and the way he said it.

She tried not to show it though. They stood and he held her and said goodbye, and then he was gone.

CHAPTER
13

It was a Sunday morning, 2 January, when Shaw arrived in Johannesburg aboard CX479. The big dive was set for Saturday: six days later, almost to the hour. Shaw didn't waste time; there was none to waste. A few hours after touchdown, he was in the water at Komati Springs with Don Shirley and Lo Vingerling, trying for the first time to use the body bag while he was in full dive gear. Don Shirley became the body. Using open-circuit equipment, he lay on a platform 10 metres below the surface, in the same face-up posture that Shaw had described after the dive in October. On the assumption that the body would be mostly skeletal, and therefore negatively buoyant, Shirley wore a belt with several one-kilo lead weights to keep him from floating away while Shaw worked.

This was a critical test. Shaw's dive plan allowed a maximum of five minutes on the bottom. Anything more would stretch his decompression times beyond the tolerable. Assuming one minute to swim each way between the shot line and the body, Shaw would have three minutes to secure the body in the bag. He had always imagined that he could complete the task in that time, but this was his first opportunity to try it under water, in full gear.

This test didn't exactly replicate the situation Shaw would face at Bushman's. The platform was free of the silt that he would encounter on the floor of the cave, and the effects of any effort would be far greater at 270 metres than at 10. If he couldn't do it under the time limit, in optimum conditions, they would have to reconsider the method for retrieving the entire body.

Shaw waited to one side as Shirley dropped to the platform and stretched out on his back. Lo Vingerling timed the trial. He floated nearby, ready to help if Shirley's mouthpiece became dislodged during the exercise.

Shaw swam over, as he would do at the bottom of the hole. He pulled off Shirley's fins, took out the bag from a pocket of his drysuit, unfurled it. Shirley tried to remain a dead weight as Shaw slipped his feet into the bag and worked it up over his knees. Shaw used shears to quickly cut through the nylon webbing straps of the harness. He pulled the bag up over Shirley's head and cinched it tight.

Time: 1 minute, 30 seconds.

*　　*　　*

They stayed that night at Komati Springs, and awoke at 4 am the next morning. It was a schedule Shirley planned to maintain through the week to come, so that by the morning of the dive he would be fully adjusted to the early start. The early wakeup suited Shaw, whose sleep rhythms were still on Hong Kong time, six hours advanced.

Before 5 am, they were on the road, westbound. Shirley drove his truck, with a trailer full of dive gear. Shaw and Lo Vingerling followed. They were headed for the farm owned by Petrus Roux, one of Shirley's former students, who lived about midway between Komati Springs and Bushman's.

Roux had been a support diver during Shaw's record dive in October, and the two men became friendly after a long conversation following a setup dive. Roux used an Inspiration rebreather. Most Inspiration divers write a name or short slogan on the cover of the machines in permanent ink. Roux's Inspiration showed the word THEOS – Greek for 'god'. Shaw asked him about it as they sat among the boulders, resting after a dive. They discovered that they shared a fervent and fundamental Christianity.

They exchanged emails after Shaw returned. Roux learned that Shaw hadn't spoken of religion with any of his other diving companions. Roux felt that it gave him a special connection with Shaw. It was a busy time on the 5000 acre farm, and his duties on the farm prevented him from joining the dive, but Petrus and his wife Sumarie had invited Shaw, Shirley and Vingerling to spend the night on their way to Bushman's.

Shirley and Vingerling went with Roux on a tour of the property, but Shaw declined. He went to sleep early after dinner. Roux was concerned for him; he thought that Shaw seemed tired and maybe a little distracted.

They were all up very early the next morning. Shirley, Shaw and Vingerling left before sunup. Four hours later, when they arrived at the hole, they were greeted by the sight of a plan made real. The police dive team had arrived the day before, and with them was the portable recompression chamber, enclosed within a large truck trailer and parked along the west side of the rim. The police had set up a large command tent and several smaller bivouac tents. And when he got out and spoke with the police, Shirley learned that the gas supplier, Afrox, had delivered dozens of tanks of oxygen and helium for use in the chamber.

It's really happening, Shirley thought.

It came together further over the next few hours, when all the divers except for Truwin Laas arrived at the hole; Laas had told Shirley that he would not arrive until late Thursday, and he did. Four members of the Modikwa mine rescue team also arrived on Tuesday.

In the end, everyone who had promised to be there was there. Every commitment was fulfilled.

Peter Herbst arrived about an hour after Shaw, Shirley and Vingerling. Even before he started down to the bottom of the pit, he heard their voices from below, carried up in the weird echo chamber produced by the steep stone walls. He clambered down and greeted them. He hadn't seen Shaw since their trip to Bushman's the previous June, but immediately the banter between them resumed.

A few minutes later, the tone turned more serious as they stood together at the edge of the pool, looking down into the water.

'This is a really good thing you're doing for the Dreyers,' Herbst said.

Shaw shook head. 'Let's face it,' he said. 'We're doing this for the hell of it.'

*   *   *

That afternoon, Shaw and Shirley made the first dive of the expedition, down to 45 metres, to put in some shallow cylinders and replace an air-filled barrel supporting the shot line. After angling down out of the upper cave, the rope hung from a ring on the barrel and dropped straight down to the bottom. This was where the cavern opened up, the point of demarcation between a standard cave dive and a plunge into the void.

Actually two lines passed through the metal ring that hung on the barrel. One was the stout white line from Verna van Schaik's dive, which ended about 40 metres short of the bottom. The other was a yellow polypropylene rope that had been put in for Shaw's dive in October. They followed the same path and were loosely intertwined for much of their length. Taken together, they were far stronger and more secure than most shot lines. This isn't usually important; most of the time, shot lines are used mainly as guides and as a means to hang cylinders, which are near-weightless in water. Divers are assumed to control their buoyancy, and seldom use the line the way a mountaineer might use a climbing rope. But before the sun set on Saturday, the lines would be used exactly that way, and their strength potentially would mean life or death for one of the men.

After their dive that afternoon, Shaw and Shirley returned to the lodge. There they found Gordon Hiles, the documentary producer, carrying equipment from his truck. Hiles had just arrived from Johannesburg, later than he had hoped. Minutes before he was to leave for Bushman's, he had gashed his forehead while replacing a light bulb and had visited a hospital emergency room for several stitches.

Now he brought out the underwater housing for the video camera and showed it to Shaw and Shirley.

'It's larger than I thought,' Shirley said. He had expected a miniaturized camera, something no bigger than his thumb. It wasn't a question of aesthetics. The bigger the housing, the greater the chance that it would interfere with the dive. Shaw was already laden with gear, the layout determined after much thought and trial.

But it was Shaw's choice, he thought.

Shaw too was sceptical, but he seemed mostly concerned about whether the housing would withstand the high pressures at 270 metres. Hiles said that he didn't expect a problem. The pressure at the bottom was 28 Bar, or about 410 pounds per square inch. The housing was sealed by an O-ring arrangement similar to the one used on diving tanks that are pumped to 200 Bar. If anything, Hiles said, pressure would compress the rings, strengthening the seal.

Hiles knew that Shaw and Shirley planned to do a setup dive to 150 metres in the morning. He urged Shaw to bring the camera along. That depth would test the integrity of the housing and Shaw would have a chance to try the camera.

Shaw agreed to try it.

That evening, and each of the next three evenings, Shirley and Shaw held a team briefing on the lawn outside the Mount Carmel lodge. Shirley hadn't yet laid out the specifics of the plan; until that afternoon he hadn't been sure who would actually be available. But he described it in general and he said that he would be Shaw's deepest support, at 220 metres.

'I don't intend to go any deeper than that unless Dave is not there,' he said, grinning. 'And I want him to be there.'

174

'Yes, I'll consider that,' Shaw said drily.

That brought chuckles all around.

'The most important aspect of this is that all the divers who go in, come out and that everyone's well,' Shirley said. 'The priority is the diver. If someone's got a problem, and if your task was to support the body, now it's not any more. It's to support the real live person. Things could flip like that.'

He added, 'I can't see anyone really having a problem.'

Shaw described what he had found in October, the position of the body, with tanks buried in the mud.

'I was actually kneeling, trying to lift him up,' Shaw said. 'I'll feed him up to about his waist, into the body bag. Because he's anchored there, and that actually makes it a lot easier for me to do.'

He mentioned that the police were interested in recovering the dive equipment, and that they would give him a wire line that he could attach to the equipment, allowing it to be hauled up with the shot line. Privately, he and Shirley had already agreed that the equipment was the lowest priority and that the wire was an unnecessary complication.

'Personal opinion,' he said, 'I don't think that's gonna work. I think the stuff is very firmly stuck in the mud.'

*   *   *

Don Shirley worked until midnight that night, mixing gas for the recompression chamber. The sixty large cylinders of donated medical gas sat in a shed near the Mount Carmel guest house, which was completely occupied by divers and others connected with the operation. Shaw and Shirley shared a large room. Many others, including the large police team and a contingent from the South African National Defence Force, were camped on the rim.

Shirley wanted everyone to prepare for a very early start on Saturday morning, so on Wednesday all the divers were at the hole before daybreak. While the support divers spent the morning with shakedown dives, becoming familiar with the arrangement of the lines, Shaw and Shirley dropped down to 150 metres and hung three cylinders, the deepest of the emergency tanks. Shaw carried the underwater camera at the end of a lanyard clipped to his harness, and while he was at 150 metres he tried it briefly before starting back up. It was their last time in the water before the big dive on Saturday.

On Thursday, while Shaw and Shirley watched from shore, the support divers went through a full rehearsal, entering the water according to a schedule that Don and Dave had worked out the previous day. All went to the same depths they had been assigned for Saturday. All brought in cylinders to be hung on the line.

Before the dive, Verna van Schaik walked among the tanks laying at the water's edge, noting each, with the gas mixture it carried and the depth for which it was intended. Throughout the week she logged every piece of equipment that went down into the cave and the diver who carried it. Van Schaik had agreed to be the surface marshal for the dive. She had never done this before, but she imagined that it would be mostly clerical. She had already picked out a book that she would bring to the hole on Saturday, something to pass the time during the long empty hours of decompression.

The rehearsal dive went well. Shirley knew there would be a jam in the shallows – probably 80 per cent of every technical dive is spent doing decompression at six and three metres. Later he slightly adjusted the start times for a couple of the divers, but in all he was pleased with the way it had come off.

On Friday, all rested except for Truwin Laas, who got in a quick familiarization dive.

For such an ambitious operation, it was a remarkably brief series of setup dives. To Shirley, this was a triumph of organization and preparation, and it was possible only with rebreathers. Open-circuit divers, going to the same depths, would have required many more cylinders in the water, each of which would have had to be hauled in and out of the hole for daily filling. More cylinders would have meant more setup dives, requiring rest days between dives. A two-week operation had been reduced to a few days.

Up on the rim, the police team had virtually taken over. Besides the four-man police dive team, Ernst Strydom was on hand with at least half a dozen support personnel. The police had set up a radio repeater link to the bottom of the hole, and cordoned off access to all but the divers. A police PR specialist was handling media relations.

The plan was good; it was all coming together.

*   *   *

A four-man team from the Modikwa mine rescue team arrived on Tuesday afternoon. They were without Reán Louw, the team captain, who wouldn't be released from his mine duties until Thursday. Working without him, the crew spent most of Wednesday setting up a pulley system that would allow them to winch a victim in a litter directly up from the bottom of the hole.

They selected a spot where a rock ledge jutted out from the side of the wall, about five metres below the rim. They bolted a plate with rollers onto the lip of the ledge and ran a line from pulleys, over the rollers, down to the bottom. The mobile recompression chamber was parked beyond the edge of the rim.

On Thursday morning the rescue team was ready for a trial run.

Time is critical in treating the bends. A recompression chamber essentially forces gas bubbles back into the blood and tissues in a dissolved state, but the longer the bubbles remain, the greater the potential for permanent damage. At Bushman's, Jack Meintjes, the diving physician, wanted a victim in the recompression chamber within 30 minutes of coming out of the water, but the sooner the better.

The miners loaded a rebreather onto a litter at the bottom – weight, about 46 kilos – and began to haul the litter up the wall. The setup required a team member to accompany the basket, clipped in below it and walking it up the wall. But the labour on the pulley didn't have to be trained, and police divers joined the rescue team on the rope behind the pulley.

They began to pull. Most of the divers were at the bottom, resting from the rehearsal dive earlier that morning, and they watched with interest; any one of them could be in that litter on Saturday.

The litter's progress was slow – excruciating to more than one of the divers who watched. After 25 minutes, the litter reached the rollers on the ledge below the rim. And there it stopped. Two men climbed down onto the ledge, and tried to pull the basket past the rollers. The trailing team member who had walked it up the wall, a burly man named François Cilliers, climbed up to help. But the three men were unable to lift the basket over the lip.

Two bolt anchors worked loose where they had been screwed into the rock. The rope was anchored to a boulder the size of a kitchen table, yet the weight on the rope caused the boulder to move almost a metre.

They lowered the basket back to the bottom.

The trial had been a failure. If an actual victim had been in the litter, the attempt would have delayed treatment, at the cost of further damage or even death. Shirley and Shaw had watched the trial. Now they faced the possibility of abandoning the system if it couldn't be put right.

Many who watched had their doubts. That afternoon one of the police divers approached a member of the mine rescue team.

'That didn't look so good,' the police diver said. 'I don't think this is going to work.'

'It'll work,' the miner said. 'Reán will make it work.'

Reán Louw was a can-do guy: not an uncommon trait in the mining business. He was a private pilot, a technical diver, and a former paratrooper who saw action in Angola. He arrived at the site Thursday night, looked at the rope and pulley arrangement, and on Friday morning he worked with the team, resetting bolts and finding a new anchor.

When Louw was finished, a police official, visiting for the day, volunteered to ride in the litter for a trial run. They strapped him in, and Louw clipped in beneath the basket and walked it up the wall while the mine crew and others winched it up.

They were on display. This was a media day with Shaw and Shirley taking questions under a tent at the rim before inviting the reporters down to the hole to look around. As the litter basket rose up the cliff face, the reporters were watching, the entire dive team was watching, the police were watching,

The litter reached the lip, the point where it hung up the day before. For a minute or more, several men struggled to get it up the last metre. Then Reán Louw braced himself beneath the litter. Louw was a small man but wiry and strong, and when he lifted it and pushed from below, the basket cleared the lip and the rollers. From there it was a short distance to the top. The trip from the water to the rim had taken 27 minutes.

CHAPTER
14

That Friday morning, shortly after the press briefing, Shaw and Shirley wandered over to the mobile recompression chamber. It sat inside a truck trailer, a steel cylinder, painted white. At one end, facing out the back of the trailer, was a round porthole with a pressure seal.

Shaw and Shirley looked around the operating panel, with numerous dials and gauges, and then Shaw climbed into the chamber and Shirley followed him in. Derek Hughes was standing nearby, shooting with a digital still camera, and he caught them in a playful moment as they peered out through the open porthole. Dave's grin is wide and eager. Don's face is genial and relaxed, with a tinge of wonderment. They do not appear to be even slightly stressed or unnerved. Never would you guess that they are both less than a day away from an enterprise so fraught with risk that nobody had ever attempted any-thing like it.

What does come through is a sense of shared closeness. They're completely at ease with one another in the cramped chamber. They are friends: you would know it even if you knew nothing about who they are and what they had done together.

It is a poignant photograph. They were at the farthest reaches of their sport, a place where even small misjudg-ments and minor shortcomings can reverberate in disaster. As they sat smiling in the chamber, they were being over-taken by events: the first a decision made two days earlier, the other a mishap that was still a few hours away.

On Wednesday afternoon, after his 150 metre dive, Shaw met Hiles and Derek Hughes at the lodge swimming pool to test the submersible video housing in the water. Hiles had mounted it to the top of a kayaking helmet lined with foam. Shaw was concerned at first about the weight of the camera; at 270 metres he didn't want to create any extra effort, even just in the muscles of his neck. But when he tested it under water, vigorously moving his head, he didn't think that the weight was a problem.

His only concern was that the helmet seemed loose and there was no way to tighten it. But Hughes had brought a climbing helmet with adjustable straps. Shaw tried that one and he liked it right away. The weight was good, the helmet was comfortable, and he could tighten it during the dive if necessary. He was ready to use it.

That left just one decision. He wasn't sure what to do about his cave light.

Dave Shaw (left) and Don Shirley at the water's edge at Bushman's, before the big dive, with some of their bailout cylinders.

left The sheer cliff wall of Bushman's Hole, with the entrance pool at the bottom, the water surface covered by an aquatic weed.

below Memorial plaque for Deon Dreyer, beside the path leading down into Bushman's Hole.

Shaw as a boy in Australia.

Shaw's certification card to use trimix gas with a closed-circuit rebreather. This certification allowed him to attempt his deepest dives.

As a young man, Shaw was an agricultural pilot in western Australia.

In later years, Shaw was a Cathay Pacific flight captain based in Hong Kong.

Police and mine rescue crew setting up the winch system at Bushman's.

South African Police Supt Ernst Strydom, a key figure in supporting the big dive and in the recovery of the bodies.

The dive team and others with medical gas cylinders in the farm shed at Mount Carmel lodge. Kneeling from left: Dusan Stojakovic, Lo Vingerling, Gerhard du Preez, Stephen Sander, police inspector Theo van Eeden and Derek Hughes. Standing from left: Gregory Stojakovic (son of Dusan), Mark Andrews, Verna van Schaik, Peter Herbst, Don Shirley, Dave Shaw and Gordon Hiles.

left Petrus Roux before his dive to recover the bodies, 12 January 2005.

Shaw submerging at the start of his dive.

Don before a dive at Komati Springs, 2006.

right Deon at about age 19, in school uniform with shooting medal.

Shaw at the entrance at Bushman's, October 2004.

Shaw descending through the entrance at Bushman's in October 2004, probably minutes before he found Deon Dreyer's body.

above The first message between Shirley and the surface after his accident. Shirley wrote this and sent it up with Stephen Sander, who rushed it to the surface.

Shirley on deco at Bushman's, October 2004.

left The front side of Shirley's slate brought to the surface by Stephen Sander: 'Dave not coming back'.

below Shirley on the litter, near the top of the wall; Reán Louw is second from left in black, Peter Herbst is at the head of the litter.

left Shirley being helped off Peter Herbst's truck on the day after the dive, with the recompression chamber in background.

below The housing of Shirley's Hammerhead controller imploded under the immense pressure at 250 metres.

Andre and Don Shirley
at their home.

Don Shirley at the
edge of the pool at
Bushman's Hole,
May 2007.

This was a high-intensity lamp that he usually wore at the back of his right hand, gripping it by a rectangular handle that slipped over his fingers. The light was powered by a battery pack that he wore at his right hip. An electrical cord, about one metre long, connected the battery pack to the light head.

Usually the lamp stayed on his hand throughout a dive. Occasionally, though, when he needed full movement with his right hand, he would slip the light and the handle off his hand, and drape the cord around the back of his neck so that the lamp head would sit at his left breast, not only out of the way but pointing down and casting light in front of him, where he needed it in the darkness.

But the helmet and the housing wouldn't allow him to do this. Instead he decided to let the cord and light head dangle free, so as to help illuminate the immediate area where he would be working.

Of all the acts and decisions that determined the outcome of the dive, this was the most important.

Friday evening, after they returned from the hole, Shaw and Shirley held a final team briefing. They had met every evening since Tuesday, gathering on the lawn outside the lodge. But this meeting, unlike the others, was closed to everyone except the divers and Verna van Schaik. Shaw threw it open to questions. Gerhard du Preez wanted to know what the support divers should do if Shaw were delayed in coming up. For the deeper support divers, the timing was close – almost to the minute. Should they wait for Shaw if he wasn't there? Should they descend below their maximum? And what should they do if they had a problem on the way down?

Shaw and Shirley were emphatic. *Dive your plan*, they both said. *Your maximum depth is your limit.*

Shaw said, 'I really must emphasize that the most important diver is you. It is not me. For me, the most important diver is me. You must look after yourselves. If you have a problem, you deal with your problem and forget about me ... It cannot be any other way. It's better to have one person dead than two. It's as simple as that.'

Shirley said, 'If you have a problem, if you see someone else having a problem, deal with that problem before you go on. Having you meet Dave is helpful but not essential. Dave is capable of doing this dive alone.'

They discussed for several minutes the possibility of bringing back Deon Dreyer's equipment. The police wanted it; Theo Dreyer wanted it, Shaw said, because he wanted to settle the question of how his son had died. But to Shaw this didn't justify the added complication.

'Leave the equipment,' Peter Herbst said. 'I wouldn't do this expedition to bring you back, and you've got good equipment.'

He meant it as a joke, but Shirley was serious when he answered.

'If Dave doesn't make it, if I don't make it, we stay there. That's the end of the story.'

'That's a given,' Shaw said quickly. 'And my wife agrees with me on that.'

'We do not want to be recovered,' Shirley said. 'If there is a problem, we stay.'

The meeting ended. Shaw took Derek Hughes aside, and gave him a paper with Michael Vickers's phone numbers.

'This is my pastor. If anything goes wrong tomorrow will you please call him?' Shaw said. 'Wait until you're sure, but don't sugarcoat it. He knows what to do.'

The request didn't faze Hughes. He didn't think that Shaw was being fatalistic or morbid; to Hughes it was a normal, rational request. ('Divers are just more matter-of-fact about death and consequences,' he said later, recalling the incident.)

Hughes took the paper.

Now they were ready. The planning, the filling of tanks, the organizing, the fretting – all finished. Shaw and Shirley planned to in bed no later than 9 pm; they would be up by 4 am They ate a light meal and changed the batteries in their electronic gear.

And suddenly, improbably, it all came apart.

It started with Shaw. He put a fresh battery into his VR3 dive computer, tried to turn it on, but it would not power up. He tried a second fresh battery. It wouldn't power up.

The VR3 was a staple of Shaw's gear. He carried two: so did Shirley. The VR3 was worn at the wrist, with an LCD display panel that showed the depth and running time of the dive and a decompression schedule that constantly updated throughout the dive. Shaw didn't rely on the computers for deco on his very deep dives, but the depth and time information was essential – so important that he wore a spare. And he wouldn't start a major dive unless both his VR3s were working.

But all of Shirley's divers used VR3s, and most had spares. Peter Herbst gave Shaw one of his, and took Shaw's malfunctioning unit. Herbst checked it, cleaned the battery terminals and turned it on.

It came to life.

That was one potential disaster avoided. But the late-hour betrayal by a critical tool was unsettling. Then minutes later came another failure, and it was not so simple. Shirley was alone at the hole, screwing down the battery cover of his Hammerhead wristset, using a coin in the slotted metal disc. As he tightened it with one last twist of the coin, he heard – or maybe just sensed – a small *tick* somewhere beneath the cover.

The unit was dead when Shirley tried to power it up.

This was serious ... it was devastating. The wristset controlled all the electronic functioning of his rebreather. He couldn't dive without it.

He opened the battery cover, slid the battery out and looked inside. He saw nothing wrong.

The controller was machined from a hefty block of Plexiglas. When strapped on, it covered much of Shirley's forearm. The front side showed an electronic display. At the back was a removable cover, secured by screws at each corner.

Shirley disconnected the controller and brought it back to the lodge. He took it to Peter Herbst's room, and the two men discussed what to do. Shirley decided to open the back of the unit so that he could look inside and trace the fault with a multimeter. He laid the unit flat, removed the screws and very carefully lifted off the back cover. The well inside was brim-filled with paraffin oil. Shirley had filled it at Komati Springs. Shaw and Shirley believed that the oil strengthened the body of the controller and helped it stand up under the pressures at depth – Shaw's own Hammerhead was filled the same way and had been to 270 metres without a problem.

186

Herbst had a clean glass tumbler from the kitchen at the lodge. Shirley very carefully lifted the wristset and poured the oil into the tumbler, letting every possible drop drain out.

He set the tumbler aside and began to examine the interior of the controller. He couldn't see a problem. The multimeter traced the fault back to the battery well, but Shirley couldn't find any broken connections.

At around 8 pm Shaw looked in on Shirley, saw that he had a problem. Shaw used his cell phone to contact Kevin Juergensen, the designer and maker of the Hammerhead. Juergensen built the Hammerhead in small batches, assembling the units at his shop in California.

Shaw reached Juergensen and spoke with him. Shaw gave the phone to Shirley, and Juergensen walked Shirley through the circuitry. But Shirley still couldn't locate the problem.

The time was now past 9 pm, and Shaw wished Shirley good luck and went off to bed. The two men didn't discuss how the problem might affect the plans for the dive. But Shirley thought he knew the answer. The dive was ready to happen. People were in place, expectations were high. For weeks it had been gaining momentum, everything pointed to 6 am on Saturday morning, 8 January. Everyone was ready; Dave was ready. Dave wouldn't like doing it without his friend, but he would go ahead if it came to that.

What Shirley had told the other divers was true for him as well. *Dave is capable of doing this dive alone.*

Shirley poked and prodded at the innards of the controller, looking for the problem. He wore a headlamp and a magnifying loupe. At about 10 pm he found the problem: a broken connection near a battery terminal, hidden from sight.

He considered his options. He could re-attach the connection with a spot of solder, but it would be tricky. The working space was tight and he risked damaging the Plexiglas. He had an alternative, a trick he had sometimes used in the military for quick fixes in the field. He sent Herbst to the kitchen for a piece of aluminium foil and he wrapped the foil around one end of the battery. He slipped the foil-capped battery down into the well. The edges of the foil touched the bare end of the broken wire. The connection was good.

To Shirley, it was a 'bodge', but he had seen it work many times. Aluminium foil was stronger than it looked.

At about quarter past ten, he held the body steady while Herbst poured the paraffin oil back into the cavity. He replaced the back of the unit and screwed it down tight.

The unit powered up when he turned it on. Herbst grinned and slapped Shirley on the back.

'Two hundred seventy metres with a fucking bit of tin foil,' Shirley said.

He tapped it hard against his palm.

'What are you doing?' Herbst said.

'I'm trying to break it,' Shirley said.

'We just fixed it, be gentle with it.'

A thin bubble, so slight that it was almost invisible, had appeared between the face of the unit and the LED display. The bubble hadn't been there before. Somehow, in the emptying and refilling, they had lost a drop or two of oil.*

Shirley stared at it thoughtfully. He looked bleary.

---

* When Shirley had first filled it at Komati Springs, he screwed the cover shut while the controller was submerged in a large bowl of oil, eliminating any chance of air being trapped inside.

'I'm just wondering what the pressure's going to do, that's all,' he said.

'It won't do anything,' Herbst said.

Derek Hughes had joined them in the room, and was videotaping.

'Why did you put so much effort into this repair?' he asked Herbst from behind the camera. It was a setup question; Hughes already knew the answer. They all knew.

''Cause Don has to do this dive, mate,' Herbst answered. 'He wants to do it. He worked too hard for it, too long for it, not to do it. Simple as that.'

The time was now half past ten. Shirley collected his tools and went to his room. Shaw was already asleep. When they woke at 4 am, Shirley told Shaw that the problem was fixed, he was good to go. At about 4:45, they walked out to Shirley's bakkie, and Shirley punched up the iPod as they drove in darkness to Bushman's Hole.

*   *   *

One of Shirley's first acts when he arrived at the bottom of the pit the next morning was to test the Hammerhead's operation on his rebreather. He screwed in the lead cable from the rebreather and switched it on. The rectangular LCD screen came to life behind the thick transparent panel. Shirley laid the controller on a towel that was spread on the gravel. With Herbst looking on, he kneeled beside it and hunched over the screen, peering at the electronic display that glowed in the near-darkness.

One after the other, the oxygen readings from each of the machine's three sensors popped onto the screen. A solenoid clicked open inside the machine, and oxygen hissed softly into the breathing loop. Over the next several seconds the oxygen readings from each sensor rose. The solenoid clicked off. The hissing stopped. The sensor readings climbed and then held.

Good to go.

A few steps away Shaw sat on a rock, stripped to the waist. He was pulling his drysuit up around his legs as Gordon Hiles approached. Shaw gave no sign that he resented the intrusion. If he was anxious, he kept the anxiety well hidden. There was barely enough light for videotaping, but Shaw began speaking for the camera, describing Shirley's problem with the electronics.

'That wasn't causing me any stress as such,' he said. 'What was causing me stress was Don's stress with the failed unit.'

Peter Herbst, who hadn't yet dressed for diving, helped both Shaw and Shirley with their gear. Shaw was in the water first, shortly before 6 am, standing about chest-high on the sloping bottom. He tucked the body bag against the side of a bailout tank, using two elastic loops, and he clipped the tank under his left arm.

Shirley stepped into the pool at about 6.06.

Several minutes later, Shaw spat into his dive mask, rubbed the saliva against the lenses – a precaution against condensation forming on the glass – and rinsed it out before he fitted the mask to his face.

'I look forward to taking that off,' he said. That would be after he surfaced at the end of the dive. Stephen Sander handed him the helmet with camera and torch, and Shaw spent about twenty seconds positioning it on his head. This was the first time he had tried it while wearing a hood, and he didn't look completely comfortable. Sander had to lean in and buckle the chin strap.

Peter Herbst, on his haunches a few feet away, spoke to Shaw in a rare serious tone: 'Have a good dive, OK?'

Shaw turned to him and flashed a quick OK. After a final handshake with Shirley, Shaw floated out into deeper water. He put his face down into the water, swam until he was over the opening, and disappeared.

Verna van Schaik reset the hands of a battery-powered wall clock to show '00:00', and she placed the clock in a shallow niche on a nearby rock where it was visible to all the divers. This was the dive's run time. It would key every other scheduled event in the dive plan.

But very little today would go according to plan.

Shirley was to go at 00:13. As he stood waiting in the water, he ate a sticky energy bar and drank from a bottle of water. Staying hydrated helps to protect against an onset of the bends and one of the iconic images of the day would be divers sitting among the boulders, tipping long swallows from plastic bottles.

Five minutes after Shaw left, Dusan Stojakovic and Mark Andrews, who were to follow Shirley, buckled into their machines and came down and entered the pool. They had been standing in drysuits for more than half an hour, and the morning air was already warm.

Marie and Theo Dreyer came climbing partway down. They had waited out of sight, near the rim, until Shaw descended. He had asked them not to come down until he was gone. Marie had had a bad moment a couple of days earlier, a feeling of guilt when she saw some divers' wives: *They must hate me,* she thought, *their husbands, risking their lives for me.* Now her face showed an expression that was both distressed and expectant, as she stood beside a boulder that overlooked the water. From here she was close enough to see what was happening, but distant enough that she wasn't quite part of it.

With minutes yet to wait, Shirley moved a few metres away from the water's edge, floating above the entry to the cave. He fidgeted, muttered a quip – 'Fewest cylinders I've had all week, this' – and turned around to have Herbst check his buoyancy wing. He had insisted on being in the water, ready to dive, before Shaw started his dive. That way Dave would know that his deep support was on schedule, and hadn't been delayed by some late problem.

With twelve and a half minutes on the run clock, Verna van Schaik called to Shirley: 'Thirty seconds.' Shirley pointed down into the water, a signal that said, *I'm going now.* Shirley immediately released gas from his buoyancy wings and sank out of sight in a blink.

Now the minutes began to drag for Dusan Stojakovic and Mark Andrews as they floated in the pool, waiting their turn to go down.

Stojakovic was worried. Too much had gone wrong in the past twelve hours. The failures of Dave's computer and Don's controller were bad enough. But Stojakovic was also concerned about the effects of those distractions so close to the dive. Technical diving is in many ways a mind game, and the evening before a major dive is often a time for mental preparation. Stojakovic thought that the distraction factor was

Strike Three. At any other time, he believed, the dive would've been postponed for a day or two. None of the divers would've argued with the decision. But this dive was different; it had acquired a momentum, fed by the attention and the expectations. They were all under pressure to perform as promised, and he felt a general air of apprehension around the hole.

Still, he was going to dive. When the run time clock reached 00:29, he and Andrews sank beneath the surface and disappeared into the opening.

Peter Herbst was next. At 00:43 he was gone.

Lo Vingerling followed at 00:55.

Five minutes later, at 01:00, four police divers headed down to 20 metres, where they expected to receive the body. Derek Hughes was already waiting in the shallows, and he followed them down to record the arrival of the body from the deep.

At 01:14 – about 7.27 am – Stephen Sander dropped through the entrance. He was the twelfth diver to descend into the cave. None had yet returned. Bushman's was swallowing up men, and so far nothing and nobody had come back.

At about the time Sander disappeared, the first chilling shadow of disaster crept over the hole. The police divers now had been down for 15 minutes. Their trip to 20 metres would require two minutes at most. Two minutes down, two to return. By now they should have been back with the body.

To those who knew the plan and the schedule, their absence suggested that something was wrong in the tenuous chain that stretched down to 270 metres.

In cave diving, there is the world above with light and air, and the one down below that is rock and water and darkness, and every cave diver knows how impossibly separate those worlds are. That day, to be in the sunlight was to be ignorant and anxious. Knowledge filtered up to the surface in bits and scraps, like pieces of flotsam from a deep shipwreck.

The first piece was about to emerge, and it was not good.

*　　*　　*

Dusan Stojakovic felt himself relaxing as he and Mark Andrews reached the end of their descent. So far, everything was perfect. Shirley had planned for them a nine minute descent to 150 metres, with a four minute hold at 150 before they began to return. Stojakovic and Andrews began to slow their descent as they reached 135 metres: they didn't want to drop below their maximum depth. So they gradually drifted down, checking the depth readout and elapsed time on their computers. At exactly nine minutes, they hit 150.

They saw nothing. This didn't alarm them at first. But two minutes passed, then three, and there was nothing.

At four minutes, they saw a single light below, along the shot line. It wasn't the bright beam of a cave light: more like a dull glow that seemed to cycle on and off. It meant that someone was down there. Stojakovic knew that one light, whatever it was, meant that something had gone wrong. Two divers down, there should be two lights.

Stojakovic and Andrews waited. They were past five minutes now. Stojakovic's backup deco plan allowed for six minutes at 150. He decided that they could stay that long, but no longer. He signalled this to Andrews. Mark nodded agreement, and swam away from the shot line. Andrews thought that a second figure might be hidden below the first on the line, blocked from their view, and he wanted to get a better look. But he saw just the one light, glowing on and off, and he showed Stojakovic a single raised digit.

Six minutes now; they had to go. Later, when he talked about that moment, Stojakovic would remember a heartsick feeling, indescribable. One man dead, one on his way back, and they had to leave without knowing who had survived.

Dusan liked Shaw, they all did, but his attachments were clear: *Please let it be Don*, he thought, when he saw the single light below.

They started up.

* * *

When Peter Herbst arrived at his assigned depth, he saw Andrews and Stojakovic coming up. When they reached him, Andrews scribbled on a slate that he showed to Herbst:

DID NOT MEET D + D
@ 150 FOR 6 MIN.
1 LIGHT BELOW?
NOT SURE D'S LIGHT OFF

Herbst peered into the depths. He saw one faint light below. How far below, he couldn't judge.

He decided to go down.

Plan your dive, dive your plan is a fundamental rule of the sport. It was also the explicit instruction of both Don and Dave at the pre-dive briefings. But Herbst felt that he wasn't taking a huge risk. The gas in his rebreather was suitable down to 150 metres. If his rebreather failed, he could run it manually and use the emergency tanks stashed at intervals along the shot line.

As for the depth, he was comfortable at 111 metres. Below that, he was in unfamiliar territory. He decided that he would just deal with it.

He began dropping in increments. About every five metres he would stop and check his dive computer. Besides showing depth and elapsed time, it also displayed a running total of his deco obligation, the time he would have to spend submerged if he began ascending at that moment. He would ask himself, *OK, are you good with this?*

Each time, he would decide to go another five metres deeper.

As he dropped, Herbst pointed his light down, trying to identify the diver below. Was it Dave, or Don? Even from close up, they were almost indistinguishable in the water.*
Both wore black drysuits and black hoods. Both used rebreathers with black covers (Don had replaced the stock yellow cover of his Inspiration). The shapes of the rebreathers differed slightly, though. Don's Inspiration had a tunnel-like hump from top to bottom; the shroud of Dave's Mark 15.5 had a slightly raised circular portion to accommo-date the scrubber canister.

Herbst's attachment to Shirley ran long and deep. As much as he liked Shaw, Herbst knew whose face he hoped to

---

* The helmet and camera would have distinguished Shaw, but he had told the support team on Friday evening that he planned to remove the helmet after he began to ascend, and hang it from his hip by a lanyard.

see when he got closer to the solitary diver below. Losing Don would crush him. He imagined himself climbing up to the rim of the hole and calling André on the cell phone to tell her that Don was dead.

He dropped to 120 metres. Now just a few metres separated him from the figure below, and Herbst was able to make out the shape of the rebreather.

Tunnel. Inspiration.

It was Don.

CHAPTER
15

Don Shirley's dive went smoothly at first.

He headed down quickly. About five minutes into his dive, he reached 120 metres. He knew that Shaw should now be returning to the shot line, beginning his long return to the surface, with or without the body. During an ascent, all rebreathers release some gas from the breathing loop to compensate for the reduced water pressure, so Shirley began to look for bubbles coming up the line.

He saw nothing. He wasn't too concerned at first. He thought that Shaw might have fallen slightly behind schedule on his descent. But when another minute or more went by, still no bubbles, Shirley knew that Dave must be in trouble. As he dropped passed the last group of four emergency tanks at 150 metres, Shirley began to prepare himself mentally: he was going to the bottom.

Some time after he passed 150 metres, Shirley glimpsed a single dim light below, at an angle off the shot line. But the light wasn't moving. Shirley – still plummeting – shone his high-intensity beam down towards the spot. If Shaw were conscious, he would certainly see it from this distance, and would respond by waving his own light.

The light didn't move.

This is bad, Shirley thought.

As he approached 220 metres, he still saw no bubbles and no movement from the light. He continued to descend, dropping about 10 metres every twenty seconds.

Past 220 metres. The light didn't move.

Past 230. The light didn't move.

Past 240. The smear of light in the blackness got bigger as he approached, but it hadn't yet moved since he first sighted it, nearly five minutes now.

Then, at about 250 metres, he heard a sharp crack down by his left forearm, followed by a thump. Shirley glanced down, but he already knew what he would see: the Hammerhead controller was dark. It had imploded under the pressure of the depth and was now flooded, the electronics ruined.

Shirley's jet fighter plane was now a crippled duck.

In the space between heartbeats, a debate played itself out in Shirley's mind. For an instant, he thought that he might continue down the last 20 metres to the bottom. He could add oxygen manually to the rebreather loop. He might yet be able to do something for Dave.

This was a contradiction of everything Shirley taught his students, everything that he believed. A critical failure always turns a dive. Always.

He thought: *But maybe ...*

The dim light still wasn't moving.

Then: *No. He's gone.*

Now he had to save himself.

With his left thumb, Shirley opened a valve to add gas to his wings, arresting his descent. With his right hand, he injected oxygen into the Inspiration's breathing loop. But this spiked the oxygen to a dangerous level, so high that a single breath could have convulsed him. His next breath had to come from one of the open-circuit bailout tanks that floated at his left side.

Shirley had simulated this emergency hundreds of times, while training his students on rebreathers. *Drills and skills,* he lectured them. Now he went through the same procedure, reflexively: exhale, twist the mouthpiece valve to prevent water from entering the loop, remove the mouthpiece and let it float free, and bring the open-circuit regulator to his mouth.

The last part brought a quick twinge of uncertainty. The regulators on Shirley's emergency tanks were from the shipment of new Scubapro gear he had received in December. They were standard issue, not modified, and only briefly tested. As his right hand reached for the regulator on the nearest tank, Shirley was about to trust his life to a piece of off-the-shelf scuba equipment that had never been designed for these depths.

He fitted the mouthpiece between his lips and inhaled.

Instantly gas flowed through the regulator, and he felt it fill his lungs.

Less than half a minute after the emergency began, Shirley was stabilized. His descent was arrested and he was breathing safely.

Shirley was now the only living being in the cave. Nearly 250 metres of water and 70 decompression stops – a total of ten and a half hours – lay between him and the surface.

He began to ascend.

With the emergency averted, Shirley now began to focus on a plan to get safely back to the surface as quickly as possible. The descent to 250 metres had increased his decompression dues – by how much he didn't yet know. He found that one of his two VR3 dive computers had flooded. But the backup unit was still operating and showed a deco time of more than eleven and a half hours to the surface.

Shirley carried a thick set of slates with half a dozen plans tailored for different depths and bottom times, based on schedules that he and Shaw had worked out in October. Each plan occupied two slates, and flipping through them was almost like paging through a book. Shirley decided to use a plan designed for three minutes at 270 metres. He hadn't quite reached 270, and he hadn't stayed for three minutes, but this would build in a margin of safety. The plan called for a first deco stop at 222 metres, for 30 seconds, and Shirley headed up, breathing from the bailout tank.

He checked the tank's gauge, and discovered that the pressure had dropped perceptibly after just a couple of minutes. One breath at this depth consumed as much gas as 25 breaths at the surface. He could see the needle of the gauge tick downwards with each inhalation.

He had brought two bailout tanks. He realized that at this rate, both tanks might be empty before he reached the emergency cylinders at 150 metres. The Hammerhead's secondary console was still operating – it monitored the machine but didn't control it – and when he checked the panel, he saw that the oxygen levels in the loop had stabilized.

He went back on the rebreather. This kept him busy: he constantly had to check the oxygen level in the breathing loop and add oxygen when the level dropped. He was also following the deco plan, ascending in increments and holding for the precise intervals. At these depths, the stops were really just pauses, thirty seconds or a minute every three metres. His main cave light was more than he needed for this close work, and he decided to use the bright screen of the VR3 for illumination whenever he needed to read the slates. In the utter darkness, that was plenty good enough.

This was the dull light that Andrews and Stojakovic saw winking on and off when they looked down from 150 metres.

Shirley saw Andrews and Stojakovic above him, but the descent to 250 had put him behind schedule, and they had left when he reached 150 metres. Shirley was now at the first set of emergency tanks. If necessary, he could complete his dive using only the cylinders on the line. There was no point in that, though. He was confident that he could manually operate the machine for as long as he needed, at least up to the shallow stops where he would find almost unlimited quantities of oxygen-rich gas and pure O_2.

According to his original plan, he should have taken one of the three cylinders here and brought it with him when he continued up. But he decided to leave them all.

Shirley still hoped that Shaw might be following him up the line. He knew that it was unrealistic, and he could see only blackness below, but he couldn't completely reconcile himself to the certainty that he was leaving behind his dead friend.

Dave might be alive, he thought. And if he was, then he would be facing a massive decompression, and he would need all the gas he could get.

He started up without the cylinder.

*   *   *

Derek Hughes, the underwater cameraman, grew concerned as he waited with the police dive crew at 20 metres. Hughes wasn't a part of Shirley's dive team; but he was an experienced technical diver and he had absorbed the details of the dive plan. When Peter Herbst didn't appear on schedule with the body, Hughes knew that there must be a serious problem below.

Hughes had been hovering around ten metres, where he had photographed each of the divers as they came down through the entrance. He was an open-circuit diver, and was staying shallow to conserve the air in his tanks. From here, a ledge blocked the view of the deepest part of the cave. Hughes kept waiting for the single light of Peter Herbst to appear over the ledge. But there was just darkness where Herbst should have been.

Finally Hughes saw a bright glare climbing over the ledge. But it was two lights, not one. Immediately Hughes swam down to about 40 metres, following the shot line along the sloping cave roof. He found Andrews and Stojakovic, resting at a deco stop near the white barrel where the line plunged down into the abyss. There was no Herbst, no body. Hughes peered down into the depths. He could make out two lights

below. He knew that these must be Herbst and Lo Vingerling.

Andrews handed Hughes the slate that he had showed to
Herbst:

DID NOT MEET D + D
@ 150 FOR 6 MIN.
1 LIGHT BELOW?
NOT SURE D'S LIGHT OFF

Hughes made his way back up the line, passing Stephen
Sander who was coming down.

Except for the divers who ascended from the depths – and
so far, none had done that – the only communication between
the cave and the surface were two ropes that dropped through
the entrance, down to about 10 metres. One rope was tied to a
capped bottle that floated on the surface. Inside the bottle
were several stones. When the rope was pulled from below,
the bottle would bob in the water, and the stones would rattle
loudly against the sides of the bottle. It was a signal to pull up
a second rope that also hung down to about 10 metres.
Hughes swam now to the two ropes. He tied Andrews's slate to
the bottom of one, and he yanked on the other.

*   *   *

The bottle's sudden banging reverberated off the walls and
startled some of the anxious onlookers around the water. Gregory Stojakovic, the 17-year-old son of Dusan Stojakovic,
bolted up to the top of the boulder and pulled up the rope
with the slate.

204

He read the slate aloud, halting as he made out the scrawled words. His expression was quizzical and stunned; Gregory had known Shirley since he was a young child, and he had quickly become drawn to Shaw in the past couple of days.

'OK, so we are on our emergency plan,' said Verna van Schaik. There was, in fact, no set plan: only an understanding that divers might try to extend their range if someone below them was overdue. This meant that Vingerling might go to 150 metres, Herbst as far as 100. She would have to account for this when she decided what to do next. Much was out of her hands; what happened below would happen. But she had two support divers on the surface, Gerhard du Preez and Truwin Laas – still in their street clothes because they hadn't expected to dive until later in the day – and she had to decide how best to use them.

For several seconds van Schaik sat alone, staring off, her face sombre. She had hoped that this would be an easy day, with little more to do than count down the divers as they waited to go in. The plan would do most of the work. Now the plan was broken and she had multiple divers in the water who would probably be going to their limits.

She stood and climbed up to where a policeman stood with a walkie-talkie, with line of sight to a radio repeater on the rim. She wanted to tell the dive physician, Jack Meintjes, what she knew. She spoke rapidly, almost breathless. Later she would recall feeling charged with adrenaline.

The police squad came up and climbed out of the water, empty-handed. Marie Dreyer had ventured down with her husband at the edge of the pool, and watched them as she held a knotted fist to her mouth. She appeared ready to weep.

Derek Hughes then came up after finishing a short decompression stop. He was struck by the shocked faces that he saw gathered around the pool. They seemed to be waiting for answers: he was the first diver to the surface who had glimpsed what was happening below.

He stood with van Schaik and the two standby divers. Dusan and Mark were fine, he said.

'To my mind, I saw two lights below, which would be Lo and Pete,' Hughes said. 'We're missing Don and Dave.'

He told Laas and du Preez to get into their gear.

* * *

Lo Vingerling was the next support diver to reach Shirley, as Shirley arrived at 118 metres for a one-minute stop. Lo gave Shirley an OK sign – intended as a question – and Don promptly returned it. Shirley was so composed that Vingerling never realized that he was manually operating the rebreather. Vingerling only learned of it a couple of hours later, when he finally surfaced.

Vingerling peered down below and saw only blackness. He was prepared to go down to 150 to look for Shaw; he had the proper gases and he was willing.

He made a 'down-there' gesture. But Shirley shook his head and drew a finger across his throat.

Vingerling nodded. He pushed a valve to add gas to his buoyancy wings and began to rise.

The next diver to drop down out of the darkness was Stephen Sander, about 18 minutes later. Shirley was now on a deco stop at 81 metres. Sander was shocked to see just one light below as he approached Shirley from above. Sander settled to a stop in front of Shirley. Sander knew from the look in Shirley's eyes that something was wrong. He also noticed that the controller on Shirley's left forearm had imploded: it was as if someone had smashed it with a big rock. He knew that Shirley must have gone beyond his planned depth.

Shirley made a pencil-on-paper scribbling motion, asking for a slate; he wanted to conserve his own. Sander gave him one of his plastic slates. Shirley wrote:

DAVE NOT COMING BACK
Cylinders all way to 150

And on the reverse, a summary of his deco profile:

Running cross between 270 and VR3 profile
VR3 shows 600 mins to surface
time now 66 mins from descent

Shirley knew that with that information, Verna van Schaik would be able to calculate his position at any time.

He handed the slate back to Sander. Before Sander left, he angled his cave light off to one side, to cut the glare and get a better look below. But he saw only blackness.

Then he kicked away towards the surface.

Sander knew that the information on the slate had to get up top as quickly as possible. His computer showed more than an hour of decompression debt. But Sander didn't think that the information should wait that long. He believed that he knew his body, what it could handle. He decided to skip some of his stops and cut some others in half. He reached the bell rope approximately 26 minutes after he had left Shirley and he sent the slate up.

* * *

The energy at the hole seemed to snap into focus when Sander's slate arrived. And immediately that focus was on Don. The certainty of Shaw's death was distressing, but it could be put aside. They now knew that Shirley was alive and apparently in control. And they knew where he was.

Now Verna van Schaik had a better idea of how to use the two fresh support divers. After she spoke by radio to Jack Meintjes, to tell him the news, she told Gerhard du Preez to go down and check on each of the divers. Herbst, Vingerling, Stojakovic and Andrews were all above Shirley, decompressing on the line.

'Make sure they're OK. If they're OK, move down to the next one,' she said to du Preez. She had become more confident and composed since the confusing early minutes when the original slate appeared. 'Spend as little time as possible, but take as much time as you need.'

She also gave du Preez a spare VR3 for Shirley, to replace the flooded unit. It would be useless for decompression, but it would serve as a backup timer and depth gauge.

Du Preez went down into the cave and a few minutes later Sander came up. After sending the slate up, he had gone to decompress on 100 per cent oxygen just below the entrance.

His legs wobbled under him as he climbed out of the water. His wrist-mounted computer continued to flash a warning at his rapid ascent. The VR3 considered him bent.

208

Jack Meintjes came down to the bottom of the hole when he heard of Sander's rapid return, Meintjes examined him, and ordered Sander into the chamber. But Sander balked. If he went in, he told Meintjes, there would be no room for someone who might really need the treatment. He promised Meintjes that he would go in if he began to feel symptoms.

Derek Hughes took Sander off to the side. He asked Sander exactly what he had seen.

'I saw Don, I saw all the other guys above him,' Sander said. 'I stayed at 80, no use going further. I saw nothing below. I put my light off to the side, I looked down, I should have seen something. I saw nothing.'

'Nothing within 50 or 60 metres?'

'Nothing, nothing, nothing,' Sander insisted.

Hughes had a reason for pressing Sander. *Wait until you're sure*, Shaw had told him. Now Hughes left Sander and began to climb out of the hole.

He reached Michael Vickers in Hong Kong, where the time was early afternoon. Hughes told Vickers what he knew.

'Are you sure that Dave's not coming back?' Vickers asked.

Hughes equivocated slightly. He hadn't completely let go of the possibility that Dave might somehow be alive, slowly working his way back up the line, alone in the black depths.

'Call me in two hours,' Vickers said.

*   *   *

André had awakened early to take Don's call at around 5 am, before he walked down into the pit. Through the early morning, she tried to go about her normal day, working in the office that they kept in their home. She knew the dive profile, and by watching the clock she was able to imagine his progress.

Eighty-five minutes into the dive, now he will be on deco at 60 metres ...

Then, the call from Derek Hughes. Don is fine but is on a deep profile. Dave is not coming back.

Her mind ran through a quick series of reactions.

Oh Dave, you should have left the body there.

But Don is all right.

Dave's wife ... she will be devastated.

But Don is all right, thank God.

An FM radio always played in the background when André was in the office. Now she heard a news report from the scene: two divers missing. (Hughes's early reading of the first slate – 'No Dave, no Don' – might have worked its way out to the press.) She knew that this would panic the families of the other diver; it would have crushed her if she hadn't heard first-hand from Hughes. So she began to call the wives who weren't already at Bushman's, to pass on the straight story. She was glad to have a task to occupy her.

Dave, we'll miss you.

At least Don is all right.

CHAPTER
16

But he wasn't. Don was in a fight for his life.

It happened suddenly, after Gerhard du Preez came down to check on him. Du Preez had worked his way down through the other divers on the line – they were all doing well – and then finally he found Shirley at about 45 metres. This was the top of the vertical shot line, just below the white barrel where the line angled along the cave roof. Shirley was due for a five minute deco stop here, and he also planned to flush the gas from his breathing loop, using one of the several cylinders that were clipped to the line at this level.

Shirley was still fine at that moment. Du Preez dropped down to him and showed him an OK sign; Shirley returned it. Du Preez handed him the spare VR3; Shirley strapped it to his wrist.

Du Preez had no reason to stay longer. He had done what he was supposed to do, and the sooner he returned to the surface the sooner he would be available to dive again. He pointed to himself and then gave a thumbs-up: *I'm going up now.* Shirley nodded and showed another OK. Du Preez swam away, up the line.

Seconds later, Shirley felt himself start to pass out. He never knew why. Possibly he was distracted by du Preez's visit, and forgot to add oxygen to the breathing loop. Whatever the reason, he felt himself start to lose consciousness.

Once again, ingrained training took over. Divers on rebreathers are taught to switch immediately to open-circuit when they start to sense a blackout. Shirley had taught it and practised it so often that it was now automatic. Without thinking, he shut the mouthpiece valve and jammed the scuba regulator into his mouth. It was instinctive. It had to be: in another couple of seconds he would have lost consciousness.

With the regulator in his mouth, he breathed.

Immediately his world turned upside down. He pitched forward and began to spin in the water, rotating beneath the roof of the cave. The sensation was surreal. The beam of his high-intensity light would sweep white across the roof, then he would rotate into the blackness of the abyss, then the hot white roof flashed past again and then he was back in the blackness. He was disoriented, no sense of direction.

Through all this, a lucid part of his mind was watching, trying to understand and react. He knew that he had to catch hold of the rope. If he didn't, he would tumble off into oblivion.

He got a brief glimpse of the rope as he rotated, then he was back in blackness. When the rope slid into sight again, he reached out for it ...

... and he snagged it and held tight.

But he continued to tumble, now spinning up the line, hand over hand. With each rotation he managed to snag a handhold before his other hand was wrenched free.

He stabilized, and he held tight to the rope. He became aware of the bright screen of the VR3. He checked his depth: 35 metres, too high too soon. He retreated back down the line, moving carefully, until he reached 46 metres again.

He was bent. It happened in a heartbeat; when he switched to open-circuit, a bubble suddenly formed within the inner ear, his left side. It was a mindblowing event, literally. The inner ear is a fulcrum for the body's sense of balance, and Shirley's was so badly disrupted that he could not sense which way was up. An inner ear bend involves a radical mismatch between the pressures of inert gases in the tissues and blood – a 'counter-diffusion'. It occurs mostly among those who ascend after breathing trimix at great depth – Nuno Gomes was afflicted during his 1994 dive at Bushman's – but nobody knows how frequently it occurs. Many victims probably spin out and drown. Even if the body is recovered, the ear 'hit' will go unnoticed in a routine postmortem, and the death will be attributed to unknown causes.

Back at 46 metres, Shirley floated motionless in the water and tried to quiet his mind, organize his thoughts. *What do I do next? What do I need? THINK!!!*

He decided that he wouldn't go back on the rebreather. He could no longer focus on the controls. But on open-circuit he would use more gas. This meant that he'd have to carry tanks with him until he got closer to the surface.

He reached for one of the cylinders on the line.

Suddenly nausea overwhelmed him. He vomited. The effluent streamed through the exhaust valve of his mouthpiece, clouding the water. He breathed a couple of times, settling himself. Then he twisted his upper body so that he could clip the cylinder to his harness.

He vomited again.

He brought his left arm up and cocked his head to read the VR3, and he vomited again. He found that every slight movement brought on a wave of nausea. He gripped the rope. It was his lifeline in every way.

The other divers on the line were too far above him to help, or even to notice; they were crammed below the narrow opening at 15 metres and above, doing long deco stops. Shirley would be alone until someone else came down to check on him. He was on his own.

The time now was about 8.30 am. His computer showed more than 11 hours before he could safely come to the surface.

He grasped the line and held tight.

Many months later, his memories of those moments were still immediate and vivid. In a letter to the author, he described his impressions from the moment he began to lose consciousness:

> I was almost in the light zone (of the cave). A long time to go but nearly out of the cave as far as I was concerned. I had just picked up a cylinder and clipped it off with ease as I have a

million times before. Turned it on. (This was the first time that I had taken cylinders from the line.) Then I began slipping out of consciousness. Have you ever fainted? You feel it coming, you know something is wrong, you don't know what it is. On land if this happens you wake up on the floor. You don't have a clue where you are, who you are, what day it is, even if you are human, alive or dead. Underwater, if this happens, generally, you don't wake up. When I felt myself going, I ran on my ingrained instinct to survive.

I closed the loop and went OC – it was an instinctive reaction, hard-wired by endless training. The next thing that I remember was the flash of brightness followed by pitch black – this repeated over and over again – I was still there, but I was not part of the events. I was trying to make sense of it. The white focused into a floor (the ceiling) the black cave, then a rope, brilliant white like a crack in a car's headlights, floor, black, bright, floor, black, bright ... The next time I saw the rope in the light again, I grabbed it. The spinning continued even though I now had a stable source. I was still in a daze, still in a body, but it was not mine to command fully. Where was I? Where is up? Where is down? No sense could tell me.

Ok, follow the rope, it was on the floor, no it was the on the roof. (I was on the part of the rope where it hit the roof). I followed it, but I could not follow it as I would do normally. I was still spinning, I held it with one hand, and spun around until I saw it again and grabbed it with my other hand. I was conscious that there was a coil of rope on the ceiling to be avoided at all cost at risk of entanglement. But I knew that I had no control of this body, it just spun and spun. I found myself back at a point where the line went away from the roof, the drum, the wrong way. I reversed my direction, spinning, past the coil of rope again. All the time in an unreal, spinning world. Then I became conscious of the VR3, the light shining in my eyes in the darkness – I could see the letters clearly – *I've got to be at 45m, have to go down deeper* – I said in my mind. My body functioned, I could drive it now. I moved down, hand over hand – not feeling the spinning so much. I got to the cylinders and my mind said, "collect cylinders, you will need three". I collected them, one by one – each movement made me vomit. Deep, gut wrenching, merciless. I did my time at the prescribed deco stop, concentrating on what had to be done next. Eventually I could make my way up the line again.

*   *   *

Once again, those in the realm of air and sunlight were completely unaware of the life-and-death struggle playing out in the black chamber below.

Gerhard du Preez never saw Shirley's sudden convulsion below him. Du Preez was already on his way up when it happened, and when he reached the surface he reported all divers well, Don OK at 46 metres.

Divers now began to emerge from below as they finished their shallow decompression stops. Peter Herbst came out and reported a sore knee, the possible sign of a DCI hit; Jack Meintjes ordered him to lie down and breathe oxygen for a while. At 9.40 am, Lo Vingerling climbed out after having spent two and a half hours in the water.

A police diver helped Vingerling out of his equipment and van Schaik handed him a bottle of water. Theo Dreyer approached him as Vingerling drank.

'What do you think the chances are?' Dreyer said.

'Nil,' Vingerling said.

They were talking about Shaw. Nobody questioned whether Shirley might be in jeopardy. To anyone who knew him, Don's safe return from 46 metres was a certainty. He still faced the long decompression, but Don did deco as easily as anyone they had ever seen. During long stops he would enter a trancelike state in which he would float motionless in the horizontal position, his body relaxed, head tucked down, seemingly unaware of his surroundings or of the passage of time. Yet he was always alert when he needed to be, and ready to move up to the next level when the time came.

They all took it for granted: at 46 metres, Don was almost home.

*   *   *

He hung below the shot line, grasping it in both hands. It was an ungainly posture for someone whose usual attitude in the water was a perfectly trimmed horizontal, but it was all Don Shirley could manage.

His world was the rope and the computer at his wrist. Each breath was a conscious effort. He tried to remain perfectly still, because every movement provoked retching dry heaves.

This was how Truwin Laas found him, down at around 40 metres. Laas was making his first dive of the day, what he expected would be a routine check of Shirley.

He hadn't expected to find this, Shirley shaking and heaving and hanging from the line in such a way that Laas feared he would fall away and disappear if he lost his grip.

With great effort, Shirley wrote a message on a slate. He was careful to keep the writing legible, and he wrote in complete sentences, avoiding the usual shorthand. He wanted everyone who saw it to know that he was lucid and still under control. He wrote:

I'M HAVING A BAD TIME
I'VE GOT NAUSEA
AND VERTIGO

Laas took the slate and read it. The clarity of the writing reassured him. But everything else he saw worried him deeply. He took one more look at Shirley, then he hurried up to deliver the message.

* * *

After he received the call from Derek Hughes, Michael Vickers contacted Harry and Pamela, the Shaws' good friends and members of the congregation. Vickers told them what they knew, and he asked them to stand by.

About two hours after he spoke to Hughes, Vickers took another call from South Africa. Hughes knew that he might be busy in the hole, so he had left Vickers' number with one of the police on site, with instructions.

No hope, the police official told Vickers.

It was early evening in Hong Kong. Around mid-day, Ann had gone for a walk down to Tseung Kwan O, one of the 'new towns' in Hong Kong, built around a group of spectacular high-rise apartment buildings. As she walked, she had thought about her phone call from David that morning. 'I'm going down to the dive site now,' he had told her. That worried her. She suspected that *I'm going down to the dive site now* actually meant *I'm going to dive today.*

The walk was mostly downhill, but long, nearly an hour. Along the way, she convinced herself that he wasn't diving today after all, and she put it out of her mind. At the moment David died, she was in a government office in Tseung Kwan O, where she was supposed to pick up her new Hong Kong identity card. Much later, she would find this ironically fitting: that as she was getting a new identity card, she was literally getting a new identity, as a woman without her husband.

The card was ready for her, and she took a taxi back up Clearwater Bay Road, to her home.

The rest of the day was a typical Saturday. She spent time with Lisa, and tended the potted flowers on her patio. She and Lisa had a meal, then Lisa went upstairs to her room.

That was when Michael Vickers arrived unannounced, with Pamela and Harry.

She opened the door and they came in. Michael told her that David had dived today, that he hadn't been seen, and was five hours overdue.

'But there's still a chance –' Vickers said.

She shook her head. No. Not after five hours. As little as she understood about David's diving, she knew that nobody comes back after five hours.

They sat with her. Ann was numbly aware of a seismic shift in her life, total and irrevocable. She had expected another 30 years with David. She had expected that they would grow old together. Now that was lost, and she couldn't even imagine what else was gone with it.

Lisa was still in the kitchen, unaware. Ann sat and felt loss and change descending around her, and she wondered how she could tell her daughter that her father was gone.

How can I ... would be a constant in her life during the weeks and months to come. It would precede hundreds of tasks and problems, some trivial and some momentous. Most were the kinds of problems that she had always left to David, because he handled challenges so well. David always had the answer for *How can I ...?*

Now she was on her own.

* * *

The sombre mood around the pool was instantly transformed when Truwin Laas arrived at the surface with Don's slate. It became a place of intense energy, and for the next nine hours Dave Shaw no longer mattered.

Extreme divers are pragmatic and purposeful individuals. If that trait isn't there already, their training and experience instils it. For the rest of that day, until the crisis was resolved, the divers at Bushman's turned all their energy and knowledge – and their love for Don Shirley – into keeping him alive and bringing him out whole.

They became so intent that their memories later were indistinct. Nobody could say exactly what had happened, or exactly when, or in what sequence. It defied cataloguing: six different men, at least a dozen dives, some for an hour or more, some in and out and back in, all without planning or calculation. Diving is almost always a deliberate activity; this was as close to a fugue state as it ever gets, and for the best of reasons. A life was in the balance. And it belonged to Don Shirley.

When he got the first report from Laas, Jack Meintjes ordered that Shirley be tied to the shot line to keep him from falling away if he lost consciousness. Someone made a tether from a metre-long piece of rope with a brass snap at each end and tossed it to Laas, who had stayed in the pool, ready to go back down again.

Meintjes was considering the possibility of bringing Shirley out of the water. With at least eight hours of decompression still to go, it would have been disastrous: inevitably crippling. But it was preferable to a certain death by drowning if Shirley wasn't able to maintain control.

'If he's there and he's conscious, leave him in,' Meintjes ordered. 'If he's unconscious but he's still breathing, bring him out. If he's not there, I don't want anyone to go after him unless they can directly see him only a few metres below them.'

Down below, Shirley was conscious and he was maintaining, barely. He was laboriously working his way up the line, waiting out stops that were growing progressively longer: eight minutes at 36 metres; 11 at 33 metres; 12 at 30 metres. The sudden nausea was still a problem, and his diaphragm was sore from the violent retching.

He didn't dwell on the hours that still stretched ahead of him, and he refused to consider the possibility that he might not come through it all safely. His immediate goal was 'the fifties', a group of cylinders at 21 metres, containing air enriched to 50 per cent oxygen. When he finally got there, he took one cylinder from the line – the movement sent waves of nausea through his body – and he clipped it to the harness belt at his right hip. Then he switched regulators and began breathing from the 50 per cent tank that he had just removed from the line.

Or so he believed.

In fact he had taken up the wrong regulator. He was breathing from one of the two tanks that he had brought with him at the start of the dive. It contained only 4 per cent oxygen, with 80 per cent helium. It was an ideal mixture below 200 metres, but at this shallow depth, the low concentration of oxygen wouldn't support life.

If he continued to use it he would soon black out and die.

That's when Truwin Laas arrived. Laas had come down to tether Shirley to the shot line. At first Shirley resisted; he thought that the tether restricted his movements. Laas wrote on a slate that the tether was doctor's orders, and Shirley relented.

Before he left, Laas paused for a last look at Shirley. Could he do anything more for Don? Had he missed something? That's when Laas noticed that the hose from Shirley's mouthpiece led to a tank that was labelled **4/80** in large black numerals on a piece of tape.

Laas was puzzled. He knew that this was Don's deep mix.

But he wasn't sure if it was really a mistake. He thought that breathing a deep mix might be some arcane decompression technique. *Don is way beyond us mere mortals. He knows things about diving the rest of us don't even think about.*

Laas tilted the tank to show Shirley the label. Don's eyes got big behind his lenses. He removed the regulator from his mouth, and took the one that Laas handed him from the tank of 50/50.

Shirley's recollection:

I was carrying a lot of cylinders. Normally I would have taken them off, but I had wanted to keep them at that point, as I did not know up from down and I did not really want to change anything. I remember getting to the 50's and taking one of the cylinders there. I remember thinking that I would clip the cylinder to myself. I picked up the cylinder and thought that I clipped it on. But I had mis-clipped it, and unknowingly dropped it instead.

Under normal circumstances I always recheck the contents label before breathing from a cylinder, but I didn't this time. Moving my head would make me vomit. I breathed the gas. Things started to shimmer. I knew something was different. The next thing I remember was Truwin holding a regulator in front of my face. Then he took the cylinder and showed me the markings. This is when I raised the eyebrow, and took the reg out, replacing it with the one Truwin was holding out for me. After this mistake, I asked Truwin to remove all unneeded cylinders.

* * *

As soon as he could get free, Derek Hughes hurried up to the rim from the water's edge, so that he could tell André of Don's plight.

When she heard the news, André felt her legs go weak. She had to sit on the floor to compose herself. She knew how bad this was. Don was hours away from being able to surface safely. She thought of being seasick, how debilitating nausea can be; then she imagined trying to deal with it for hours underwater.

The idea made her ill, just to think of it.

Hughes told her that other divers were in the water with Don, helping him through it. But André knew that other divers could only do so much. They couldn't breathe for him. They couldn't give him a time out from the vertigo and take his place on the line. Don was on his own, and the slow trip to the surface would be an unrelenting test of will.

He would literally have to hang in there.

She knew her husband: he could do it, she thought. He *would* do it. But it would be the hardest thing he had ever done.

*   *   *

Verna van Schaik wanted a diver in the water with Shirley at all times. She thought that this would be a problem, since all except Laas and Gerhard du Preez had dived to their limits and beyond that morning.

But she found divers volunteering – competing – to go down. Andrews and Stojakovic had been down more than four and a half hours during their 150 metre dive, and were definitely done for the day. But everyone else wanted to be in.

Herbst, with a suspected DCI hit in his knee, insisted on diving again. She held him off for much of the day, but he got in for one dive in the late afternoon.

Vingerling wanted to go (and did) after resting from his 108 metre dive.

Eventually Laas and du Preez busted their own limits as well, diving three or four times each.

Stephen Sander did multiple dives after his crazy ascent from 80 metres. 'When it's your friend, you don't think about what you're doing,' he explained later. 'You just do it.'

From the time Truwin went in to tether him to the line until he finally emerged, Shirley had someone with him at all times. He was becoming cold, weak and dehydrated. The nausea abated somewhat; after one visit of several minutes Derek Hughes reported that 'he only vomited twice while I was with him this time'.

The chill came in part from breathing the cooler gases from the open-circuit gear. To reduce the hypothermia, Herbst brought down a spare rebreather so that Shirley could breathe from it while it sat in front of him. But Shirley had to refuse: he couldn't vomit through a rebreather's mouthpiece, as he did with the open-circuit regulator.

He was becoming weak. He unable to maintain his usual horizontal position, where gas flows directly into the lungs. Breathing while vertical was more work, and the hours of added effort were sapping him. Occasionally he would ask for help in angling his legs upward, but each time the nausea would come on hard. This was desperate: he was truly reaching a point that he no longer had strength to breathe.

Stephen Sander went down with anti-nausea medicine in a syringe. He squirted some in between Shirley's lips but it came back up moments later. Sander tried again after a few minutes and this time the medicine stayed down. It seemed to help somewhat, but when Shirley asked him to lift his legs, Don began to retch again.

Meintjes sent down a slate suggesting that Don come out early. Shirley refused. Sander thought that Shirley was reluctant to leave because it would have meant putting his fate into someone else's hands. He didn't know what was waiting for him at the surface, and he would be relying on others to get him into the chamber and save his life. As pitiful as he was now, Shirley down here was still in control.

Sander understood that. He thought that he might've done the same in Shirley's place. Later, in an email to the author, he described being with Shirley:

> Don would close his eyes and concentrate on breathing in and exhaling. Every breath was an effort and I was wondering if he would hold up ... Occasionally I would tap Don lightly on his shoulder. He would open his eyes and look at me, convulsing all the time. He was shivering from the cold, even though he was in his drysuit. He was dehydrating from all the vomit and his body was starting to go into shock ...
>
> Remarkably, Don knew what was going on, he knew what he had to do to survive ... I felt for him there. I wished in a way that it was me and not him although I know I could not have handled it any better. He was just my friend and it was not pleasant to see him suffer like this.

As he left the 15 metre stop, still with several hours remaining, Shirley found that his inhalations were too weak to open the demand valve of the regulator. But even now he refused to come up. He began to operate the valve with the regulator's purge button: a light touch sends air bursting out in an uncontrolled stream. He did this with every breath he drew in. It meant that he had to skip breaths in order to use his right hand for anything else. At the 6 metre level he alternated breathing and writing three times to compose a note asking that the Poseidon regulators on the oxygen tanks there be replaced with Scubapro gear, which he considered easier to breathe.

Derek Hughes brought the slate to the surface and announced it with a grin.

'Don may be in the shit,' Hughes said, 'but he's still fussy about his kit.'

As the afternoon wore on, Shirley moved to levels where he was breathing 100 per cent oxygen to hasten decompression. Meintjes became concerned about Shirley's long exposure to oxygen. If he stayed down too long he would risk pulmonary damage during the long treatment in the chamber, when he would be breathing 100 per cent oxygen under pressure for hours.

While he breathed at the 6 metre stop, Shirley began to feel a pain in his left knee, a classic DCS symptom. He knew that it should be treated. At around 6 pm, Shirley agreed to skip his stop at the 3 metre level. But he had about half an hour remaining at 6 metres, and he wanted to finish it.

Meintjes agreed.

There was one further delay. A critical gas mix needed for the treatment was not on hand at the chamber. It would have to be mixed at the farm warehouse where the large cylinders of helium and oxygen were stored.

All afternoon, Meintjes had been urging Shirley out of the cave. Now he had to tell him to stay down until the correct gases were available.

Peter Herbst scrambled up to the rim and hurried back to the lodge in a pickup truck. He mixed four large cylinders with the proper gas – 20 per cent oxygen, the rest helium – then raced back to the hole. During the delay, Shirley finished his 6 metre stay and moved up to 3 metres, where the pain in his leg increased, another sign that he had been bent.

Sander came down and showed Shirley a slate:

I'M HERE TO BRING YOU HOME

At 6.59 pm Meintjes sent down word that the chamber was ready. Don had been underwater for twelve and a half hours, incapacitated about ten hours of that time.

Laas and Sander began to haul Shirley out through the opening, face up, with a boost from below. But something seemed to be stuck; they looked and found Shirley still gripping the shot line with one hand. Laas remembers prying Shirley's fingers off, one by one.

But Shirley recalls that he was still in control:

> All of my actions were deliberate. To move over the 6m line I had to pull it out from between a rock and the line, where it is tied around a big boulder. I had to then locate and follow a line up the wall. This was no mean feat – it was tight. I jammed my hand deliberately in the rope again. Steve and Truwin came into view, I said I was OK to go up. They unclipped my computers and consoles, so that my arms were free of instruments, and I undid my drysuit power inflator – this to save time on the surface. When all was clear, I let them take me. I still did not know up from down, in my body, but I knew where it was in my head. Getting to the surface was a relief. I could breathe naturally. I relaxed and let them take me.

They carried him through the shallows. They held him while Gerhard du Preez cut the harness, and when it was free they laid him at the side of the pool.

His skin was pale, his eyes unfocused. His head lolled to one side; to Shirley his skull felt as heavy as lead. They peeled away his drysuit. A medic immediately gave him a injection to control his nausea. Then half a dozen people carried him to a shelter where they laid him in a litter basket. A medic took his vital signs – blood pressure strong, pulse rate 88, temperature too low: 34.8°C (94.6°F).

At 7.13 pm volunteers began to work the rope-and-pulley system up on the rim, and the litter basket lifted off from the gravel floor, with Shirley inside and Reán Louw riding it from beneath, kicking it away from the wall.

At 7.19 pm it reached the overhanging lip of rock that had stymied the rescue crew during their test run on Thursday. This time the crew waiting at the edge lifted it past the lip in a few seconds, and it continued up.

A group of police, and Peter Herbst, carried the litter from the rim of the hole to the chamber. Less than 24 minutes had elapsed since Shirley's head first broke water at the surface of the pool.

Shirley was immediately placed in the chamber, head first, laid out on a rigid spine board. Meintjes had already climbed into the chamber. Herbst carried the foot of the board and he pushed it inside, leaning into the steel capsule of the chamber for a few words with Shirley. Then he backed out and pulled the door shut behind him, and sealed it.

Gas, 50/50 HeliOx, began to hiss. Herbst went to the control panel at the side of the capsule. He briefly watched needles rise on pressure gauges, and when he was satisfied he walked outside and stood beneath a sky that was livid with sunset reds and purples.

He thought about all that had happened here since sunup, how for a few hours the extraordinary had become the norm, one magnificent act after another. He thought about Shaw at the bottom of the cave and about Shirley inside the chamber, and his ordeal and all that he had done to survive.

That's diving, he thought.

CHAPTER
17

Just that quickly it was over. For ten hours the hole
had been a place of focused energy, all of it directed at
getting Shirley out of the water alive and into the chamber.
In the months and years to come, when they spoke of it,
those who had been there would marvel at the intensity
and efficiency they had all brought to the task. *Everyone
operating at one hundred per cent, everyone going the limit,
you don't see that very often,* Peter Herbst would say later.
Anything less, he thought, and Don would not have
survived.

But with the closing of the chamber door, the urgency that
had sustained them through the day was suddenly gone, and
nobody seemed quite sure what to do next. The fact of Shaw's
death began to settle over them too. Herbst thought that they
had put it aside to deal with Shirley's crisis. Now the crisis

had passed and they were all confronting the reality that Dave was not coming back.

The police and the rescue team drifted back to their camps. Shirley's divers gathered their belongings and made their way back to the lodge. They showered, made phone calls, rested. At around 8 pm they came to the dining room for a meal that Debbie van Zyl and her kitchen staff had prepared. Besides the dive team, there were some family and friends, and Marie and Theo Dreyer. The room was crowded, the mood sombre. Around the table there was already speculation that the helmet-mounted camera figured in the disaster.

Herbst noticed that reporters had joined what he had thought was a private gathering. A woman whom he recognized as a magazine writer asked a speculative question about how Shaw had died.

Herbst began to shout, berating the writer. ('I lost all sense of decorum,' was how he put it later). The situation was coming apart, he thought. He believed that, even with Shaw's death, they had all been part of something special today. The dive belonged to all of them, but it was in danger of being co-opted by those who knew nothing. Conclusions were being formed in haste and ignorance. Nobody knew what had happened down in the hole.

He pushed his plate away and stood. He called a private meeting of the divers and Verna van Schaik and he walked out of the room

After dinner they all gathered in the darkness around a fire ring outside. Herbst spoke first. He told them that someone had to take charge until Shirley was ready to take over. He would do it or he would step aside for someone else.

232

'No, you do it, *boutie*,' said Lo Vingerling, using an affectionate Afrikaans term for 'little brother'. Nobody objected.

Herbst began by telling them that there should be no serious diving on Sunday – at most, a quick dive to 6 metres to retrieve gear in the shallow neck of the cave. Instead they would go to the hole and begin to pack and remove their equipment.

Herbst said that they should stop speculating about what had happened at the bottom.

'Let's not talk about things that might have happened,' he said. 'Let's not talk of how Dave died. The only person who knows that is Dave, and he's not here tonight.' His voice became husky. 'The camera, we all looked at it, nobody said don't take the camera. We all thought it was a cool idea, we all wanted to watch the movie it made. We lost a great friend to all of us, fuck it, he died the way he wanted to go.'

Derek Hughes said that the police wanted to speak to them all the next day. Hughes also suggested that he schedule a press briefing in the morning.

Agreed, Herbst said. But he said that they needed a coherent account, something based on fact instead of speculation. He suggested that since they were all together now, they should try to recount individually what they had seen and done. They all had a piece of the truth, Herbst believed, and when their accounts were put together with Shirley's, they would have the whole truth, as close as anyone could know it.

One by one, they told their stories, fitting together the pieces. They seemed hesitant at first. Then enthusiasm and emotion came into their voices as they remembered messages on slates, moments of despair and tension and exhilaration. Like Peter Herbst, they knew that they had been a part of something special, and they wanted to get it right.

* * *

Herbst returned to the hole some time after the meeting broke up. Since early Friday morning, he had slept no more than four or five hours. But he felt restless and he wanted to be closer to Don.

An attendant sat at the control panel of the chamber. Herbst looked in at Shirley, resting in the chamber. Shirley was due to come out of the chamber shortly before 3 am Herbst phoned André and told her that Don was doing well. André had planned to speak to Don when he got out of the chamber, but Herbst told her that she should try to get a full night's sleep. He said that he would bring Don back to the room, and that André could talk to him later in the morning.

Herbst found a mattress nearby. He moved it under the truck bed that held the chamber. He lay down on it but he wasn't able to sleep. The night was very warm and the chamber's diesel-powered generator was loud in his ears. Herbst thought of Shaw at the bottom of the hole, and he thought of Shirley directly above him, and he waited for the chamber door to open.

* * *

From the moment she learned that Don was in trouble in the water, André knew that she would travel to Bushman's. She

234

would have left immediately but gaps in cell phone coverage during the long, desolate stretches west of Johannesburg would have left her out of contact, and she wanted to be able to monitor his progress up the line.

Once she learned that Don was safe in the chamber, she made plans to leave. An immediate departure would have meant an all-night drive alone. She decided, instead, to wait until she spoke to Don when he left the chamber. She was in contact with the attendant operating the chamber and asked him to phone her when Don emerged. This would be her wake-up call. The only vehicle left for her was a Land Rover that she didn't consider fast enough, so she arranged to borrow a BMW from a friend in Johannesburg who was also a student of Peter Herbst.

She packed a bag and tried to get to sleep early, but calls kept coming through the evening from different members of the dive team and others on the scene at Bushman's. They all told her that Don was resting and was doing well and that there was no need for her to come to Bushman's.

To André they seemed to be reassuring themselves as much as her, saying what they all hoped to be true. But none of them could really know, she thought. She told nobody of her plans to drive to Bushman's. She wanted to see for herself, she wanted to be near Don and she didn't want any resistance.

The last call of the night was the one that Herbst made from beside the chamber, advising her to skip the 3 am call and sleep through the night. She didn't argue with him. But when the call ended, she waited a couple of minutes and then phoned the chamber attendant.

'Don't pay attention to what anyone else says,' she told him. 'I want to talk to my husband as soon as he's out.'

The call woke her. The attendant said that Don was out, that he had come through the treatment well. Then he handed the phone to Don.

'I'm alive,' Shirley said. It was his standard greeting whenever he called André after a dive. He said that he was doing OK, but was tired.

'We should probably cancel the course schedule for a while,' he said, a wan joke.

They spoke briefly; she told him that he should sleep, that she would call in the morning. She didn't mention her plan to start driving to Bushman's. She was reassured when she put the phone down. He sounded like the Don she knew, and she felt sure that he was on his way to a full recovery.

I'm a wife, she thought, *not a widow*.

It brought her a euphoria that stayed with her for hours.

But Peter Herbst knew that his friend had a serious problem. Shirley wasn't able to crawl out of the chamber on his own; he needed Herbst to pull him out and then half-carry him down the steps to the ground. He was wobbly, even without trying to walk. The DCI 'hit' had ravaged the delicate mechanisms of equilibrium of his inner ear, a labyrinth of tiny chambers and membranes. Though his hearing was not affected, he had lost all sense of balance on one side. He couldn't hold his head up, and his eyes were askew, pointing off in different directions. He would have toppled to the ground if Herbst hadn't held him upright.

Herbst hadn't imagined this. He had expected a whole man to emerge from the chamber: not chipper maybe, but sound. Herbst had seen many divers go into recompression chambers, but he had never seen one come out looking like this.

He had planned to drive Shirley back to the room at the lodge but that was impractical. Don would never be able to keep himself upright in the seat.

Herbst lowered Shirley down to the mattress beneath the chamber and lay down beside him. Herbst couldn't look at Shirley's face – the crazy, unfocused eye was too disturbing – but he pulled Don close and held him tight, and they slept that way until the sun came up.

* * *

Gordon Hiles, the documentary producer, continued to shoot video footage. The story had changed but he intended to gather material until someone told him to stop.

Nobody ever did and he went around the lodge on Sunday morning, doing interviews. His camera caught the moment that Shirley and Herbst returned from the hole. Hiles was interviewing Jack Meintjes when Herbst and Paul Grindrod, a friend of Herbst, walked past, with Shirley between them, hanging onto their arms, leaning against them.

'How are you feeling?' Meintjes asked him. 'What are your legs like?'

'Fine,' Shirley said. 'I can walk if – I think I can walk.' (In fact, he could not stand without support.) 'If I just get my balance back, I'll be fine.'

They spoke for a few moments, Meintjes giving him a schedule of chamber treatments through Monday.

'I think I'd better go lie down now,' Shirley said. With Herbst and Grindrod flanking him, he moved away haltingly, not so much walking as being dragged.

Herbst and Grindrod took Shirley to his room. Herbst brought him some food. Don wanted a bath; Herbst filled the tub, helped Shirley to climb in, and dried him when he came out. Shirley insisted on doing as much for himself as he could, but Herbst helped him to dress in a T-shirt and shorts, and led him over to the bed.

The floor felt like a sponge beneath Shirley, and the mattress seemed to wobble beneath him as he pulled himself into bed.

Shirley was sitting up in bed, head against a pillow, when Hiles entered and set up his camera for an interview. Over the next thirty minutes, without prompting or interruption from Hiles, Shirley gave a lucid running account of the previous day, from floating in the pool with Shaw at the start of the dive to his entry in the chamber. His voice seemed slightly dull and weary. He spoke without hesitation, and his recollection seemed certain. His tone was almost matter-of-fact, completely without self-pity or pathos. It was a remarkable performance for a physically debilitated man who had spent much of the past twenty-four hours in a moment-to-moment struggle to survive.

Near the end, he spoke about Shaw and about a possible attempt to recover the two bodies.

'The camera would tell us exactly what happened. I'm sure that Dave would want to get that video. Apart from that, I would prefer to leave Dave where he is, as he is, end of story. That was Dave's express wish. Same thing I would like to have happen to me in the same situation. I don't see a cave as a nasty place and neither did Dave. A cave is where we lived. It's where life happened. That would be a fitting end. Like an Egyptian's tomb. That's the way Dave would see it.'

* * *

André arrived at the game farm around midday, having picked up a fine of more than 3,000 Rand (£220) in speeding tickets along the way. She was told that Don had gone to the chamber for a second treatment and hadn't yet returned.

She drove towards the hole. About halfway there she met Peter Herbst's truck coming the other way. Don was in the passenger seat, arms wrapped around his head. An odd posture, she thought. As she got closer, she understood: he was supporting his own head. This was the only way he could keep it from lolling to one side. His eyes were pointed in different directions. He seemed unable to focus.

She was shocked. This was much worse than anyone had led her to believe.

She followed them to the lodge and helped Don walk back to the room, stabilizing him at one arm while Herbst walked on the other side.

Don seemed to be acting as if all were well, and she tried to go along with that, to act natural. She knew that Don needed to believe that he was well; believing it was the first essential step to actually being well. But inwardly she was dismayed.

Are you ever going to be right? she thought. *Because if you can't dive again, your life will be hell. And mine too.*

She would not have been reassured by the interview that Jack Meintjes gave to Gordon Hiles that morning. As he watched Shirley stagger towards his room, Meintjes said that Don actually appeared to be in better shape than he had expected when he first saw him in the litter. But clearly, he added, there were residual symptoms, a loss of balance.

'These symptoms are very, very hard to treat,' he said.

'Could they be permanent?' Hiles asked.

'They can be permanent, yeah,' Meintjes said. 'One sort of gets used to the symptoms, so you can lead a fairly normal life. But obviously you can't dive.'

*　*　*

When André entered the room that Don and Dave had shared at the lodge, she was struck by the sight of Shaw's watch and cell phone and car keys, sitting on the bedside table as if he might walk through the door at any moment. *So sad*, she thought. As soon as Don was resting and fed after his second chamber treatment, she began to gather Shaw's belongings. She packed them in his suitcase and put it away in his rental car, along with a PC and a bag of spare diving gear. Later that week, a policeman drove the car to Johannesburg and the belongings went off to Hong Kong on a Cathay Pacific flight.

At the hole, others were picking up the pieces.

The Proto team and the Netcare medics packed their equipment and left.

Most of Shirley's divers were due back at their job on Monday morning. On Sunday, they went back to the hole to gather equipment and personal gear that they had left the previous evening. Nearly two dozen emergency cylinders still hung from the shot line, at depths between 6 metres and 150 metres. Several divers went in briefly to bring up the shallowest of the cylinders, but that still left about 18 to be retrieved, and by Monday morning Peter Herbst was the last of the team still at the site.

Ernst Strydom, the police superintendent, decided that his squad – and the recompression chamber by regulation – would remain on site until the last of the equipment had been cleared from the cave. Strydom felt that the experience of diving with Shirley's group had been valuable for his men and he wanted them to take part in any dives to recover the emergency tanks.

Derek Hughes returned to Johannesburg but Gordon Hiles decided to stay on. He wanted to document the recovery dive from the surface. Another impulse kept him at the hole too: he couldn't stop thinking about the underwater camera. He imagined it at the bottom of the cavern, the secrets that it must hold. Hiles was confident that the housing hadn't leaked, even after days under pressure, and he believed that if it could be raised, the tape inside would be preserved and would show exactly what had happened to Dave Shaw.

Don Shirley took a third chamber treatment on Sunday afternoon, then more on Monday and Tuesday morning. He showed incremental improvement after each session, though he still couldn't walk without help. After the last treatment, André drove him to Pretoria, to continue treatments at the hyperbaric medicine department of Eugene Marais Hospital.

Before he left, Shirley asked Peter Herbst to take charge of recovering the emergency tanks that still hung on the line. This hadn't been part of the plan. If all had gone well on

Saturday, support divers would have removed most of the tanks during the dive itself. Shirley and Shaw would have retrieved the rest after recuperating for a day or two. Now it was Herbst's job and it was not a trivial task.

On Monday Herbst did a solo dive to remove a group of nine tanks at 50 metres. That left 10 cylinders in the water: four at 80 metres, three at 95 metres, and the three deepest at 150. The three hanging at 150 metres were the most problematic. Shaw and Shirley had dropped off those tanks during their shakedown dive the previous Wednesday. A shakedown for Shaw and Shirley was an epic dive for almost anyone else, and 150 was beyond Herbst's range.

Shirley advised him to attach a lift bag to the line at 100 metres. When inflated, the bag – a nylon bladder with a slit opening at the bottom – would pull the deepest tanks up to a depth where Herbst could work more safely.

Herbst knew that it would be a drastic, dangerous operation. He would be deep in a cave, working hard, with multiple cylinders ascending around him, connected by the shot line and gathering speed as they rose. The upper levels of the cave would be festooned with loops of line. *Scary shit*, he thought.

An incident during his dive on Monday showed the dangers. Some slack had come into the shot line that ran across the roof. Herbst removed the nine 50-metre cylinders from the line, and as he began to ascend, the slack line worked its way up into a narrow slot between his rebreather and an auxiliary tank that he used to inflate his drysuit. Herbst was caught. He reached back to free himself, but even with his left arm at full extension he wasn't able to push the line out of the gap where it had snagged.

A police diver was in the water about 30 metres above, at his depth limit. Herbst signalled to him, a side-to-side movement of his cave light, the universal distress sign for most technical divers. But the police divers, who almost always operated in zero visibility, had never learned the signals. When Herbst saw that the police diver wasn't coming down, he began to pull himself up, laboriously working the line through the slot with his left arm. Finally, as Herbst approached 20 metres this way, the police diver saw the difficulty, came over, and pulled the line free.

At 50 metres the incident was an inconvenience. At 100 metres it would be much more serious. Herbst knew he would need help for the recovery.

Call Petrus Roux, Shirley said.

This was not a good time for Roux. It was a critical period in the farm year and he was working long hours every day in the fields. He was also disturbed by Shaw's death. Though they hadn't been close friends in the usual sense, he had felt a kinship with Shaw because of their shared faith, and was saddened to think of him dead at the bottom of Bushman's and of his widow grieving in Hong Kong.

The recovery dive itself, as Herbst described it, made Roux uneasy. He recognized the hazards. Petrus knew Herbst, but had never dived with him. Roux was subdued and sensitive, the opposite in temperament of Herbst's roaring force of nature. They would likely never have chosen one another as dive partners. But Herbst was asking for help and he was doing it in Shirley's name. Like almost all of his former students, Roux was devoted to Don Shirley.

Roux decided that he would do it: for Don, for Dave.

He approached his father, Boet, and asked to leave the farm and his duties. He said that it would require a day and a half: a substantial loss of time for a South African farmer in the middle of the growing season. Petrus explained the dive and why it mattered.

Boet seemed to sense Petrus's apprehension about the dive. In ten years the father had never showed much interest in his son's passion for the sport, and had never seen him dive. So his answer was astonishing.

'You can go,' he said, 'and I will go with you.'

They worked a long half-day on Tuesday and then they quit. It was an odd sight, Petrus thought: the farm equipment parked in sheds while the sun shone bright on a summer day. He loaded his gear, and together father and son set off for the four-hour drive to Bushman's Hole.

*　　*　　*

The next morning was grey and gloomy, leaden clouds hanging low over the southern Kalahari. Thunder rumbled as Herbst and Roux and the police team suited up for the recovery dive around 10.30 am. The theatrical atmospherics matched the mood around the water's edge.

The police superintendent, Ernst Strydom, suggested a brief reading before the divers entered the water. It seemed appropriate; the gathering at the water's edge had the solemn feel of a gathering beside a fresh gravesite. This was a good-bye. Petrus Roux read a passage from an Afrikaans-language Bible that he had brought with him. Ernst Strydom also read a passage. As they spoke, Herbst stood with hands on his hips, staring into the water. When Strydom finished his reading, Herbst began to speak. It was an unplanned moment. Earlier that morning, as he passed the plaque for Deon Dreyer on his way down from the rim, Herbst had told himself that there should be a new plaque soon with Dave Shaw's name on it, and he had wondered what the new plaque should say. Standing beside the water, the words came to him, and he spoke them aloud.

'You're in a good place. You're where you wanted to be,' he said in a quavering voice. 'I know you're there, and you'll be in our hearts with us. We're gonna miss you, mate.'

Strydom began to sing the hymn 'Amazing Grace' and the others picked it up, about a dozen voices including the police crew and some acquaintances, and Boet Roux.

Then they went diving. Rain began to pock the surface of the pond as Herbst and Roux disappeared down into the opening. Immediately all thoughts of Shaw left Herbst. He was alert, completely in the here-and-now of the operation, as they dropped down the shot line. They stopped at 80 metres to remove four cylinders. They stopped again at 95 metre to remove three more. Though it was their first time diving together, Herbst felt no awkwardness between them in the water. They had both trained under Shirley, learning the same procedures.

They had agreed earlier that Roux would attach the lift bag, and as they reached 100 metres Herbst drifted several metres off to one side. He watched Roux inflate the bag with gas from one of the emergency tanks. The bag ballooned. Roux released it, and the bag began to climb, pulling the shot line up behind it – slowly at first, then picking up speed. Herbst and Roux ascended beside the rising line. They attached a rope from the surface to the slack line. Up at the surface, one of the police stood atop the large exposed boulder and began hauling up the rope from below while two of the police divers guided it through the throat of the cave, up through the opening.

At one point, the rising line snagged in a crevice along the wall of the cavern, at about 70 metres. Herbst and Roux had to descend again to free it. Herbst didn't like this. Reversing an ascent is dangerous: it means reloading nitrogen and helium, complicating decompression and increasing the risk of the bends. To Herbst it was one more crazy wrinkle in a dive that already held too many wild cards.

But there was no choice. The line was stuck. Herbst and Roux dropped down to release the snag. As they were pulling it out, Herbst saw the three 150 metre tanks rise up from the depths. He reached out, grabbed the tanks, quickly removed them from the shot line and clipped them onto his harness. These were the last of the cylinders on the line.

At about this time, Herbst's handheld cave light flashed on braided white line – the shot line – hanging straight up and down in the darkness behind Roux, running up from the depths toward the roof of the cavern. This surprised Herbst, since he wasn't expecting to find any line behind Petrus. It hadn't been there a few minutes earlier. Herbst pulled Petrus away, to keep him from tangling in it. But he gave it no more thought. The job was finished and he was glad to be done with it. He and Roux began a slow ascent, first to 50 metres and then along a series of decompression stops dictated by their dive computers. Herbst hoped that the VR3s would be able to cope with the unorthodox dive.

Herbst had been in the water for two and a half hours when the VR3 finally ticked down the last of his decompression. Roux's computer still showed several minutes. Herbst floated up the last 3 metres, broke the surface, swam in towards shore until he could stand on solid footing.

He was still waist deep in the water when Gert Nel approached him and leaned in close. Sound behaves strangely at Bushman's. Normal conversations sometimes can be heard up on the rim, the words carrying up eerily from below. Several journalists were watching from the rim, and Nel didn't want anyone else to hear what he was about to say.

He spoke in a low voice, in Afrikaans:

'*Big B, ons het hulle gesien.*' (Big B, we saw them.)

Herbst didn't understand. '*Wat het julle gesien?*' (You saw what?)

'*Ons het vir Dave, en dit lyk soos nog iemand onder hom, teen die dak sien dryf, hier naby!*' (We saw Dave, and it looks like someone under him, floating against the roof, close by.)

Herbst was incredulous.

'*Is julle seker?*' (Are you sure?)

'*Ja! Dit was twee mense, Dave is bo en reg onder hom hang iets wat lyk soos n ligaam.*' (Yes, it was two people. Dave is on top and right below him hangs something that looks like a body.)

When Roux came to the surface, Herbst told him what the police had seen. Then Herbst followed Nel and a second police diver, 'Fires' van Vuuren, to the ledge beside the pool, Shaw's favoured spot, where the overhang would muffle their words. The police repeated what they had seen: two bodies, one against the roof of the cave, the other hanging beneath the first, both in plain sight at about 30 metres.

At that depth they were below the police divers' limit. Herbst told them that he would go down to bring out the bodies, but only after they had rested for three or four hours. Though he didn't say so, he thought even that was risky. At 30 metres they would again be loading up nitrogen. After a crazy dive like the one they had just done, they really ought to have an overnight recovery.

But he couldn't be sure that the bodies would be there in the morning. Whatever had brought them to the roof probably wouldn't keep them there indefinitely. The bodies were there *now*.

Herbst went to Petrus Roux, sitting in the shade of a canopy that the police had erected near the edge of the pool. Roux believed that Nel and van Vuuren were probably mistaken. He and Herbst had passed through that area while doing their decompression stops, and they hadn't seen anything. But he agreed to go back in with Herbst later that afternoon.

The time now was about 1.30 pm

*   *   *

Days later, when he thought about it, Peter Herbst realized that the bodies had passed within a couple of metres of him and Petrus Roux. It must have happened while they were at 70 metres, shortly after they had removed the last three cylinders from the line.

Pulled off the floor by the rising shot line, the two corpses had risen to the top of the chamber, probably no more than a few seconds behind the cylinders. If Herbst had looked towards Roux at the right moment, he would have seen the bodies floating up behind Petrus, close enough to touch. Instead, he saw only the length of shot line that trailed behind the corpses – the hanging white line that had momentarily puzzled him before he and Roux started back to the surface.

Another couple of metres, the bodies would have come up around him and Petrus, rather than behind them. It would have been a horrific moment, the two divers and the two bodies wrapped up together in a web of rope and string at 70 metres.

CHAPTER
18

Bushman's did not relinquish its dead without a struggle.

Peter Herbst and Petrus Roux both felt uneasy as they stepped into the pool to begin their second dive. Herbst was concerned about the residual effects of their morning dive. Roux's anxiety was less specific. He just didn't feel right about it, but he decided to ignore the feeling and get on with it.

Then, as he checked his gear one last time, seconds before his descent, he saw his rebreather's electronic display go blank.

He unshouldered the machine, carried it out, and sat it against a nearby boulder. He felt pressure from the situation. Evening was closing in on the hole, and they didn't want to finish this dive in darkness. The police were already laying out body bags. Herbst was standing in the water, watching him. Everyone was watching him.

Anxiety over an ostensibly minor dive may seem puzzling: surely, going to 30 metres is trivial to anyone who visits one hundred. But improbable depths and stunning heroics tend to obscure the difficulties of even a routine cave dive. In essence, Herbst and Roux were standing on the roof of a ten-storey office building, preparing to descend a flooded elevator shaft, in darkness, so as to search for two bodies in the bottomless basement. Some routine.

As Petrus examined the machine, Boet Roux approached his son.

'Listen, you don't have to do this,' the father said. 'You can leave it.'

Petrus was on the verge of telling Herbst that he wanted to do just that. Tomorrow would be better, he thought. But then he imagined Shaw on the roof of the cave.

'If it's Dave, I want to get him,' he said.

Petrus tried a fresh battery in the controller. The machine powered up. He pulled himself into the harness, stepped back into the pool. He walked out into deeper water and was the first diver through the opening.

Gert Nel followed Roux into the cave, with Herbst behind them both. Nel shone his light off to their right. Roux saw a faint object at the roof. Like a stalactite, he thought. But there are no stalactites in Bushman's. He swept his own cave light towards the object, a much brighter beam, and then they could all see it clearly.

Dave Shaw was flat against the ceiling, face in, arms extended outward. The headless corpse of Deon Dreyer seemed to float beneath Shaw, suspended in a cradle of thin cave line wrapped twice around the body. As Roux swam

251

closer, he saw that the string was wrapped around the head of Shaw's cave light, which hung from his waist. Unlike many experienced technical divers, Roux had never before encountered a dead body underwater. But he wasn't shaken. The presence of Shaw's body brought him some calm and comfort as he approached. He found himself mentally addressing Shaw: *You did it, Dave. You said you'd bring him back, and you did.*

Roux saw that the strand of string hung by two turns around the head of the cave light. It was a tenuous attachment. Roux feared that if he jostled it, Dreyer's body – still in dive gear, with a tank strapped to the back – would sink back to the bottom. He carefully attached a lift bag to the tank valve.

Beside Roux, Peter Herbst seemed stricken. His heart raced, and he felt palpitations in his chest. Unlike Roux, Herbst did have experience handling corpses under water, and he didn't believe that the sight of the two bodies could have produced the reaction. But *something* was happening to him. He wanted out.

He touched Roux on the shoulder – Roux would later say that Herbst tried to pull him back from the bodies. Roux turned and saw that Herbst was badly shaken. His eyes were red behind the lenses of his dive mask. Roux thought that Herbst might be weeping.

Herbst gave a small goodbye wave, then turned and swam away.

Roux went back to work. He inflated the lift bag slightly, just enough to support the body, then cut away the cradle of string. He swam a short distance up to the police divers and passed the body up to them before turning back to Shaw.

Herbst was now on the shot line, headed up. When he looked back, he saw Petrus handing off Deon Dreyer's body to the police divers, with the lift bag attached. Herbst took the body and headed for the surface. As he ascended, the lift bag became more buoyant, expanding against the reduced pressure in the shallows. It pulled up Herbst and the body. Herbst guided the lift bag and the body through the opening. He delivered the body to policemen waiting on shore.

Herbst immediately asked for oxygen. A headache was ripping through his skull. He was convinced that he had been bent during the rapid ascent.

A few feet away, the policemen handling Deon Dreyer's body were encountering a surprise. They felt a solid mass inside the wetsuit. This was no bag of bones: it had shape and weight. It was solid.

Down below, Petrus Roux had begun to deal with Shaw's body, which was so greatly buoyant that Roux could not budge it from the ceiling. All of Shaw's dive gear was still in place, exactly as it had been on Saturday morning, and Roux went through all the usual procedures to reduce buoyancy. He removed the four bailout cylinders slung at the sides of the body; the gas mixture in the tanks, 80 per cent helium, was so light that the tanks would float. Roux deflated the wings at the back of the rebreather, and he vented air from the rebreather and the drysuit. Still the body seemed to cling to the stone.

Roux was concerned about the helmet and camera. Knowing what had happened to Shaw was important to all the divers, and Roux thought that Ann might be better able to accept her husband's death if she understood how it had occurred. But Roux worried that the helmet might be dislodged as he tried to pull it to the shot line. He also knew that he didn't want to look into Shaw's face.

So far Roux had been working at arm's length from the body, keeping his eyes averted from the head. That didn't bother him. But with the body still resisting his efforts to move it, he decided that he had to get closer. He embraced the body from behind, one arm around the torso, another around the neck, and he began to wrestle it toward the shot line. This was a grim and heartrending exercise. Moving the corpse along the roof required all of Roux's considerable strength. As he approached the line, the roof rose in a series of ledges, and the buoyant corpse shot up quickly from one to the other, in Roux's tight embrace.

At the surface, Peter Herbst's headache was abating. He began to think that his distress was more mental than physiological. He thought about Petrus Roux, down in the cave with Dave's body. He berated himself: *Don't be a wimp!* He put away the oxygen, climbed back into his rebreather, and entered the pool again. The headache seemed to vanish as his head dipped below the surface.

He dropped through the opening beside the large boulder. Seconds later, a dark form rocketed up from below. It was the body of Dave Shaw, with Petrus clinging to it. Roux and the body slammed into a ledge below the opening, jammed against the stone. Clouds of silt rose as Roux struggled to free the body. Multiple loose strands of rope hung down through the entrance. A nightmare scene.

Herbst floated up and got Roux's attention. Herbst gave an I've-got-him gesture. Roux nodded. He pulled his arms away and backed off to give Herbst room.

Herbst tried to shift the body. He found that it was massively buoyant. The drysuit was deflated, the wings were empty, yet he had to grapple with it as he moved it towards the nearest opening to the top. This was not the usual entrance but a narrower slit off to the side. Its odd shape made it inconvenient to enter from above, but Shaw sometimes used it as an exit if other divers were floating above the main entrance. The slit opened at a corner of the pool, where Shaw would pop up unexpectedly, sometimes surprising those who stood nearby. Now Herbst guided the body there. He positioned it under the opening and when he released the body, it surged up towards the light.

Gordon Hiles was videotaping the police as they worked on Deon Dreyer's body, removing his equipment. Hiles occasionally glanced at the spot beside the large boulder where divers usually appeared from below. Then he heard a bubbling to one side and he saw Shaw's body bob up from below and drift slowly towards the edge of the pool.

Herbst and Roux ascended. Hiles, watching them through the camera's view screen as he taped, thought that Roux seemed shaken. But Roux kept himself under control as he helped Herbst catalogue Shaw's equipment. An evidence technician took notes as they removed equipment piece by piece, checking its condition, noting the position of switches and valves and the readings of pressure gauges. It was all intact, apparently in working order. Nothing was amiss. Even with the jostling at the roof of the cave, the rebreather's mouthpiece was still in place between Shaw's lips.

Gordon Hiles stood a few feet away, videotaping. At one point he swung the camera to the housing on top of the helmet. He zoomed in on the circular lens window, looking for signs of water inside the housing. He saw none.

When all the other equipment had been removed, Herbst cut the helmet strap and pulled the helmet from Shaw's head. Hiles spoke up: he said that the housing and the camera were his property and that only he should open it. While Shaw's body was zipped into a bag, a police official carried the helmet up to the rim, with Herbst and Hiles beside him.

They went to Hiles's vehicle where he got a wrench and removed the two hex-head bolts that secured the back cover of the housing. The camera was dry when he pulled it out. The interior of the housing was dry. The camera's battery indicator light was flashing, a sign that the battery was exhausted but that the circuitry was otherwise functioning.

Hiles opened the camera and found that the one-hour tape had run through to the end.

Hiles fitted a fresh battery and rewound the tape. Several of the police had gathered around him now, and Hiles suggested that he immediately make a copy of the tape. He had equipment to duplicate the tape while they watched it.

They set up the equipment in the police command tent. Hiles's gear included a video monitor but no speakers. There was a single audio output jack. Hiles plugged in a pair of headphones and handed them to Herbst, and the tape began to roll.

*　*　*

No other diving accident has ever been so closely scrutinized as the death of Dave Shaw at Bushman's. The existence of the helmet video made that possible. Though Shirley and Hiles tried to control its distribution, long segments appeared on Internet video sharing sites, captured from an Australian documentary film that used some of the footage. It was discussed on Web forums devoted to rebreathers and tech diving, including at least one where Shaw had participated when he was alive.

This was not all macabre curiosity. The number of dives ever recorded below 250 metres is so slight that any new attempt has the potential to illuminate the performance of gear and the reaction of the human body. And near-death and death – representing limits reached and breached – are often more instructive than success. In a real sense, advances in diving are built on the agonies of those who have gone before.

No video was necessary to glean at least the outline of what had happened at the bottom of Bushman's. The story was there in the bizarre tableau that Herbst and Petrus Roux and the police divers had found on the roof of the chamber. The cradle of string that held the body of Deon Dreyer was hanging from the head of Dave Shaw's cave light, wrapped twice around it. And the light head, which Shaw usually wore at the back of his right hand, was hanging free.

Don Shirley and every other cave diver understood what that meant: Shaw at some point had slipped his hand from the light's rectangular grip and had allowed it to hang loose. The trailing light head had tangled in the cave line that led from the shot line to the body, the line which Shaw had run during his dive in October. Shaw had become victim of one of the simplest and most insidious errors in cave diving: he had become tangled in the guide line.

Shirley was stunned when he first learned of it. Shaw was always careful to keep his gear 'clean': nothing loose, no protrusions, no flyaway hoses. But because the camera housing prevented him from hanging the light head around his neck, as he usually would, Shaw allowed the light to hang down by his side. It tangled in the guide line, which trapped him when he tried to leave.

Shaw apparently mentioned his plans to trail the light head only once, during the pool session on Wednesday afternoon before the dive, when he tried the helmet. But Shirley wasn't there.

Many months later, when he talked about it, Shirley was unequivocal about how he would have reacted if he had known Shaw's plans to let the light head hang free: 'I'd have said, "Don't do that."'

There was another surprise in the post mortem of Deon Dreyer's remains. The flesh in the exposed areas outside the wetsuit – head and neck, hands, ankles – had decomposed normally. But the portions of the body enclosed in the wetsuit were a solid mass of a soaplike substance known as adipocere, which is often formed when bodies are left in wet environments without free oxygen. The process is known as saponification. Rather than the skeleton that Shaw had expected to find, he had encountered a soap mummy.

It was the first time Shirley had heard of such a thing. None of the pathologists he had consulted ever mentioned adipocere or saponification. Many months later, an undertone of bitterness crept into his voice when he talked about it.

'Before the dive, nobody could tell me what the body was going to look like,' he said. 'Once it came up, everybody knew.'

Adipocere is positively buoyant: that is, it will float on water. That explained why the body rose up in front of Shaw when he jostled it in attempting to slide the bag over the legs. What has never been explained is why the body *didn't* float when Shaw tried to move it during his dive in October. When he returned from that dive, he described how he had pulled at it, trying to free the tanks from the mud. He pulled so hard that he began to pant. The tanks were stuck there: he was sure of it.

Yet he hadn't been able to budge it.

If it had floated then, he could have pulled it up at the end of his cave line, or else allowed it to float free to the ceiling of the cavern. Either way, the dive on 8 January wouldn't have been necessary.

*　*　*

On a day two years after Shaw's death, Don Shirley watched the tape with a visitor who had never before seen its full length. The very first time Shirley watched the video, several days after it surfaced, he believed that he understood exactly how Dave Shaw had died. Nothing since then has changed his mind, and after his first couple of viewings, he watched it again only to guide others through it.

Run time 11:33.
At the end of a fast, smooth descent, Shaw reaches the bottom. He now has a maximum of six minutes to find the body, secure it in the bag, and return to the shot line.

His light briefly hunts the thin cave line, partly covered in mud on the floor; then he begins to swim towards the body.

The torch is still on his right hand, and its bright spot of light tracks purposefully across the floor as he follows the line.

Run time 12:35.

As Shaw approaches the body, the bright spot suddenly swings out of sight: he has let go of the light and allowed it to swing down. Shaw pulls out the body bag and it billows in front of him. Shirley at this moment is dropping through the entrance, 270 metres above.

The knee of a drysuit appears in the frame, out of the darkness; Shaw's right hand, without the light, reaches out and finds the body.

Run time 13:25.

Shaw's hands move in and out of the frame as he pushes the bag up over the legs of the body. Shaw's breathing can be heard, slightly heavy; Shirley compares it to the effort of jogging at the surface.

Run time 13:47.

Suddenly a regulator and a light-coloured tank rise up into the frame. The body – headless – is now floating off the floor, hovering in Shaw's face, slowly turning so that Shaw is looking at the back of the corpse.

This is the crucial moment, where every knowledgeable diver begins internally urging Shaw to back away from the body and leave. The plan has gone off track, unexpectedly but serendipitously. If the body floats, it can easily be pulled up with the shot line when Shaw returns to the surface. He can leave now: job all but done.

But Shaw doesn't leave. He begins handling the body, turning it, trying to pull the bag up. He flicks a quick look at the computer on his right wrist, checking his elapsed time. He has 3 minutes 40 seconds before he must begin to return to the surface.

His breathing is heavier and more rapid. The jog is now a hard run.

'It's easy to sit here in an armchair and say that he should be leaving,' Shirley says at this point as he watches the video. 'Down there, it's different. You go down there with a plan in mind, that's your focus. You shut out everything else.'

Run time 14:29.

The taut cave line appears in front of Shaw's face, inches away, between his head and the bag. The cave light briefly flares off to the left, no longer hanging from his side, but apparently snagged on the line, which has become tangled around the body.

Shaw lifts the light off the line, lets it fall, and works at clearing the tangle.

Three minutes of bottom time remain, and he is breathing harder.

Run time 15:05.

He tries to open a pair of shears that he takes from a pocket at his belt. He fumbles with the shears for a few seconds, and then snaps a safety catch. The jaws of the shears pop open.

He slips on the slick, sloping floor, steadies himself with both hands, checks the wrist display.

The head of the corpse appears out of the murk in the lower left of the frame. Shaw's left hand appears to be resting on the skull.

Shaw isn't yet caught up in the line: he still can leave. But the body is caught up in the string.

'He's thinking, do I take the body or do I take the head?' Shirley says as he watches. 'Now he's going to cut the line. The problem with cutting the line is that if you lose it, you have no way back to the shot line. That would cause a real serious problem in that silt, because you've got to find the line again to know which way to go.'

Shaw checks the wrist display. Seventy-five seconds of bottom time remain, but with a one minute swim back to the shot line, he should be leaving the body now.

Run time 16:15.

Once more the head appears in the frame. The bag floats beside it, now no longer around the legs. Shaw pauses and seems to look at the head, considering it. He moves, as if to swim off.

But he's caught. He works to untangle himself. With the shears still in his right hand, he paws at the line. His movements are rapid.

His breathing now is very hard, very fast.

He's past his departure time, behind schedule.

Run time 17:10.

Shaw tries to move away from the body, pushing his way back up the slope, dragging the body behind him. He holds the line in one hand, shears in the other.

The shears wave ineffectively in front of him.

One last check of the display on his wrist.

His breathing is rapid and shallow, short, sharp inhalations; there's a gurgle as Shaw flushes his breathing loop and adds fresh gas.

Run time 20:41.

The breathing seems choked. It has become a desperate gasping that's hard to listen to.

He grasps the line, but his movements seem vague and ineffectual.

Shirley now was eight minutes into his dive, past 150 metres, and probably just now sighting the light below. But it wasn't Shaw's main light; the bulb was now broken from being dragged along the floor of the cave. The light Shirley spotted was from the smaller torch attached to the helmet, beside the camera.

The breathing trails away.

From the first time he saw the video, Shirley was convinced that Shaw had died from an excess of carbon dioxide – CO_2. The breathing tells the story. One of the effects of CO_2 in the body is to trigger the breathing response. As the concentration of CO_2 climbs, the breathing rate increases. The breathing reflex isn't a voluntary response: once concentrations of CO_2 start to build, you cannot will yourself to slow down and breathe more deeply.

With the faster rate, the breathing becomes shallower. The volume of each breath becomes increasingly small, creating a 'dead space' in the lungs in which the gas is stagnant, so that

CO_2 continues to build up in the blood. This in turn provokes an even greater urgency to breathe, so that breathing becomes even more rapid and shallow: it's a death spiral.

At the same time, the shallow breathing creates increased resistance in the loop: it's comparable to breathing in and out of a paper bag held over the nose and mouth.

Eventually almost no gas is being moved in and out of the lungs. Although the rebreather is still perfectly functional, the concentration of carbon dioxide in the lungs and the blood becomes lethally high. At high levels, CO_2 is a sedative, and can cause unconsciousness within 10 to 12 minutes; for Shaw, that corresponds to the time when he began to exert himself with the corpse.

In the weeks following the accident, an Australian physician and tech diving expert, Simon Mitchell, examined photos of Shaw's rebreather, taken when Shirley opened it for the first time since Shaw had finished preparing it before the dive. Mitchell found certain details that might have restricted the flow of gas through the loop. One of the criticisms of rebreathers is that they require a greater effort to draw a breath. Unlike open-circuit gear, which delivers gas at pressure, the pressure of the breathing loop is always equal to that of the lungs, so inhaling gas requires a certain muscular effort. Shaw's use of a fine-grained scrubber absorbent, his method of packing the material, and the use of a felt pad atop the absorbent canister all might have added to the work of breathing, especially given the added density of his breathing gas at 270 metres.

Yet Shaw had used the same setup during his dive in October without a problem.

Shirley points to a test that he conducted with the DAN diving physician, Frans Cronje, at Eugene Marais Hospital about a week after the dive. Shirley played the video, and timed his breaths to match the sounds of Shaw's breathing while a breath counter – called a capnograph – measured his breathing rate and carbon dioxide levels. Cronje found that Shaw's rate of respiration reached 36 breaths per minute. Although Shirley was voluntarily hyperventilating rather than gradually suffocating, as was the case with Dave, the abnormal breathing pattern nearly caused Shirley to pass out at a point where Shaw was still struggling to free himself from entanglement.

Shirley's recollection of the test:

After initially watching the tape in the early morning on Gordon's small screen, I watched it on a large screen. This was part of the formal analysis that Frans Cronje was doing. We watched it forwards and backwards, frame by frame, trying to work out what happened. I found that I was breathing to the sounds of Dave's breath, every time he died – 'I died' with him, empathising involuntarily. Frans then suggested that we try an experiment. I lay on the bed, breathing through a CO_2 monitor, with a pulse being taken on my finger. I followed the breathing, breath for breath, with headphones on. I had to mentally push myself to take full breaths, very difficult when you are so loaded with CO_2. By the time Dave came to the last breaths, I could barely move. It took me 30 minutes to get the use of my arms and legs properly after that.

I died with Dave. It was not closure, but it was knowledge.

CO_2 also exacerbates narcosis; Shaw planned his gas mixture to give him the effect of a 46 metre dive on air, the amount that he was willing to tolerate based on his own experience. But Shirley says that the heightened CO_2 probably increased the equivalent air depth to about 55 metres. Whether the narcosis affected his judgment, and dulled his reaction to the unexpected floating of the body, is impossible to say. On the video there is no indication of the aimlessness and stupefaction that's associated with the most severe narcosis. Shaw remains active, apparently aware, and engaged in what he is doing.

'If he had just given up, I would have said that he was too badly narcosed,' Shirley says. 'But he didn't give up. He was working his way through it. He knew what he was doing. He knew what he wanted to do. My biggest annoyance with this whole thing is the fact that the torch wasn't where it was supposed to be, which was around his neck. He was moving away, but he couldn't get loose. If he hadn't got caught up, he would have swum out to the shot line and he would have come out, and none of the rest of this would have mattered.'

*   *   *

Cronje, Mitchell, Meintjes and South African diving physician Hermie Britz discussed the incident for months. They dismissed the possibility that the rebreather had failed, and focused on the likelihood of a downward spiral of increased CO_2 and rapid breathing. In February 2007 they jointly published an article on the incident in the *Journal of Aviation, Space, and Environmental Medicine*.

The stress and modest exertion associated with entanglement at the point of leaving the site precipitated a spiralling crisis of increased respiratory demand which could not be met because of flow limitation. Futile attempts to do so only resulted in a vicious cycle of wasted work and accumulation of more CO_2. Once established, this cycle would have been hard to break unless resistance to breathing could be rapidly reduced.

They suggested that Shaw might have been able to break the breathing cycle by bailing out to his open-circuit backup. They noted the irregularities in his rebreather setup and the possible effects of narcosis, but weren't able to say how these might have influenced the outcome.

Extreme divers are almost always optimistic about the outcome of their next big dive, but the physicians who treat them are rarely so sanguine. All four of the report's authors have advised against the most extreme attempts, and they ended their article on a dry but plaintive note:

This case provides a tragic but timely and salient lesson to a growing population of deep 'technical' divers that there are physiological limitations that must be understood and considered in planning extreme dives.

In an interview several months later, Cronje spoke of Shaw's death, and of extreme deep diving.

(Shaw) was continuously monitoring his depth, he was continuously aware of his time. He aborted, and he followed procedure down to the last, with the possible exception of not bailing out to the open-circuit. We know that when people are already breathless, they are notoriously reluctant to give up a known source of breathing gas for an unknown source. But apart from that, he did everything that one could hope. It was just an interplay of a number of little incidents leading to a major incident in an extremely hostile environment.

The number of people who have survived dives to 250 metres without injuries is about ten per cent, and at least half have lost their lives. We can't endorse that. But we know that people do it. There is a silent admiration for what they do, because we know that they dedicate themselves to it. We have a pervasive concern that they aren't always aware of the true physiological limitations.

If you're doing deep diving, don't make it complicated. As futile as it seems to tell people, 150 metres is a reasonable limit. The undefined depths are not the boundary; 150 should be the boundary. But if they do continue to dive beyond that boundary – and they will – they should keep their dives very simple, and they should be very conscious of the issues of breathing, particularly if they use rebreathers, where breathing resistance is such an issue. They should realize that if they go beyond 150 metres, the chances are high that they will get seriously hurt, and if they go beyond 250 metres the chances are high that they will not survive. The advice is, don't do it, but if you're going to do it, keep it simple.

After his experiences at Bushman's, Jack Meintjes became pointedly critical of extreme attempts by sport divers. Meintjes had been frustrated at being unable to deal directly with Don Shirley's crisis, and he came to believe that the lack of constant communication between divers and the surface, and the absence of an in-water decompression chamber – both standard elements in commercial diving, but virtually unheard-of in sport diving – leave sport divers vulnerable to the emergencies that are almost inevitable in dives to great depth.

At the time of the Bushman's dive, DAN-South Africa routinely insured the treatment of sport divers for dives as deep as 250 metres. In 2007, the group reduced that limit to 100 metres. Divers who wished to be insured for deeper attempts are now required to submit an advance dive plan for specific approval.

CHAPTER
19

In his years as a minister, Michael Vickers had many times comforted the bereaved. Only once before had he ever seen anyone so utterly grief-stricken as Ann was that Saturday evening when she learned of David's death.

They sat in the living room: Ann and Lisa, Harry and Pamela and Michael Vickers, and after a few minutes Ann brought up the question of how others in the family should be notified. Vickers called David's parents in Perth. He spoke with Ann's older brother in Melbourne, who said that he would visit Ann's mother and father early in the morning; then they would all go to see Steven to tell him what had happened.

Over the next several days, Ann's family and friends gathered around her. Her parents and David's father and sister arrived from Australia with Steven. Sharon and Grant Dixon, whom the Shaws had known well in New Guinea – she was a midwife at Steven's birth – also flew in immediately after they learned the news. Acquaintances from the church brought meals, answered the phone, and kept company with Ann.

Plans began to take shape for a memorial service in Hong Kong. Because the congregation didn't have a church building, Vickers arranged for the service to be held at an Episcopal church in Hong Kong.

Ann was existing from day to day, hour to hour, taking part in the decisions where she was needed, leaving the rest to others. In this greatest crisis of her life, she felt oddly reassured, as if God was looking after her, providing for her.

Then she learned that David's body had been found.

It was night in Hong Kong; Lisa was in the shower. Lisa's boyfriend at the time, Roger, was in the living room with Ann when the call came.

Ann came apart when she heard the news. She began sobbing on Roger's shoulder. When Lisa came out, she found her mother nearly incoherent. Lisa phoned Peter Herbst for more details, then called Pamela and Harry, who came over and spent the night. The family members who weren't in Hong Kong, including David's mother, learned the news from radio and TV.

Ann, by her own account, was 'not worth very much' that night and the next day. She was distraught at the discovery of the body. Ann had reconciled herself to David's remains staying forever at the bottom of Bushman's. She didn't need closure; she knew very well that David was gone, and she didn't need his body to confirm it. Even with the help of Michael Vickers and her family and friends, she had barely been able to negotiate her way through the practicalities so far: the phone calls and the arrangements for the memorial service.

Dealing with a body added many more difficulties and decisions and burdens. From the repatriation of the remains, through cremation, Hong Kong law would have required at least three different identifications of the body by next of kin. It would have been beyond her ability to cope. She thought that the funeral customs in Hong Kong were ghastly; she had been appalled by the recent funeral for one of the students at her school – overblown and impersonal – and she wanted to avoid that.

And the body simply didn't matter to her. She had no sentimental attachment to the corpse. It was not David, she thought. He was in heaven.

She decided that the body should be cremated in South Africa, and that the ashes should stay there. She discussed it with Steven and Lisa, and David's parents. They all agreed. Peter Herbst handled the arrangements in Pretoria, including cremation, with a memorial service one week later.

Two years later, Ann was certain that it was one of the best decisions she had ever made.

Though they had never met in life, Dave Shaw and Deon Dreyer were now forever linked in death. Yet their families' reactions to the discovery of the bodies were as different as could be. Theo and Marie Dreyer were eager to see Deon's corpse before the post-mortem. Though it had no head, Marie immediately knew her son's muscular body. She even recognized the underwear she had washed for him a couple of days before he left for Bushman's.

On impulse, she embraced the corpse. She wasn't disgusted; this was her son, and she later said that the moment brought her peace. Ten years after he walked out the door of their home and drove off with his friends, Deon had finally returned.

*   *   *

Ann forbade the wearing of black to the memorial service in Hong Kong. She didn't want it to be a lugubrious affair. She chose a hymn that had been a favourite of David and her.

Ann and Steven both felt that they wouldn't be able to speak at the service. Lisa felt that someone should speak for the family and say what they all felt, and she told Michael Vickers that she would speak.

The previous August, she had planned to write an appreciation that she would deliver to her father on his 50th birthday. But she wasn't able to come to Hong Kong. She had thought that she might deliver it at Christmas, but the opportunity never seemed to come up. Now she decided to say to him in death what she had never said in life.

She wasn't in the church when the service began; she was outside on the steps, trying to work up the courage to go in.

But she did go in, and she spoke, reading from the paper without looking up, afraid that she wouldn't be able to go on if she looked into the faces of the several hundred people in the pews:

My father was honest ...
    He was also incredibly hard-working ...
    He had very strong values and morals ...

My father was young at heart. He approached the world with the desires of a 20-year-old but with the wisdom of a 50-year-old, always striving to learn new skills and discover new things ...

I am at peace with my father's death and I hope that many of you here are or will be too. I am at peace because I know, having faced death before, that my father was unafraid and was completely at peace with the prospect. I know and he knew that the Lord would be right there ready to take him onto new adventures. I am also at peace because he died doing something he loved. Very few of us will ever get that privilege, and I thank the Lord that my father did, because, let's be honest, my dad was not the sort of person who was going to take to old age gracefully ...

I can see God in the actual manner and circumstances that surrounded his death. He has gone out with a bit of a bang, and I cannot think of anything more fitting or anyone more deserving of such a departure ...*

A week later, Steven and Michael Vickers flew to Johannesburg for an emotional funeral service that most of the dive team attended (Don and André were in England for a long-planned trip to clear up his late father's affairs). After the funeral, Stephen Sander drove Vickers and Steven to Bushman's.

Peter Herbst took custody of Shaw's ashes.

A few days later, Ann and Lisa flew to Australia for another memorial. After the service, Ann returned alone to Hong Kong, and she tried to resume normal life.

---

* See Appendix C for full text of Lisa Shaw's eulogy.

She had always believed that she was prepared for suddenly losing David: at least as prepared as anyone could be. From his days as an agricultural pilot, she had always lived with the possibility that he might go away some time and never return. She had even made certain plans in advance, so that some of the big decisions would already be in place if the time ever came.

The question of where she would live was one of those decisions. She knew that she would stay in Hong Kong for at least two years. She remembered the widows of two MAF pilots who had been killed in a landing accident in Australia. One of the widows had returned to her family in England shortly after the accident, and didn't seem to reconcile herself to the loss for years. The other woman had remained in Australia, and had worked through her grief while surrounded by supportive friends and the church. So Ann already knew that she would stay in Hong Kong. She returned home and resumed her work at the school, and she waited for her grief to subside.

After the two services, it would start to happen, she thought. But it didn't. Several weeks passed, and she didn't feel better at all. Just the opposite: she felt her grasp of life slipping away.

*   *   *

For Don and André, the year 2005 was supposed to be a time when life turned a corner. After years of work, their business had begun to thrive, and Don expected to train an instructor who could take over much of the daily responsibility. He looked forward to spending more time with André, and to diving with Dave Shaw. If all went well, Don would retire in 2007. The big dive occupied him for two months, and though he gladly took on the responsibility, he had looked forward to getting on with his life and his plans when it was done.

The accident ended all that. Three days after he was pulled from the water, on the Tuesday morning when André placed him in the passenger seat and drove him from Bushman's, many who knew him questioned whether he would ever truly recover. His diving career was in grave jeopardy, and there was doubt whether he would even be able to walk normally. His future had become a salvage operation.

When he left Bushman's he was still unsteady on his feet. If he sat up from a chair too quickly, he would lose his balance. He could hold his head up straight, but a sudden movement would cause him to lose his balance. He could walk a few steps in a straight line, but only if he focused on the task and kept his eyes fixed forward. Any distraction would throw him off.

A week-long series of chamber treatments in Pretoria alleviated some of the symptoms but couldn't restore the mechanisms of balance in his left ear. Those were gone forever. His return to normal functioning would depend on how well he could compensate for this diminished capacity. Frans Cronje compared it to the loss of one engine in a twin-engine airplane. A skilled pilot could continue to fly, but he would have to adjust his techniques. Everything would be different, and it would require total concentration.

With his usual confidence, Don declared that he would recover fully. He didn't just say it: he began to act as if he were already there, pushing against limitations, as if his incapacity were a passing nuisance. André thought that he needed less pushing, and more rest. She watched his struggles to walk and move about, saw him sway and fight for balance. It was as if he had had several glasses of wine, and was in a woozy state where he had to focus on everything that he did.

They had long planned a trip to England in mid-January, to visit Don's family and arrange his father's estate. They decided to go through with the trip. Don insisted. They boarded a flight to London a few hours after his last chamber treatment. He took a powerful sedative before the plane lifted off and he woke shortly before landing.

He found England difficult. He had expected it to seem bleak and cramped, and it was. It was also crowded and noisy, distracting for someone who needed all of his attention to execute simple motor tasks. He visited a friend in Oxford and was spooked by all the people and the commotion on the pavements. Stepping on and off an escalator was the equivalent of an amusement park thrill ride.

At first André drove Don wherever he needed to go. But she would be returning to South Africa ahead of him, and Don decided that he wanted to try driving. André went along, gripped the seat tightly, and tried not to show her anxiety. He had to focus straight ahead; cross traffic was a problem because he would get dizzy if he swung his head too quickly to one side. He knew that he would drive off the road in a moment if he even glanced down to tune a radio or check the shift lever. But he managed, and she felt reassured about leaving him when she returned home.

When he got back to South Africa, he continued to recover by increments. There was never a formal rehabilitation. The way to walk straight, he decided, was to get on with the job of walking. He simply kept working at what he wanted to do, thinking his way through acts that he used to perform unconsciously. He devised small tests, looking for signs of improvement, small milestones. One day he put one foot in front of the other and stood for a few seconds without wobbling. That was a victory, because he hadn't been able to do that the week before.

The progress came at a price. Though he insisted that the accident hadn't affected him mentally, André knew that he wasn't himself. He seemed to exist in a fog. The problem wasn't a direct effect of the accident; he was just completely absorbed. He spent his days focused on the minutiae of individual acts, devoting all his attention to executing simple motor skills.

'You're completely stuffed if you don't have your balance,' he said, many months later. 'You don't realize how much it matters until you've lost it.'

The year that was supposed to mean so much was being ground away by his moment-to-moment struggle to restore himself. The business was totally at a standstill.

And many months later, Shirley realized that he hadn't properly mourned Dave. He hadn't had the chance. From the moment he suddenly spun out of control during his decompression, Shirley was absorbed in the struggle first to survive and then to make himself whole. For ten and a half hours down in the cave, he had lived from moment to moment, gripping the rope, seeing no further than the computer display on his wrist and the next pressing task that had to be performed if he was to get out alive. And really, that hadn't changed much even after he was dragged out of the water and hauled up the face of the hole. He was still captive to the moment, riveted to the next immediate task in the seemingly endless sequence of tasks that had to be performed before he could truly say that he had returned to normal life.

*　　*　　*

For Shirley, life wasn't normal if it didn't include serious diving. Don insisted that he would be able to dive again, but the truth was that nobody knew what would happen when he tried to return to the water. Would he have to relearn all of his movements under water, as he was doing on land? And what would he do with himself, if he couldn't return to the kind of diving he loved?

André couldn't even contemplate the possibility. They could survive financially, she thought. But Don would be miserable and it would inevitably affect their life together.

The weeks after the accident became an enforced glimpse of life without diving. He felt it most sharply on weekends, previously his busiest days. He would stand in the sunshine outside his home, looking out over the rippling grasslands of the Komati valley, and he would think about the cool dark depths of the mine a few kilometres away. He knew that that was his true element, and he wondered whether he would ever be back there, doing what meant most to him.

About four months after the accident, he decided to find out. It was a weekend, and Peter Herbst and Lo Vingerling were visiting Komati Springs from Pretoria and Johannesburg. Shirley pulled on the drysuit that he had last worn at Bushman's. He strapped on a twin set of cylinders, open-circuit scuba gear: there would be no need for a rebreather today. Vingerling and Herbst waited for him at the surface as Shirley climbed down the steel ladder that descends from the top of the pit, down into the water. When he was torso-deep, he released his grip on the ladder and pushed himself away from the wall.

He floated.

It felt great.

Herbst and Vingerling followed him as he descended a few metres. Still great. He was as sure and stable and controlled as he had ever been: in fact, he was much more sure in the water than he was on land. This was as if he had leapfrogged all the hard work and tedium that movement on land still required. When he walked on land, he had to fix his eyes to a spot, to keep himself oriented. But here, he didn't need any reference. The water seemed to cushion his movements and hold him where he wanted to be.

He laid out flat in the water, floating horizontal, the position that had automatically provoked violent retching in January. Now, nothing.

He rocked his shoulders and let the motion carry him through a slow roll. He levered his torso forward until he was almost vertical, as if standing on his head, and after a few seconds he returned to the horizontal, hitting the position perfectly.

The ballet: he had it again.

They didn't go deep and they didn't stay long. There would be no decompression today. Shirley's kind of diving is built on deco, but decompression had caused the accident in January, and while the circumstances then were extreme even by his own standards, he still wanted to approach it cautiously.

In the following days, he began with a couple of dives that didn't really require deco; but he did it anyway, stopping at three metres for a few minutes before coming to the surface. Then, a couple more dives, slightly deeper and longer, gradually extending himself. He returned to teaching entry-level tech courses. No dives below 40 metres, very conservative deco profiles. At first Peter Herbst accompanied him on these dives, until Don became more confident.

Out of the water, he continued to make progress. He drove with increasing assurance. He would occasionally stumble when walking on rough ground, but his awkwardness in walking and moving was much less apparent. In his own self-prescribed therapy, he and André began taking weekly private dance lessons from one of his former diving students. The dance studio was in Nelspruit, the capital of Mpumalanga, about an hour away from their home, and they would spend the rest of the day in the city. It was the first time they had regularly taken days off since they were married.

CHAPTER
20

Ann made plans to travel to South Africa during her Easter vacation. Easter was early that year, barely three months since David's death, and her emotions were still raw. But she wanted to meet Don and André and the other divers, and to get a sense of David's life when he was in South Africa. She also wanted to give Don the crates of diving gear that were sitting in the downstairs room where David had kept an office.

Around this time she began to sense how the dive and its outcome had affected others around the world. An Australian weekly TV news magazine contacted her about doing a half-hour segment on David and the dive, and she agreed to allow the producer and a video crew to accompany her and Lisa on the trip.

She flew alone from Hong Kong; Lisa and the others were to arrive from Australia later that day. Ann became tense during the flight. The tension increased when a customs officer questioned her sharply about the ten crates of diving gear stacked on three baggage carts.

'Whose equipment is this?' the officer said.

'It's mine.'

'What is the value?'

'I don't know.'

'Do you plan to take it back with you when you leave?'

'No. It's staying here,' she said. 'I'm going to give it away.'

The officer kept repeating the questions, and soon Ann found herself at the ragged edge of self-control, struggling to maintain her composure.

'This equipment belonged to my husband,' she said finally, brimming with emotion, 'and he died here trying to help one of your citizens.'

He waved her through.

Gordon Hiles drove her to the Shirleys' home in Mpumalanga, and she stayed with Lisa in the guest cottage. They visited Komati Springs, where David had dived so often, and they went with the Shirleys down to a rocky ford of the Komati River where Dave and Don and André had spent several happy afternoons. Ann liked Don; she found him gentle and genuine. She could see why David had liked him.

There was discussion of a trip to Bushman's. She was apprehensive about visiting the place, but she also sensed that this was something she had to do, for her own sake. She agreed to go.

They drove to Bushman's with the Australian documentary crew, and arrived late evening. The van Zyls were gone but they had arranged for Ann and Lisa to stay in the room where David and Don had stayed before the big dive. The others gathered for a *braai* (South African version of a barbeque) but Ann wandered off alone, and she sat and began to cry. She couldn't face the room where David had spent his last night. She wept for a long time, then while the others were still eating, she summoned her resolve, walked to the room, took a sleeping pill, and had a shower. She was soon asleep.

The next morning, she was reluctant to drive to the site. She was sure that she would become emotional, and she didn't want that on tape: the Australian crew followed her everywhere. But the producer agreed not to videotape down in the hole, and Ann acceded. They drove to the site. This was also Shirley's first visit since his accident, and he had recovered enough to lead Ann and Lisa down the steep path through the boulders.

The place was as tranquil as it had ever been. The green duckweed had grown back over the surface of the pool, except for one patch over the main entry hole that always seems to remain clear. Don led them to the ledge that Dave had always staked out for himself, and where he had geared up for his last dive. Ann and Lisa clambered around the rocks and then Ann sat close beside Don for a few minutes, and they listened to the birds and looked out onto the water. It was more beautiful than she had expected. She didn't feel distraught – just the opposite.

'Is it underneath us now?' she asked. She meant the big cavern, the deep and distant floor where David had died.

Shirley said no, not exactly. The throat of the cave slopes away, he told her, and the main chamber is beneath the far wall on the other side of the pool. She followed his hand where it pointed, and stared out across the water, and she imagined David disappearing into that cavity and heading for the bottom with that great mass of stone over his head. The resolve that it would have required. The courage.

She put her head on Don's shoulder and wept silently: not the desperate and mournful keening of the night before, but a quiet sadness at the thought of leaving the place. She hadn't wanted to come at all, and now she felt that she would be leaving a part of herself behind.

They sat that way for a few more minutes, and then they walked out together. But the leaving was the only difficult part. She was glad that she had come.

*   *   *

On the last day of her visit, shortly before she left for the airport, Ann briefly met Marie and Theo Dreyer in the coffee shop of her hotel. It was a moment of well-intentioned awkwardness.

Theo seemed jovial and likeable, but Marie struck Ann as somewhat distant. Ann didn't expect any apologies; David had died doing what he wanted to do, of his own choice, but Ann thought that Marie ought to be a little more forthcoming.

Marie, though, felt that she didn't know what to say: even before the dive, she had harboured feelings of guilt and obligation. She literally didn't know what to say to the wife of the man who had died trying to bring back her son's body.

Ann seemed fragile to Marie.

But for Ann, this was a moment of strength. David had told her that Marie tended to be emotional even at the best of times. Ann was determined not to let this dissolve into an exercise in mutual wailing, and she had promised herself that she would remain strong and composed. And she did.

Ann became aroused once, when Theo seemed to imply that David and Deon had died equals in the sport. This annoyed her. Ann had come late to an appreciation of what David did underwater, but she was now proud of his accomplishments and protective of his legacy as a diver. She had also learned enough about the sport to realize that a novice heedlessly diving to 70 metres on air couldn't be compared to David, with his careful planning and thoughtful analysis.

She resented the comparison, but she kept it to herself.

The Dreyers stayed only long enough for a cup of coffee, then they all said a cordial goodbye, and Ann left for the airport and her return to the empty home in Hong Kong.

*   *   *

Ann returned home and waited for the healing to begin. It hadn't happened yet. Her sense of loss was even more overpowering than it had been the night she learned that David was dead. The pain was every bit as sharp.

In those first few days after his death, she had told herself that things would start to get better after the two memorial services. But nothing got better. She told herself that the grief would start to recede after the trip to South Africa. But that didn't happen, either.

For a while, she immersed herself in work. She was responsible for writing the next year's timetable for the secondary section of the school, a difficult and stressful job, and when it was complete, she thought that now she would begin to adjust to David's absence. But it didn't happen. She wasn't getting better: she was crumbling. One afternoon, while driving home from school, she nearly drove into the back of a truck. She quit driving after that. She no longer trusted herself behind the wheel.

One morning when she was due in school, she simply wasn't able to get out of bed. There was still nearly a month of class left, but gathering herself up and presenting a normal face to the world was now more effort than she could manage. She took more time off. She simply couldn't function.

A doctor put her on sleeping pills and antidepressants.

She spent much of the summer in Australia, some of it visiting family, some travelling to investment property that David had bought. She knew that it existed because David always discussed it with her, but she hadn't seen most of it, and she wanted an idea of what she actually owned. But this required driving in a car and she was uneasy about that, so her father agreed to accompany her.

At first she did feel some relief from the constant sense of pain and loss. David's birthday was in July, and she got through that by spending the day with his parents. Her own birthday was in August, and she got through it by spending the day with her parents. She would be returning to Hong Kong shortly before the start of the new school year, and she told herself that this would be a truly new start, and now the healing could really begin.

But it didn't happen that way. As the time drew near, the prospect of returning to Hong Kong filled her with a leaden dread. Her time in Australia had been an escape. But Hong Kong meant daily life – real life – without David. And she wasn't ready to face that.

She cried most of the morning on the day of her flight. At the airport, she wept so piteously that Lisa didn't want to say goodbye at the security counter. As she waited to board the flight, Ann again burst into tears, alarming the employee at the check-in desk; the woman re-arranged seating so that Ann would be by herself in business class.

When she returned, she spent only a night or two alone in the house. She couldn't stand the place any longer; she couldn't bring herself to look at the family photos on the walls. She called several friends, including Harry and Pamela, and asked to sleep in their homes. All of them invited her to stay with them, but when they spoke among themselves, they all agreed that this couldn't last long. She was beyond their help and needed more than they could give her.

The start of school was just a few days away when she decided that she couldn't face work any longer. She resigned in an email to the headmaster. Physically, emotionally, she was drained. Simple tasks overwhelmed her. She had been touch-typing since she was a teenager, but now the act of typing at a keyboard required her to concentrate on each letter. She was unable to do simple arithmetic. Even laying in bed, turning her head on the pillow, required an effort of will.

She stopped going to church: the music, the thought of being there without David – it was too much to handle.

Lisa realized what was happening, and flew in hurriedly from Australia, just to stay with her in the house.

One day after Lisa arrived, Ann went to meet a friend in the city. Lisa dropped her off nearby, but as soon as Lisa left, Ann became confused and started to wander the streets. She didn't recognize where she was – her brain would not engage – but it was a street full of fast-moving vehicles. She began to imagine herself walking in front of a speeding car. One step off the kerb, that's all it would take, the end of her misery.

Eventually she used a taxi to get to the restaurant where she was meeting the friend. Later the friend tried to drive her home, but they got lost because Ann literally couldn't find her way back.

It was a frightening experience. Ann truly didn't know how she could continue this way: she felt that she had fallen off the edge of the universe, into a place where God didn't exist.

It was an evening of emotional upheaval in the house. Ann called her brother in Australia and told him what had happened. Alarmed, he phoned their parents, and her mother bought a seat on a flight to Hong Kong the following day. Lisa called Pamela and Michael Vickers, and they both came over to pray with Ann. But Ann was so distraught that she bruised her hand while striking a piece of furniture in the living room, an outburst so out of character that those who know her would have refused to believe it if she hadn't later told them of it.

Lisa couldn't watch this: she left the room, and Ann watched her hurry up the stairs to close herself in her bedroom.

Ann remembered later:

I don't think I have ever been so frightened in all my life, because it seemed I was facing the rest of my life, and eternity, without God. Michael just asked me if I thought there was any faint possible chance that God could reach me where I was at that moment. And I thought about Lisa up in her bedroom, her mother off the deep end, and I thought that poor Lisa doesn't want a mother like this. And I said to Michael, '... Yes.' And that was the turning point.

I thought my mother was going to find a basket case when she came the next day. But that next morning, I was immediately better. I opened the Bible to read a passage, and I opened it to Psalm 30, which talks about restoring your life when you've been in the pit. And that was how it felt to me. I was in a pit, and God picked me up.

From that moment, things started to change. I still had bad days, but I was getting better.

She returned to school later that year, working part time, but at the end of that school year she left officially. She travelled, visiting Australia and the UK and South Africa for a second time.

People began to tell her that she had changed since David's death. Even Lisa said it one day. Ann thought that she was the same person she had always been, but she was using parts of herself that she had never before had to exercise when David was alive. He had always taken care of so much: the money, legal matters, dealing with tradesmen or banks. Anything that required confidence and assertiveness fell automatically under his domain. Now Ann often had to do these things, and she often amazed herself by actually finding a way to make it happen.

All this created the beginnings of a self-possession that spilled over into other parts of her life.

During her second trip to South Africa, she asked André to help her learn to snorkel.

290

Ann had never been comfortable around water. Though she had had some lessons as a young teenager, she swam poorly, too tense to be effective. When David began to dive, she asked him to help her learn to snorkel. He brought her to a swimming pool, and after fitting her with a dive mask and a snorkel, he encouraged her to lower her head slowly into the water. But it was no good. Before she even submerged the top of her head, the mask began to leak, and she panicked and stood up and pulled the mask away. She tried it several more times, each time with the same result. David saw that she was grimacing tightly, clenching the muscles around her eyes and opening gaps between her face and the mask, allowing water to rush in. After a few tries she gave up.

André found a mask that fit properly, and a self-draining snorkel, and they went to a heated pool at a resort in the nearby town. André patiently led her first to submerge her face and breathe through the snorkel, then to swim short distances. It was unpleasant for Ann at first – *this is awful, why am I putting myself through this, I can't do this.*

Then gradually she relaxed. She was doing it.

*   *   *

Petrus Roux didn't return to the water for almost half a year after his dive to bring out the bodies. His struggle to pull out Shaw's body had been harrowing. He had dragged it up a series of ledges, ending with the uncontrolled ascent that jammed him into a corner with the corpse. For one moment, he came eye to eye with it, exactly what he had hoped to avoid.

When Petrus finally climbed out of the pool, he felt a sharp pain in his lower back. *Bent* was the first thought that came to him. He climbed to the rim, and went into the chamber. The back pain disappeared during a treatment that lasted three and a half hours. It never returned and he has had no lasting effects. He stayed the night at the Mount Carmel lodge. The next morning, before he and his father returned home, he watched the entire video with the audio; like all the other divers he badly wanted – perhaps he needed – to know what had happened at the bottom of the hole.

It was a mistake. The sound of Shaw's last breaths disturbed him. And Roux was horrified by Shaw's attempt to cut the floating cave line.

For the next week he had trouble sleeping. He was badly rattled by the memory of that grim moment when he looked into the lifeless eyes of his friend. And he couldn't get over the image of the shears in Shaw's trembling hand as he tried to free himself.

Five months passed before Roux dived again. He went to Komati Springs with a friend, his regular dive partner who was also a cave diver. They entered a tunnel where there was no permanent line. His friend swam ahead of Roux, spooling out line from a reel and occasionally stopping to tie off to a rock or some other object in order to keep it tight. When they reached their turnaround point, his friend handed Roux the reel, to lead them out.

Roux froze at the sight of the cave line floating in front of him. He realized that he was deep in a dark cave, a place where people sometimes die. His felt his apprehension snowballing, and he was on the verge of panic before he finally brought himself under control and began to swim out, reeling up the line as he went.

After that, he was again comfortable in the water. As time passed, he believed that Dave's death had made diving more meaningful to him. He became meticulous in his diving: he realized what he could lose, and he didn't want his wife to suffer what Ann had endured. When he entered a dark, silent place, he would often think of Shaw. He would see Dave's face; he would see Dave's trembling hands. But that was all right now. It was all right.

Epilogue

On a very early morning in May 2007, I rode with Don Shirley through the darkness at the Mount Carmel farm. He parked the bakkie near the edge of the rim at Bushman's Hole and we got out and stood and waited for the sun to come up. The air was see-your-breath chilly. The time was about 5.15. The sky above the eastern horizon was darker than the starlit landscape below it, so the sun was still a long way off.

I was standing there in the darkness, waiting for sunrise, because Don Shirley said I should. 'You have to get the feeling,' he said. Shirley is a very bright and intuitive guy who almost always knows what he's talking about. And something in his voice said that it was important.

He was right.

I was in South Africa to meet the people involved in the dive at Bushman's, to learn who they were and how it had affected their lives. It was a pleasure in many ways. Divers at this level are usually intelligent; the sport demands it. The divers I met in South Africa were typically quick-witted, also unfailingly friendly, open and helpful. Long unrecognized by the public, even the greatest don't get much chance to become full of themselves.

I especially liked Don Shirley. I liked his gentle nature, his patience, his unaffected passion for the sport and for bringing others to the sport. His calm is almost supernatural. I can't imagine a more ideal diving instructor. I would put my life in his hands without hesitation.

I never met Dave Shaw. I wish I had, for many reasons. But I came to know him by his acts and by the way he was reflected in the people who knew him and loved him. I am certain that he was a rare man, with a rare combination of qualities: ambitious and highly focused, yet giving and considerate; confident but humble; self-possessed yet self-effacing. I know that I would have liked him – who didn't?

For a while, I was less sure about the way he approached diving. A career of 333 dives from the deep end of a swimming pool to an attempted body recovery at the bottom of Bushman's Hole is an arc of almost unimaginable steepness, and he could not have accomplished it if he had not sometimes been willing to suspend prudence. He was sure that he would be able to complete his task at the bottom of Bushman's and to return safely. But at such extremes, risk becomes almost impossible to assess. There is so little precedent. I admired his courage and his determination. But his loss seemed such a waste.

Then at Komati Springs I met Edrich Smook, a tech diver studying for a Master's degree in psychology at the University of Pretoria. Diving, he said, is not an adrenaline sport. The appeal is more profound. In a cave, during a challenging dive, the most minor act becomes crucial; simply tying a knot on a line is absorbing. You are completely in the moment. You are living fully.

A high fence encloses the Mount Carmel farm, but it's a big place, rich with wild animals, and it feels primal. Around us as I stood with Shirley in the darkness I heard the rattling of brush, a snort, a feral grunt. I was aware of the hole a few metres away. I imagined the vast chamber below the surface, all that had happened there beyond the sight of the world.

So subtly that I didn't realize it at first, some colour leaked into the sky to the east. At first it was just a smudge of dark blue against the black, but gradually it became a bulge of light, stunning tones of salmon and teal and aqua, pushing upward by degrees. And then a fantastic occurrence: a thin cobalt band appeared at the horizon. It started in the east, then extended in both directions, as if undercutting the night. A low rise blocked my view to the west, but everywhere I could see, maybe 270°, the band of intense electric blue encircled the horizon. It was as if the dome of night were being pried loose from the earth.

It was as striking and eerily beautiful as any sight I have ever seen in nature.

As we stood watching the glow slowly suck the stars from the sky, I thought of all the sunrises I had missed because I was occupied with other things. Because of Don Shirley, I was watching the sun come up over the Kalahari – imagine!

I didn't know how many more sunrises might be left for me, but I sensed that facing the end of them would be that much easier for having experienced this one.

I thought of Dave Shaw and the instant of his departure down at the bottom of the cavern. The phrase 'he died doing what he loved' usually sounds trite and hollow. Maybe 'he died living fully' is closer to the truth. At the bottom of Bushman's he entered a world and a reality that almost nobody on earth has ever known. He got there because he decided to make it matter, and he died at the absolute apex of life and experience.

I don't believe that he went out feeling cheated.

The amazing display in the sky continued, with the glow in the east spreading and pushing back the night. Nearly an hour after the black sky first began to lighten, the top of the sun finally pushed into sight, a searing red sliver at the edge of the world. When it finally lifted entirely into sight, we got into Don Shirley's bakkie, and he started back up the dusty trail to the lodge. He reached for the iPod.

'Let's have a little *Dark Side of the Moon*,' he said.

APPENDIX A

Dave Shaw's
iPod playlists

Deepcave 1

Isn't Life Strange	(The Moody Blues)
Ted the Mechanic	(Deep Purple)
Sunshine of Your Love	(Cream)
On the Turning Away	(Pink Floyd)
Jealous Guy	(John Lennon and the Plastic Ono Band)
Whole Lotta Love	(Led Zeppelin)
I Heard It Through the Grapevine	(Creedence Clearwater Revival)
Comfortably Numb	(Pink Floyd)
With a Little Help from My Friends	(Joe Cocker)
Hallelujiah	(Jeff Buckley)
Hey Jude	(The Beatles)
Black Night	(Deep Purple)
A Day in the Life	(The Beatles)

Deepcave 2

While My Guitar Gentle Weeps	(The Beatles)
Drive	(REM)
I Am the Walrus	(The Beatles)
Everybody Hurts	(REM)
Time	(Pink Floyd)
Telegraph Road	(Dire Straits)
Child in Time	(Deep Purple)
Stairway to Heaven	(Led Zeppelin)
Let It Be	(Joe Cocker)
Hey Tonight	(Creedence Clearwater Revival)
Sympathy for the Devil	(The Rolling Stones)
Speed King	(Deep Purple)

APPENDIX B

Don Shirley's advice to a novice diver

If you want to dive well you need to think like a fish. OK, I don't mean go round in circles and open and close your mouth – though I have seen divers do it!

My world ... I live under the water, away from the terrestrial world, away from air, often away from light, often with no noise, not even bubbles, often a very long time away from the surface. It's my world, I live under the sea. I live deep in the water, deep in a cave. A fish would rather be under water than on the surface – so would I!

For a land dweller to relate to the fish can be difficult.

First, you must behave as a fish does. You must be completely happy in your environment. That's water. The terrestrial world is for humans. They can keep it! The response of a human is keyed to this terrestrial world. Under water the response is different. You can't run back to the surface. You must solve any problem where it happens. In order to do this you must be happy in the water. This comes from mental attitude and becoming accustomed to the water. You can't learn to dive from theory. You can only do it in the water. If there is something that you don't want to happen, practise it in your mind until it is no longer a problem.

Breathing. Have you ever seen a fish short of breath, breathing hard? I have not. So breathe like a fish. Don't breathe normally; breath properly, using the diaphragm. Long slow inhalation, short pause, long slow exhalation, full breaths. If you can breathe, all is fine, if you have no gas supply then, unfortunately you have an issue. But where is that next gas supply? If you have planned your world correctly, there will be spare gas in a cylinder on your side, or a close buddy. The surface? Not an option.

I don't see fish blowing bubbles, and I prefer not to. Rebreathing the gas you exhale is efficient, and gives you many extra options when things go wrong.

Buoyancy. When a fish stops swimming, he does not sink! He generally will not lay on the bottom. He will not grab hold of something to support him! So as a diver you should not do so these things either. Your buoyancy should be such that if you stop swimming, you float neutrally.

Ascent. When you must come back to the surface, do it slowly, under control.

Movement. Move like a fish, gracefully, with seemingly no effort. Make your gear work for you, not against you. Conserve energy in your fin strokes, directing the energy for propulsion, forward, backwards or sideways. Efficiency and duration is the aim. If you want to go fast – get a scooter!

Depth. You won't find a shallow-dwelling fish in deep water. If you are a shallow-dwelling diver, you must evolve to go deeper. That means skills, drills, knowledge and equipment, all working together.

APPENDIX C

Lisa Shaw's eulogy

I feel it is important that I say a few things about my father to honour him and the life that he led, not just as a father, but also as a friend to everyone here today.

It is only with his death that I have come to realize the profound effect that my father has had on so many people's lives. I am overwhelmed by how many people he has individually touched or influenced. People from different countries and walks of life, some of whom had never even met him face to face, and yet they all seem to have an individual story to tell about my father's positive, and in many cases powerful, influence in their lives.

It really was only over the last four years that I feel I truly began to appreciate how lucky I was to have a father like I did, and it was over these last few years that I feel I really got to know him, not just as a father, but as a friend. I think he did

have a few bad points. He was occasionally a little bit stub-
born, but he more than made up for these points with the
many other qualities he possessed. I would like to take the
time to reflect on a few of these, as I believe he demonstrated
them not just as a father, but also as a husband, son and
friend to many here.

My father was honest. I know there were many times in
his life where this would have been tested. The industrial ten-
sions and difficulties that were a common part of his job are
just one example. It always amazed me, however, that no
matter what the difficulties, no matter what the consequences and no matter how hard it would be, he always
maintained his stance of honesty and truthfulness.

He was also incredibly hard working, not just for himself,
but for others too. He started with nothing and yet always
trusted God that He would provide. And in the last few years
of his life when he had worked his way to having plenty, he
never took that for granted. I believe he was not only grateful
to God, but knew that what he had worked for and what God
had provided was meant to be shared with others. Such com-
passion and generosity I hope that I too will be capable of one
day.

He had very strong values and morals by which he conducted his life and by which he and my mother raised my
brother and me. Many of these values are difficult to find
nowadays, but by conducting his life by such morals and values I was, and am still, able to see that it is possible to con-
duct mine in such a way too.

It may sound like a cliché but it was always said to me that
the greatest gift a father could give his children was to love

their mother, and with that in mind Steven and I were very lucky children. The love and respect my parents had for each other was always present and I am incredibly grateful to the both of them for the safe and secure home and family that this brought with it. I too hope that after 30 years of marriage my future husband will love me as much as my father loved my mother.

My father was very humble. It impressed me that a man who I felt was so intelligent was also never afraid to ask advice or seek help from others. This humbleness meant that it is only now, from others, that I have learnt just how remarkably talented he was as a pilot and as a diver, for he never boasted about what he had done, but rather only shared some of the highlights of his adventures to those of us who were interested.

My father was young at heart. He approached the world with the desires of a 20-year-old but with the wisdom of a 50-year-old, always striving to learn new skills and discover new things. (Although I would just like to say that I find it very odd that a man who could master two very difficult and technical professions with such skill was completely incapable of undertaking a simple task such as making a sandwich.) He had a fantastic, if not somewhat warped, sense of humour, he was adventurous and he truly loved a challenge. He did not dive for the recognition, he dived so that he could go where no man had explored before; the recognition, much to his embarrassment, just seemed to come with it.

I am at peace with my father's death and I hope that many of you here are or will be too. I am at peace because I know, having faced death before, that my father was unafraid and was completely at peace with the prospect. I know and he knew that the Lord would be right there ready to take him onto new adventures. I am also at peace because he died doing something he loved. Very few of us will ever get that privilege, and I thank the Lord that my father did, because let's be honest, my dad was not the sort of person who was going to take to old age gracefully. (He would not exactly have been happy withering away in a nursing home.)

We cannot always see God's hand in things, or the reasons why He allows some things to happen, but I can see God's hand in so many aspects of my father's death and because of this I do not seek a reason behind it. I can see it in the jokes and humour that my father and I shared before he left, something which was so typical of him and which has enabled me to laugh and smile even in this difficult time. I can see it in the timing of his death because although I will miss him in future challenges and moments in my life, he died having provided for and prepared me to the best of his ability for anything I wish to pursue in the future. And finally I can see God in the actual manner and circumstances that surrounded his death. He has gone out with a bit of a bang and I cannot think of anything more fitting or anyone more deserving of such a departure than my father.

Index

307

309